EXPLORING THE AFRO-TEXAS EXPERIENCE: A BIBLIOGRAPHY OF SECONDARY SOURCES ABOUT BLACK TEXANS

EXPLORING THE AFRO-TEXAS EXPERIENCE: A BIBLIOGRAPHY OF SECONDARY SOURCES ABOUT BLACK TEXANS

by
Bruce A. Glasrud
and Laurie Champion

Sul Ross State University
A Member of the Texas State University System
Center for Big Bend Studies
Occasional Papers No. 5

ISBN 0-9647629-7-8

Center for Big Bend Studies, Occasional Papers No. 5

Robert J. Mallouf, *Series Editor*
Kelly S. García, *Technical Editor*

TABLE OF CONTENTS

FOREWORD

In 1998 the Center for Big Bend Studies at Sul Ross State University published Bruce A. Glasrud's *African Americans in the West: A Bibliography of Secondary Sources.* This broad-based compilation of source material on African American history, folkways, fiction, films, and politics has proven an essential reference not only for scholars, but for teachers, students, and the interested public as well. Thus, it is with considerable pleasure that we now offer the Glasrud and Laurie Champion companion volume entitled *Exploring the Afro-Texas Experience: A Bibliography of Secondary Sources About Black Texans*. As was the case with *African Americans in the West*, individual entries in this second effort often defy easy classification into one category or another, but Glasrud and Champion have nevertheless performed a masterful job of creating a highly coherent and usable compendium that greatly expands upon Texas entries found in the first volume. And like its predecessor, *Exploring the Afro-Texas Experience* takes us a large step forward in the promotion of multicultural scholarship both within and beyond the artificial borders of the state.

It should come as no surprise that the term "African American" comprises many smaller, culturally diverse groups and individuals that are reflected in Glasrud and Champion's topical arrangement. The same phenomena of historical circumstance that resulted in the creation of a black African presence in Texas and other regions has led the members of this ethnic group down many diverse pathways, and resulted in group variation that defies the stereotypes of the past. The simplistic global racial categorizations of eighteenth and nineteenth century physicians such as Johann Blumenbach and Samuel Morton have slowly given way to reasoned scrutiny, but we must marvel over why issues of "race" continue to plague American society. *Exploring the Afro-Texas Experience* and its predecessor volume indirectly reveal the great social complexity and diverse heritage of the African American community. Perhaps by doing so, these important compendiums can help counteract the forces of ethnocentrism and generate better understanding of this uniquely American culture.

Robert J. Mallouf
Director, Center for Big Bend Studies
Sul Ross State University

PREFACE

In 1998, the compilers[1] of this current bibliography, *Exploring the Afro-Texas Experience*, also cooperated in the publication of *African Americans in the West: A Bibliography of Secondary Sources*—Bruce A. Glasrud as compiler and Laurie Champion as "Fiction" contributor. The book, edited by Sheron Smith-Savage, was well received; Augusta State University professor Michael N. Searles, for example, sent an e-mail message exclaiming "your bibliography made my day."

Perhaps because we reside in Texas, because our own research interests lie in the Lone Star state, and because we enjoyed our previous collaborative efforts, we wanted to add to the less than complete Texas section of *African Americans in the West.* Glasrud's earlier decision to leave such a void was purposeful; as he noted in the "Preface:" "the Texas compilation is incomplete because investigators can discover most of the works I omitted in two first-rate historiographical articles prepared by Alwyn Barr, and by reviewing a very recent listing of theses and dissertations on black Texans prepared by Paul Lucko."[2] Despite the accuracy of the above comment, we decided that it remains necessary to produce a complete bibliographical work on black Texas. Texas' situation as both a southern and a western state has meant that its experiences are more varied, that a larger number of blacks resided in the state, and that a much more formidable body of literature has emerged depicting and investigating the African-American presence in the Lone Star state. For those reasons, as well as those mentioned earlier, we prepared this text. It is our assumption that it will prove invaluable for Texas buffs, scholars, teachers, graduate students, and classroom use.

For the purposes of this essay, we follow the four chronological/ideological schools of western African-American history previously noted by Glasrud: (1) the participant, romantic school includes those who wrote prior to 1910 about their exploits and those who idealistically portrayed blacks in the West; (2) the pioneering school (who wrote from approximately 1910 to the late 1960s) who explicated the presence of black westerners by pointing out the many contributions of African Americans in the development of the West. Lawrence B. de Graaf[3] referred to many of these writers as belonging to the "recognition" school of historiography; (3) the early school (who wrote from the late 1960s to the late 1980s) includes principally those who were products of the student revolt, civil rights movement, and Vietnam War era of the 1960s. These scholars were among the first to depict discrimination and other difficulties encountered by African Americans (and other peoples of color) in the West and to discuss black reaction to their situations. De Graaf referred to these writers as the "racism" school; and (4) the inclusive, multicultural school (who began writing in the late 1980s and continue today) who vividly portray the entire aura of blacks in the West by focusing on the twentieth-century urban habitat, relations among western peoples of color, and innovative and creative methods African Americans employed to succeed and flourish amidst their continual struggle against sometimes hostile forces.

Years earlier, when historians began to investigate Texas black history, they covered any lead that seemed feasible, with little guidance from other scholars or secondary sources because so little had then been written. More recently, historians often were aware that a considerable number of essays and stories had been published about black Texans, but easily and promptly locating them was another matter. Considerable time was spent in perusing articles, theses, books, and bibliographical aids in efforts to locate citations. A comprehensive compilation of secondary sources that covered the Afro-Texan Experience was unavailable. That situation provided a primary impetus for the preparation of this bibliography.

Another motive for compiling this bibliography of secondary materials is that, although the bibliography is substantial, there are omissions that will become evident to the reader—some are purposeful, some exist because scholars have not yet covered specific topics, and some perhaps accidental. Fortunately, scholars continue to research, prepare, and publish additional works on the history of black Texans. We suspect that the activity we help set in motion will continue to flourish, so that when another generation of scholars produces a bibliographical tome it will require multi-volume treatment. And, even more importantly, we hope further research continues to unveil clearer understandings of the lives of African Americans in the Lone Star state.

The reader will also note some purposeful duplication of titles; for example, Marvin Dulaney's "Whatever Happened to the Civil Rights Movement in Dallas, Texas?" is listed in both the section on "Civil Rights" and in the section on "Urban Communities." Virtually all selections focus directly and specifically on blacks in Texas. If broader studies mention, but do not focus on black Texans, they are not included. On the other hand, if a chapter of a book concerns African Americans in Texas, then it is included.

Answers to the obvious question "why include principally secondary sources?" reveal another basis for this bibliography. A review of the secondary literature can demonstrate faulty concepts, outmoded explorations, and gaps in areas of research. Perhaps more importantly, there is a need to pull together in a single reference the extensive group of publications that have appeared in the past 30 years. Such a bibliography will also serve to show the wealth and diversity of publications regarding the history of Afro-Texans. Finally, this secondary bibliography will provide an orderly and systematic research compilation for anyone interested in discovering more about black Texans.

This is not to say that primary sources are unimportant—we do include a section on "fiction" which is a primary source. Obviously, the secondary materials included could not have been written without extensive research of primary sources. For locating primary sources, check works cited in dissertations, published works, and refer to published bibliographies. The bulk of primary sources consist of federal, state, and local government documents, diaries and letters, newspaper and magazine articles, autobiographies, photographs, and census records. Virtually all the national government materials can be located in the National Archives; for suggestions on using those documents, refer to Barry A. Crouch's "Freedmen's Bureau Records: Texas, A Case Study."[4]

However, as noted, this bibliography concentrates on secondary sources. The approach and organization of this bibliographical effort is designed to be helpful. It is divided into eighteen chapters which are organized into three basic areas:

1. **General and bibliographical**—This material is included in chapter one, and consists of bibliographies and general works covering African Americans in the West as well as in Texas.
2. **Chronological**—This section includes eleven chapters, which take the researcher from Estevan in 1528 to the present. There are a few explanations to make—chapter three includes free blacks; chapter nine excludes (obviously?) Black Seminoles, soldiers, and cowboys; chapter eleven essentially covers the years from 1954 to 1968, but it does provide background selections.
3. **Topical**—This section contains six chapters that cover specific subjects—culture, economics, education, fiction, urbanism, and women.

As this bibliography indicates, and as a survey of some of the materials in the bibliography will illustrate, blacks assumed a key relationship to the development, settlement, and life of Texas. Opportunities, though frequently limited compared to those of whites, were available. On the other hand, they faced varied prejudice and discrimination, fought for their rights, established communities, and developed social, economic, cultural, and political activities. This resulting bibliography of Afro-Texans should be especially important now, because as Alwyn Barr remarked in *Black Texans* "the longer span of black history and the greater variety of African-American experiences under several flags, suggest the value of a separate volume of Black Texans."[5]

NOTES

1. Please note: there is no way we found everything; we tried, but—please send additions, corrections, and suggestions, either snail mail or e-mail, to: Bruce A. Glasrud, School of Arts and Sciences, Sul Ross State University, Alpine, Texas 79832; bglasrud@sulross.edu.
2. Bruce A. Glasrud, "Preface," *African Americans in the West: A Bibliography of Secondary Sources* (Alpine, Tex.: Center for Big Bend Studies, 1998): *x*; Alwyn Barr, "African Americans in Texas: From Stereotypes to Diverse Roles," *Texas Through Time: Evolving Interpretations*, edited by Walter L. Buenger and Robert A. Calvert (College Station: Texas A&M University Press, 1991): 50–80; Alwyn Barr, "Black Texans," *A Guide to the History of Texas*, edited by Light Townsend Cummins and Alvin R. Bailey Jr. (Westport, Conn.: Greenwood Press, 1988): 107–121; Paul M. Lucko, "Dissertations and Theses Relating to African American Studies in Texas: A Selected Bibliography, 1904–1990," *Southwestern Historical Quarterly* 96 (1992): 547–573.
3. Lawrence B. de Graaf, "Recognition, Racism, and Reflections on the Writing of Western Black History," *Pacific Historical Review* 44 (1975): 22–51.
4. Barry A. Crouch, "Freedmen's Bureau Records: Texas, A Case Study," *Afro-American History: Sources for Research*, edited by Robert L. Clarke (Washington, D.C.: Howard University Press, 1981): 74–94.
5. Alwyn Barr, *Black Texans: A History of African Americans in Texas, 1528–1995,* second edition (Norman: University of Oklahoma Press, 1996): *v–vi*.

ACKNOWLEDGMENTS

As is always the case when preparing a work of this magnitude, the compilers have incurred many debts. We would like to thank Robert Mallouf, Director of the Center for Big Bend Studies at Sul Ross State University, for his interest in our project. The services of Sul Ross State University librarians Eleanor Wilson, Mike Robinson, and Pam Spooner were essential to our efforts. These librarians saved us countless hours by helping us locate page numbers, find dates of publications, and even uncover complete citations we might have otherwise overlooked.

We also appreciate the host of scholars who responded to our queries, encouraged our efforts, and offered us advice. They provided lists of their writings on black Texans, suggested other authors, and provided the proverbial encouragement so frequently needed by authors. The assistance we received from some of these scholars went beyond collegial duty: W. Marvin Dulaney sent a copy of his bibliography on Black Dallasites and gave permission to "use it in your publication;" Michael N. Searles allowed us to reprint a photograph of Cowboy Mike. Before moving to New Mexico, Sheron Smith-Savage provided many critical references. We list the citations for the works of numerous fine scholars, and we appreciate the support so many of them offered us.

Special thanks go to Kelly García, for proofreading, preparing an index, and editing our manuscript. We very much appreciate her efforts to polish this work.

While those mentioned above provided valuable assistance, we are solely responsible for errors and/or omissions.

Bruce A. Glasrud
Laurie Champion

"Cowboy Mike" aka author
Michael N. Searles

1. Bibliography/General

Man and ox plowing a field.

The UT Institute of Texan Cultures, No. 68-1301
Library of Congress, Prints and Photo Division

Abajian, James de T., comp. *Blacks and Their Contributions to the American West: A Bibliography and Union List of Library Holdings through 1970.* Boston: G. K. Hall, 1974.

Abernethy, Francis Edward, Carolyn Fiedler Satterwhite, Patrick B. Mullen, and Alan B. Govenar, eds. *Juneteenth Texas: Essays in African-American Folklore.* Publication of the Texas Folklore Society No. 54. Denton: University of North Texas Press, 1996.

Adams, Effie Kaye. *Tall Black Texans: Men of Courage.* Dubuque, Iowa: Kendall/Hunt, 1972.

Adele, Lynne. *Black History/Black Vision: The Visionary Image in Texas.* Austin: University of Texas Press, 1989.

Alexander, Charles C. *The Ku Klux Klan in the Southwest.* Lexington: University of Kentucky Press, 1965.

Barnes, Marian. *Black Texans: They Overcame.* Austin: Eakin Press, 1996. [Children's book]

Barr, Alwyn. "African Americans in Texas: From Stereotypes to Diverse Roles." In *Texas through Time: Evolving Interpretations*, edited by Walter L. Buenger and Robert A. Calvert, 50–80. College Station: Texas A&M University Press, 1991.

_______. "Black Migration into Southwestern Cities, 1865–1900." In *Essays on Southern History: Written in Honor of Barnes F. Lathrop*, edited by Gary W. Gallagher, 15–38. Austin: General Libraries of University of Texas, 1980.

_______. "The Black Militia of the New South: Texas as a Case Study." *Journal of Negro History* 63 (1978): 209–219.

_______. "Black Texans." In *A Guide to the History of Texas,* edited by Light Townsend Cummins and Alvin R. Bailey Jr., 107–121. Westport, Conn.: Greenwood Press, 1988.

_______. *Black Texans: A History of African Americans in Texas, 1528–1995.* Second edition. Norman: University of Oklahoma Press, 1996.

_______. *Black Texans: A History of Negroes in Texas, 1528-1971.* Austin: Jenkins Publishing, 1973.

_______. "The Negro in American History Texts." *Indiana Social Studies Quarterly* 22 (Autumn 1969): 28–34.

Barr, Alwyn, and Robert A. Calvert, eds. *Black Leaders: Texans for Their Times.* Austin: Texas State Historical Association, 1981.

Barrett, Anna Pearl. *Juneteenth: Celebrating Freedom in Texas.* Austin: Eakin Press, 1999.

Behrends, Carey F. "Historic Tour of Historic Fort Stockton, Texas: A Milestone in Black History." *Heritage* 11 (Winter 1993): 24–25.

Benedict, H. Y., and John A. Lomax. "The Negro in Texas." In *The Book of Texas*, 325–335. New York: Doubleday, Page and Company, 1928.

Berardi, Gayle K., and Thomas W. Segady. "Community Identification and Cultural Transformation: The Role of African-American Newspapers in Texas, 1868–1970." Ph.D. dissertation, University of Texas at Austin, 1972.

Billington, Monroe Lee, and Roger D. Hardaway, eds. *African Americans on the Western Frontier*. Niwot, Colo.: University Press of Colorado, 1998.

Black, Doris. "The Black Chinese." *Sepia Record* 24 (January 1975): 18–24.

Bowman, Bob, ed. "The Black Heritage." In *Land of the Little Angel: A History of Angelina County, Texas*, compiled by Angelina County Historical Survey Committee, 197–202. Lufkin, Tex.: Lufkin Printing Company, 1976.

Brewer, J. Mason. *An Historical Outline of the Negro in Travis County [Texas]*. Austin: Samuel Huston College, 1940.

Bryan, Marilyn T. "The Economic, Political and Social Status of the Negro in El Paso." *Password* 13 (1968): 74–86.

Bryant, Ira B. Jr. "The Need for Negro History in the Schools of Texas." *Negro History Bulletin* 20 (January 1957): 77–78.

_______. *The Texas Negro Under Six Flags*. Houston: Houston College for Negroes, [1936].

Bunch, Lonnie G. III. "African Americans." In *Encyclopedia of the American West*, edited by Charles Phillips and Alan Axelrod, vol. 1, 8–11. New York: Simon and Schuster, 1996.

Byrd, James W. "Afro-American Writers in the West." In *A Literary History of the West*, sponsored by the Western Literature Association, 1139–1147. Fort Worth: Texas Christian University Press, 1987.

Campbell, Jeff H. "Negro." In *Southwestern American Literature: A Bibliography*, edited by John Q. Anderson, Edwin W. Gaston Jr., and James W. Lee, 48–50. Chicago: Swallow Press, 1980.

Carlson, Paul. "The Texas Background—Spanish or American?" *West Texas Historical Association Year Book* 52 (1976): 61–70.

Carrigan, William Dean. "Between South and West: Race, Violence, and Power in Central Texas, 1836–1916." Ph.D. dissertation, Emory University, 1999.

Christian, Garna L. "Adding on Fort Bliss to Black Military Historiography." *West Texas Historical Association Year Book* 54 (1978): 41–54.

Cotton, Walter, comp. *History of Negroes of Limestone County from 1860 to 1939*. Mexia, Tex.: J. A. Chatman and S. M. Merriwether, 1939.

Cripps, Thomas R. "*The Birth of a Race*: A Lost Film Rediscovered in Texas." *Texas Humanist* 5 (March-April 1983): 10–11.

Crouch, Barry A. "'Unmanacling' Texas Reconstruction: A Twenty-Year Perspective." *Southwestern Historical Quarterly* 93 (1989): 275–302.

Davidson, Chandler. "African Americans and Politics." In *The New Handbook of Texas*, edited by Ron Tyler, Douglas E. Barnett, Roy R. Barkley, Penelope C. Anderson, and Mark F. Odintz, vol. 1, 51–55. Austin: Texas State Historical Association, 1996.

Davidson, James M. "The Oldest Cemetery in Dallas Rediscovered: The Lost Location of Dallas's Slave Burials." *African-American Archaeology, Newsletter of the African-American Archaeology Network* 22 (Fall 1998): 4, 7.

de Graaf, Lawrence B. "Recognition, Racism, and Reflections on the Writing of Western Black History." *Pacific Historical Review* 44 (1975): 22-51.

Delta Sigma Theta Sorority. *The Black Heritage Exhibit: A Pictorial History of Austin, Travis County, Texas' Black Community, 1839–1920.* Austin: Delta Sigma Theta Sorority, c.1973.

Du Bois, W. E. B. *What the Negro has done for the United States and Texas*. Washington, D.C.: Government Printing Office, 1936.

Dulaney, W. Marvin. "African Americans." In *The New Handbook of Texas*, edited by Ron Tyler, Douglas E. Barnett, Roy R. Barkley, Penelope C. Anderson, and Mark F. Odintz, vol. 1, 46–51. Austin: Texas State Historical Association, 1996.

_______. "African Americans in Dallas: A Bibliography of Sources." Unpublished paper, in possession of compiler.

_______. *Black Police in America*. Bloomington: Indiana University Press, 1996.

Emerson, C., and Gwendolyn M. Jackson. *The History of the Negro, Wichita Falls, Texas, 1880–1982*. Wichita Falls: Antioch Baptist Church, 1998.

Foley, Neil Francis. "The New South in the Southwest: Anglos, Blacks, and Mexicans in Central Texas, 1880–1930." Ph.D. dissertation, University of Michigan, 1990.

_______. *The White Scourge: Mexicans, Blacks, and Poor Whites in Texas Cotton Culture.* Berkeley: University of California Press, 1997.

Gillette, Michael L. "National Association for the Advancement of Colored People." In *The New Handbook of Texas*, edited by Ron Tyler, Douglas E. Barnett, Roy R. Barkley, Penelope C. Anderson, and Mark F. Odintz, vol. 4, 941–942. Austin: Texas State Historical Association, 1996.

Glasrud, Bruce A., comp. *African Americans in the West: A Bibliography of Secondary Sources*. Occasional Papers No. 2. Alpine, Tex.: Center for Big Bend Studies, Sul Ross State University, 1998.

_______. "Jim Crow's Emergence in Texas." *American Studies* 15 (1974): 47–60.

Glasrud, Bruce A., and Laurie Champion. "African Americans in the West: A Short Story Tradition." *Journal of Big Bend Studies* 10 (1998): 221–242.

Glasrud, Bruce A., and James A. Halseth, eds. *The Northwest Mosaic: Minority Conflicts in Pacific Northwest History*. Boulder: Pruett Publishing Company, 1977.

Glasrud, Bruce A., and Alan M. Smith, eds. *Promises To Keep: A Portrayal of Nonwhites in the United States*. Chicago: Rand McNally, 1972.

_______, eds. *Race Relations in British North America, 1607-1783.* Chicago: Nelson-Hall Publishers, 1981.

Gordon, John Ramsey. "The Negro in McLennan County, Texas." Master's thesis, Baylor University, 1932.

Govenar, Alan B., and Jay E. Brakefield. *Deep Ellum and Central Track: Where the Black and White Worlds of Dallas Converged.* Denton: University of North Texas Press, 1998.

Graham, Donald. "Red, White, and Black: An Interpretation of Ethnic and Racial Attitudes of American Radicals in Texas and Oklahoma, 1880–1920." Ph.D. dissertation, University of Saskatchewan, 1973.

Greene, Harry W. "Negro Colleges in the Southwest." *Opportunity* 5 (November 1927): 322–325.

Griffin, Marvin C. *Texas African-American Baptists: The Story of the Baptist General Convention of Texas*. Austin: Publisher's Marketing House, 1994.

Grose, Charles William. "Black Newspapers in Texas, 1868–1970." Ph.D. dissertation, University of Texas at Austin, 1972.

Hall, Charles E. *Progress of the Negro in Texas*. Washington: Government Printing Office, 1936.

Hartley, Margaret L. "Black Boundaries in Big Texas." *Southwest Review* 37 (1952): 68– 71.

Hayes, Roland C. "Blacks in Texas." In *Texas: A Sesquicentennial Celebration,* edited by Donald W. Whisenhunt, 327–337. Austin: Eakin Press, 1984.

Hayman, Bettie. "A Short History of the Negro of Walker County, 1860–1942." Master's thesis, Sam Houston State Teachers College, 1942.

Haynes, Rose Mary F. "Some Features of Negro Participation in Texas History through 1879." Master's thesis, Texas A&I University, 1948.

Heintze, Michael R. *Private Black Colleges in Texas, 1865–1954.* College Station: Texas A&M University Press, 1985.

Hollingsworth, James Selwyn. "An Analysis of Selected Demographic Characteristics of the Texas Nonwhite Population." Master's thesis, Texas A&M University, 1964.

Hornsby, Alton Jr. "The 'Colored Branch University' Issue in Texas—Prelude to *Sweatt v. Painter*." *Journal of Negro History* 61 (1976): 51–60.

Institute of Texan Cultures. *The Afro-American Texans*. San Antonio: The Institute, 1975.

Jackson, A. W. *A Sure Foundation and a Sketch of Negro Life in Texas*. Houston: A. W. Jackson, 1940.

Jones, Howard. *The Red Diary: A Chronological History of Black Americans in Houston and Some Neighboring Harris County Communities—122 Years Later*. Austin: Nortex Press, 1991.

Jones, Vonciel. "Born a Black Bastard . . . The Education and Organization of Houston's Black Lawyers, 1947–1967." Master's thesis, Rice University, 1976.

Jordan, Edna Hidell. *Black Tracks to Texas*. Corpus Christi: Golden Banner Press, 1977.

Junne, George H. Jr. *The Black American West: A Bibliography*. Greeley, Colo.: University of Northern Colorado, 1999.

Katz, William Loren. *The Black West: A Documentary and Pictorial History of the African American Role in the Westward Expansion of the United States*. Rev. ed. New York: Simon and Schuster, 1996.

Kirven, Lamar L. "A Century of Warfare: Black Texans." Ph.D. dissertation, Indiana University, 1974.

Kuhr, Nancy Jane Newton. "Segregated Public Schools in Texas, 1876–1940." Master's thesis, University of Texas at Austin, 1971.

Lipsitz, George. "'Goin' On': Afro-American Imagery in Texas Film and Folklore." *Southwest Media Review* 3 (Spring 1985): 42–45.

Lucko, Paul M. "Dissertations and Theses Relating to African American Studies in Texas: A Selected Bibliography, 1904–1990." *Southwestern Historical Quarterly* 96 (1993): 547–573.

MacGregor, Karen, and Tammy Wiloth. "Black Pioneers of Shackelford County." *Old Timer Magazine* 7 (1980): 10–13.

Mardis, Jas., ed. *KenteCloth: Southwest Voices of the African Diaspora, The Oral Tradition Comes to the Page*. Denton: University of North Texas Press, 1997.

Margot, Louis III. "The *Dallas Express*: A Negro Newspaper: Its History, 1892–1971, and Its Point of View." Master's thesis, East Texas State University, 1971.

Mason, Kenneth. *African Americans and Race Relations in San Antonio, Texas, 1867–1937*. New York: Garland Publishing, 1998.

_______. "Paternal Continuity: African Americans and Race Relations in San Antonio, Texas, 1867–1937." Ph.D. dissertation, University of Texas at Austin, 1994.

Meeks, Walter A. "The Black American in Texas after the Civil War." *Negro History Bulletin* 37 (1974): 241–242.

Miles, Merle Yvonne. "'Born and Bred' in Texas: Three Generations of Black Females: A Critique of Social Science Perceptions on the Black Female." Ph.D. dissertation, University of Texas at Austin, 1986.

Morrison, Dorothy, and Rebecca Buard. *The Black Citizen in American Democracy: Black Culture in Harrison County, Past, Present, and Future*, 2 volumes. Marshall, Tex.: Marshall Public Library, 1976, 1979.

Munchus-Forde, Lady George. "History of the Negro in Fort Worth—Syllabus for a High School Course." Master's thesis, Fisk University, 1941.

Murphy, Leonard B. "A History of Negro Segregation Practices in Texas, 1865–1958." Master's thesis, Southern Methodist University, 1958.

Murray, Pauli, comp. "Texas." In *States' Laws on Race and Color*, 442–456, 660–664. Cincinnati: Woman's Division of Christian Service, Methodist Church, 1952.

Nash, Kwame M. *Cologne: The History and Anthropology of a Rural Texas African American Community*. San Antonio: M. C. Nash, 1990.

Pitre, Merline. "The Evolution of a Black University in Texas." *Western Journal of Black Studies* 3 (Fall 1979): 210–223.

Porter, Kenneth Wiggins. *The Negro on the American Frontier*. New York: Arno Press, 1971.

Pyle, Philip Alan, and George McElroy. "The Black Press in Texas: A Short Overview." *The Black Presence in the Texas Sesquicentennial*, edited by Jesse E. Gloster and Hunter O. Brooks, 33–47. Houston: D. Armstrong Company, 1986.

Ravage, John W. *Black Pioneers: Images of the Black Experience on the North American Frontier*. Salt Lake City: University of Utah Press, 1997.

Redwine, W.A. "Brief History of the Negro in Five Counties." *Chronicles of Smith County* [Texas] 11 (Fall 1972): 13–70. Originally published as a book (Tyler, Tex.: Privately printed, 1901).

Reese, James V. "Negroes in Texas." In *The Handbook of Texas: A Supplement*, edited by Eldon Stephen Branda, 643–645. Austin: Texas State Historical Association, 1976.

Richardson, Chad. "Black, Brown, and White: Race and Ethnicity in South Texas." In *Batos, Bolillos, Pochos, and Pelados: Class and Culture on the South Texas Border*, 211–245. Austin: University of Texas Press, 1999.

Ross, John R. "Lynching." In *The New Handbook of Texas*, edited by Ron Tyler, Douglas E. Barnett, Roy R. Barkley, Penelope C. Anderson, and Mark F. Odintz, vol. 4, 346–347. Austin: Texas State Historical Association, 1996.

Sance, Melvin M. Jr. *The Afro-American Texans*. San Antonio: Institute of Texan Cultures, 1987.

Savage, W. Sherman. *Blacks in the West, 1830-1890*. Westport, Conn.: Greenwood Press, 1976.

_______."The Negro in the Westward Movement." *Journal of Negro History* 25 (1940): 531–539.

Schaffer, Ruth C. "The Health and Social Functions of Black Midwives on the Texas Brazos Bottom, 1920–1985." *Rural Sociology* 56 (Spring 1991): 89–105.

Shabazz, Amilcar. "The Opening of the Southern Mind: The Desegregation of Higher Education in Texas, 1865–1965." Ph.D. dissertation, University of Houston, 1996.

Shimkin, Demitri B. "Texas indeed is Different: Some Historical and Demographic Observations." In *The Extended Family in Black Societies*, edited by Demitri B. Shimkin, Edith M. Shimkin, and Dennis A. Frate, 363–378. The Hague: Mouton Publishers, 1978.

Simond, Ada DeBlanc. "A History of African-American Catholicism in Texas." In *Bricks Without Straw: A Comprehensive History of African Americans in Texas*, edited by David A. Williams, 309–322. Austin: Eakin Press, 1997.

Smallwood, James M. *A Century of Achievement: Blacks in Cooke County, Texas*. Gainesville: American Revolution Bicentennial Committee, 1975.

_______. *The Struggle for Equality: Blacks in Texas*. Boston: American Press, 1981.

_______. "Texas." In *The Black Press in the South, 1865–1979,* edited by Henry Lewis Suggs, 357–377. Westport, Conn.: Greenwood Publishers, 1983.

_______. "The Woodward Thesis Revisited: The Origins of Social Segregation in Texas." *Negro History Bulletin* 47 (1984): 6–9.

Smith, Ralph A. "The Mamelukes of West Texas and Mexico." *West Texas Historical Association Year Book* 39 (1963): 65–88.

Taylor, Quintard. "Bibliographic Essay on the African American West." *Montana: The Magazine of Western History* 46 (Winter 1996): 18–23.

_______. "Blacks in the American West: An Overview." *Western Journal of Black Studies* 1 (March 1977): 4-10.

_______. "From Esteban to Rodney King: Five Centuries of African American History in the West." *Montana: The Magazine of Western History* 46 (Winter 1996): 2–17.

_______. *In Search of the Racial Frontier: African Americans in the American West, 1528–1990.* New York: W. W. Norton, 1998.

Texas Historical Commission. *African Americans in Texas: Historical and Cultural Legacies.* Austin: Texas Historical Commission, c. 1998.

Vlach, John Michael. "Afro-American Folk Crafts in Nineteenth Century Texas." *Western Folklore* 40 (1981): 149–161.

Walker, May. *The History of the Black Police Officers in the Houston Police Department, 1878–1988.* Dallas: Taylor Publishing Company, 1988.

Williams, David Alvernon, ed. *Bricks Without Straw: A Comprehensive History of African Americans in Texas.* Austin: Eakin Press, 1997.

_______. "A History of Higher Education for African-American Texans, 1872–1977." In *Bricks Without Straw: A Comprehensive History of African Americans in Texas,* edited by David A. Williams, 208–278. Austin: Eakin Press, 1997.

_______. "The History of Higher Education for Black Texans, 1872–1977." Ed.D. dissertation, Baylor University, 1978.

_______. "A Sin of Omission: Documenting African American History in the Lone Star State." *Medallion* 29 (February 1992): 4.

Williams, L. V. "Teaching Negro Life and History in Texas High Schools." *Journal of Negro History* 20 (1935): 13–18.

Williams, Patrick G. "Texas." In *Encyclopedia of African-American Culture and History,* edited by Jack Salzman, David Lionel Smith, and Cornel West, vol. 5, 2633–2636. New York: Simon and Schuster, 1996.

Wilson, C. W. "The Negro in Walker County." Master's thesis, Sam Houston State Teachers College, 1934.

Wintz, Cary D. "Blacks." In *The Ethnic Groups of Houston,* edited by Fred R. von der Mehden, 9–40. Houston: Rice University Studies, 1984.

Woolfolk, George R. *The Free Negro in Texas, 1800–1860: A Study in Cultural Compromise.* Ann Arbor: University Microfilms, 1976.

_______. *Prairie View: A Study in Public Conscience, 1878–1946.* New York: Pageant Press, 1962.

_______. "Sources of the History of the Negro in Texas, with Special Reference to Their Implications for Research in Slavery." *Journal of Negro History* 42 (1957): 38–47.

_______. "Turner's Safety Valve and Free Negro Westward Migration." *Pacific Northwest Quarterly* 56 (1965): 125–130.

Wooten, Mattie Lloyd. "Racial, National, and Nativity Trends in Texas, 1870–1930." *Southwestern Social Science Quarterly* 14 (1933): 62–69.

2. Spanish Origins/ Mexico

George "7D George" Adams, resident cowhand on the Coleman Foster Cox Sr. Ranch, Brewster County, Texas, and his horse, Baquet. Photo taken 1920s.

The UT Institute of Texan Cultures, No. 98-613
Courtesy of James W. Davis

Aguirre Beltrán, Gonzalo. "The Integration of the Negro into the National Society of Mexico." In *Race and Class in Latin America*, edited by Magnus Mörner, 11–27. New York: Columbia University Press, 1970.

_______. *La población negra de México, 1519–1810*. 2d ed. México, D.F.: Fondo de Cultura Economica, 1972.

_______. "Races in Seventeenth Century Mexico." *Phylon* 6 (1945): 212–218.

_______. "The Slave Trade in Mexico." *Hispanic American Historical Review* 24 (1944): 412–431.

_______. "The Tribal Origins of Slaves in Mexico." *Journal of Negro History* 31 (1956): 269–351.

Arrington, Carolyn. *Estevanico—Black Explorer in Spanish Texas*. Austin: Eakin Press, 1986.

Barnes, Thomas C., Thomas H. Naylor, and Charles W. Polzer. "Racial Terminology." In *Northern New Spain: A Research Guide*, 90–93. Tucson: University of Arizona Press, 1981.

Bennett, Herman L. "A Research Note: Race, Slavery, and the Ambiguity of Corporate Consciousness." *Colonial Latin American Historical Review* 3 (Spring 1994): 207–213.

Boyd-Bowman, Peter. "Negro Slaves in Early Colonial Mexico." *The Americas* 26 (1969): 134–153.

Brady, Robert La Don. "The Domestic Slave Trade in Sixteenth Century Mexico." *The Americas* 24 (1968): 281–289.

Buchanan, William J. "The Legend of the Black Conquistador." *Mankind Magazine* 1 (February 1968): 21–24, 93.

Buchholz, Michael. "Racial References in the Texas Press, 1813–1836." *Journalism Quarterly* 67 (1990): 586–591.

Carroll, Patrick J. "Mandinga: The Evolution of a Mexican Runaway Slave Community, 1735–1827." *Comparative Studies in Society and History* 19 (1977): 488–505.

Chipman, Donald E. "Estevanico." In *The New Handbook of Texas*, edited by Ron Tyler, Douglas E. Barnett, Roy R. Barkley, Penelope C. Anderson, and Mark F. Odintz, vol. 2, 899. Austin: Texas State Historical Association, 1996.

_______. "In Search of Cabeza de Vaca's Route Across Texas: An Historiographical Survey." *Southwestern Historical Quarterly* 91 (1987): 127–148.

Clemence, Stella Risley. "Deed of Emancipation of a Negro Woman Slave, Dated Mexico, September 14, 1585." *Hispanic American Historical Review* 11 (1930): 51–57.

Davidson, David M. "Negro Slave Control and Resistance in Colonial Mexico, 1519–1650." *Hispanic American Historical Review* 46 (1966): 235–253.

Diggs, Irene. "Color in Colonial Spanish America." *Journal of Negro History* 28 (1953): 403–427.

Goodwyn, Frank. "Estevanico." In *Handbook of Texas*, edited by Walter Prescott Webb, H. Bailey Carroll, Llerena B. Friend, Mary Jane Carroll, and Louise Nolen, vol. 1, 574. Austin: Texas State Historical Association, 1952.

Heald, Weldon F. "Black Pathfinder of the Deserts." *The Crisis* 57 (1950): 703–708.

Howren, Alleine. "Causes and Origins of the Decree of April 6, 1830." *Southwestern Historical Quarterly* 16 (1913): 378–422.

Ibrahim, Shirley D. "Estevan, the Moor of New Mexico: An Experiment in Point of View." Ed.D. dissertation, East Texas State University, 1978.

King, James Ferguson. "Descriptive Data on Negro Slaves in Spanish Importation Records and Bills of Sale." *Journal of Negro History* 28 (1943): 7–23.

_______. "Evolution of the Free Slave Trade Principle in Spanish Colonial Administration." *Hispanic American Historical Review* 22 (1942): 45–53.

_______. "Negro History in Continental Spanish America." *Journal of Negro History* 29 (1944): 7–23.

_______. "Negro Slavery in Viceroyalty of New Granda." MS dissertation, University of California, Berkeley, 1939.

Logan, Rayford W. "Estevanico, Negro Discoverer of the Southwest: A Critical Reexamination." *Phylon* 1 (1940): 305–314.

Love, Edgar F. "Legal Restrictions on Afro-Indian Relations in Colonial Mexico." *Journal of Negro History* 55 (1970): 131–139.

_______. "Marriage Patterns of Persons of African Descent in a Colonial Mexico City Parish." *Hispanic American Historical Review* 51 (1971): 79–91.

_______. "Negro Resistance to Spanish Rule in Colonial Mexico." *Journal of Negro History* 52 (1967): 89–103.

Mirsky, Jeannette. "Zeroing in on a Fugitive Figure: The First Negro in America." *Midway* 8 (June 1967): 1–17.

Palmer, Colin A. *Slaves of the White God: Blacks in Mexico, 1570–1650.* Cambridge: Harvard University Press, 1976.

Panger, Daniel. *Black Ulysses*. Athens, Ohio: Ohio University Press, 1982. [Fiction]

Parish, Helen Rand. *Estebanico.* New York: Viking Press, 1974. [Fiction]

Pi-Sunyer, Oriol. "The Historical Background to the Negro in Mexico." *Journal of Negro History* 42 (1957): 237–246.

Porter, Kenneth W. "Seminole in Mexico, 1850–1861." *Chronicles of Oklahoma* 29 (1951): 153–168.

_______. "The Seminole [and Seminole-Negroes] in Mexico, 1850–1861." *Hispanic American Historical Review* 31 (1951): 1–36.

Rippy, J. Fred. "The Negro and the Spanish Pioneer in the New World." *Journal of Negro History* 6 (1921): 183–189.

Rout, Leslie B. Jr. *The African Experience in Spanish America, 1502 to the Present Day.* London: Cambridge University Press, 1977.

Sanchez, Joseph P. "African Freedmen and the *Fuero Militar*: A Historical Overview of *Pardo* and *Moreno* Militiamen in the Late Spanish Empire." *Colonial Latin American Historical Review* 3 (Spring 1994): 165–184.

Shepherd, Elizabeth. *The Discoveries of Esteban the Black.* New York: Dodd, Mead, 1970.

Smith, Ralph A. "The Mamelukes of West Texas and Mexico." *West Texas Historical Association Year Book* 39 (1963): 65–88.

Stern, Peter. "*Gente de color quebrado*: Africans and Afromestizos in Colonial Mexico." *Colonial Latin American Historical Review* 3 (Spring 1994): 185–205.

Terrell, John Upton. *Estevanico the Black.* Los Angeles: Westernlore Press Publishers, 1968.

Tjarks, Alicia V. "Cooperative Demographic Analysis of Texas, 1777–1793." *Southwestern Historical Quarterly* 77 (1974): 291–338.

Tyler, Ronnie C. "Fugitive Slaves in Mexico." *Journal of Negro History* 57 (1972): 1–12.

Valdés, Dennis N. "The Decline of Slavery in Mexico." *The Americas* 44 (1987): 167–194.

Wortham, Sue Clark. "The Role of the Negro on the Texas Frontier, 1821–1836." Master's thesis, Southwest Texas State University, 1970.

Zochert, Donald. "'This Nation Never Saw a Black Man Before.'" *American Heritage* 22 (February 1971): 8–9.

3. Republic; Antebellum Texas, 1835–1860

Frank Palfry with his black nursemaid, ca. 1890s.

The UT Institute of Texan Cultures, No. 85-129
Courtesy of Mrs. Charles C. Bush III

Baker, Robin E., and Dale Baum. "The Texas Voter and the Crisis of the Union, 1859–1861." *Journal of Southern History* 53 (1987): 395–420.

Bornholst, Jacquelyn Wooley. "Plantation Settlement in the Brazos River Valley, 1820–1860." Master's thesis, Texas A&M University, 1971.

Campbell, Randolph B. "Antebellum Texas: From Union to Disunion, 1846–1861." In *A Guide to the History of Texas*, edited by Light T. Cummins and Alvin R. Bailey Jr., 21–35. Westport, Conn.: Greenwood Press, 1988.

_______. "Planters and Plain Folk: Harrison County, Texas, as a Test Case, 1850–1860." *Journal of Southern History* 40 (1974): 369–398.

_______. *A Southern Community in Crisis: Harrison County, Texas, 1850–1880*. Austin: Texas State Historical Association, 1983.

_______. "Statehood, Civil War, and Reconstruction, 1846–76." In *Texas Through Time: Evolving Interpretations,* edited by Walter L. Buenger and Robert A. Calvert, 163–196. College Station: Texas A&M University Press, 1991.

Dillon, Merton L. "Benjamin Lundy in Texas." *Southwestern Historical Quarterly* 63 (1959): 46–62.

Douglas, LaNelle S. "Religious Work Done by the Texas Baptists Among the Negroes in Texas from 1836 to 1873." Master's thesis, Sam Houston State University, 1967.

Drake, David. "'Joe,' Alamo Hero." *Negro History Bulletin* 44 (1981): 34–35.

Everett, Mary. "A Texas Plantation: Then and Now." *Sewanee Review* 44 (October-December 1936): 386–404.

Ewing, Floyd F. Jr. "Origins of Unionist Sentiment on the West Texas Frontier." *West Texas Historical Association Year Book* 32 (1956): 3–29.

Hunter, J. Marvin. "Faithful Negro Wields Axe in Big Fight." *Frontier Times* 1 (1934): 1–2.

_______. "Hendrick Arnold, Negro, a Texas Patriot." *Frontier Times* 15 (1937): 42–43.

_______. "White Men Ate Nigger Meat." *Frontier Times* 26 (1949): 208.

Israel, Charles A. "From Biracial to Segregated Churches: Black and White Protestants in Houston, Texas, 1840–1870." *Southwestern Historical Quarterly* 101 (1998): 429–458.

Jones, Marie Beth. *Peach Point Plantation: The First 150 Years*. Waco: Texian Press, 1982.

Katz, William Loren. "William Goings and Greenbury Logan—Patriots of the Lone Star Republic." In *Black People Who Made the Old West*, 45–48. Trenton, N.J.: Africa World Press, 1992.

Kilman, Ed. "Negroes at San Jacinto." *Frontier Times* 24 (1947): 472–474.

Kubiak, Daniel James. *Monument to a Black Man.* San Antonio: Naylor Company, 1972.

Lale, Max S., and Randolph B. Campbell, eds. "The Plantation Journal of John B. Webster, February 17, 1858–November 5, 1859." *Southwestern Historical Quarterly* 84 (1980): 58–77.

Ledbetter, Barbara A. Neal. *Fort Belknap Frontier Saga: Indians, Negroes, and Anglo-Americans on the Texas Frontier.* Burnet, Tex.: Eakin Press, 1982.

Ledbetter, Billy D. "Slavery, Fear, and Disunion in the Lone Star State: Texas' Attitude toward Secession and the Union, 1846–1861. Ph.D. dissertation, North Texas State University, 1972.

_______. "White Over Black in Texas: Racial Attitudes in the Ante-Bellum Period." *Phylon* 34 (1973): 406–418.

Marten, James. *Texas Divided: Loyalty and Dissent in the Lone Star State, 1856–1874.* Lexington: University Press of Kentucky, 1990.

Moorer, Virginia C. "The Free Negro in Texas, 1845–1860." Master's thesis, Lamar State College of Technology, 1969.

Muir, Andrew Forest. "The Free Negro in Fort Bend County, Texas." *Journal of Negro History* 33 (1948): 79–85.

_______. "The Free Negro in Galveston County, Texas." *Negro History Bulletin* 22 (1958): 68–70.

_______. "The Free Negro in Harris County, Texas." *Southwestern Historical Quarterly* 46 (1943): 214–238.

_______. "The Free Negro in Jefferson and Orange Counties, Texas." *Journal of Negro History* 35 (1950): 183–206.

Nash, A. E. Keir. "Texas Justice in the Age of Slavery: Appeals Concerning Blacks and the Antebellum State Supreme Court." *Houston Law Review* 8 (January 1971): 438–456.

_______. "The Texas Supreme Court and Trial Rights of Blacks, 1845–1860." *Journal of American History* 58 (1971): 622–642.

Newsome, Zoie Odom. "Antislavery Sentiment in Texas, 1821–1861." Master's thesis, Texas Technological College, 1968.

Norton, Wesley. "The Methodist Episcopal Church and the Civil Disturbances in North Texas in 1859 and 1860." *Southwestern Historical Quarterly* 68 (1965): 317–341.

Platter, Allen Andrew. "Educational, Social, and Economic Characteristics of the Plantation Culture in Brazoria County." Ed. D. dissertation, University of Houston, 1962.

Porter, Kenneth Wiggins. *The Negro on the American Frontier.* New York: Arno Press, 1971.

_______. "Negroes and Indians on the Texas Frontier, 1834–1874." *Southwestern Historical Quarterly* 53 (1949): 151–163.

_______. "Negroes and Indians on the Texas Frontier, 1831–1876: A Study in Race and Culture, I." *Journal of Negro History* 41 (1956): 185–214.

_______. "Negroes and Indians on the Texas Frontier, 1831–1876: A Study in Race and Culture, II." *Journal of Negro History* 41 (1956): 285–310.

Prather, Patricia Smith, and Jane Clements Monday. *From Slave to Statesman: The Legacy of Joshua Houston, Servant to Sam Houston.* Denton: University of North Texas Press, 1993.

Prince, Diane Elizabeth. "William Goyens, Free Black on the Texas Frontier." In *The Bicentennial Commemorative History of Nacogdoches*, 73–76. Nacogdoches, Tex.: Nacogdoches Jaycees, 1976.

_______. "William Goyens, Free Negro on the Texas Frontier." Master's thesis, Stephen F. Austin State College, 1967.

Rippy, J. Fred. "Border Troubles along the Rio Grande, 1848–1860." *Southwestern Historical Quarterly* 23 (1919): 91–111.

Robinson, Richard R. "Racism as an Aspect of the Violent History of the State of Texas in the 1830s and 1840s." Master's thesis, Kean College of New Jersey, 1979.

Roper, Laura W. "Frederick Law Olmsted and the Western Texas Free-Soil Movement." *American Historical Review* 56 (1950): 58–64.

Schoen, Harold R. "The Free Negro in the Republic of Texas." Master's thesis, University of Texas, 1933.

_______. "The Free Negro in the Republic of Texas." Ph.D. dissertation, University of Texas, 1938.

_______. "The Free Negro in the Republic of Texas: The Extent of Discrimination and Its Effects." *Southwestern Historical Quarterly* 41 (1937): 83–108.

_______. "The Free Negro in the Republic of Texas: The Free Negro and the Texas Revolution." *Southwestern Historical Quarterly* 40 (1936): 26–34.

_______. "The Free Negro in the Republic of Texas: The Law in Practice." *Southwestern Historical Quarterly* 40 (1937): 267–289.

_______. "The Free Negro in the Republic of Texas: Legal Status." *Southwestern Historical Quarterly* 40 (1937): 169–199.

_______. "The Free Negro in the Republic of Texas: Manumission." *Southwestern Historical Quarterly* 40 (1936): 85–113.

_______. "The Free Negro in the Republic of Texas: Origin of the Free Negro in the Republic of Texas." *Southwestern Historical Quarterly* 39 (1936): 292–308.

Schwartz, Rosalie. *Across the Rio to Freedom: United States Negroes in Mexico*. El Paso: Texas Western Press, 1975.

_______. "Runaway Negroes: Mexico as an Alternative for United States Blacks, 1825–1860." Master's thesis, San Diego State University, 1974.

Shively, Charles. "An Option for Freedom in Texas, 1840–1844." *Journal of Negro History* 50 (1965): 77–96.

Silverthorne, Elizabeth. *Plantation Life in Texas*. College Station: Texas A&M University Press, 1986.

Smallwood, James M. "Blacks in Antebellum Texas: A Reappraisal." *Red River Valley Historical Review* 2 (Winter 1975): 443–466.

Smyrl, Frank H. "Unionism, Abolitionism, and Vigilantism in Texas, 1856–1865." Master's thesis, University of Texas, 1961.

Stern, Madeline B. "Stephen Pearl Andrews, Abolitionist, and the Annexation of Texas." *Southwestern Historical Quarterly* 67 (1964): 491–523.

Strobel, Abner. *The Old Plantations and their Owners of Brazoria County*. Houston: Privately printed, 1926.

Trammell, Camilla Davis. *Seven Pines, its Occupants and their Letters, 1825–1872*. Houston: Privately printed, 1986.

Treat, Victor H. "William Goyens: Free Negro Entrepreneur." In *Black Leaders: Texans for Their Times*, edited by Alwyn Barr and Robert A. Calvert, 19–47. Austin: Texas State Historical Association, 1981.

Tyler, Ronnie C. "The Callahan Expedition of 1855: Indians or Negroes?" *Southwestern Historical Quarterly* 70 (1967): 574–585.

Vlach, John Michael. "Black Folk Crafts in Antebellum Texas." In *Texana I: The Frontier*, Proceedings of a Humanities Forum Held at Round Top, Texas, May 1–3, 1980, edited by LeRoy Johnson Jr., 33–36. Austin: Texas Historical Commission, 1983.

Winegarten, Ruthe. "Free Women of Color." In *Black Texas Women: 150 Years of Trial and Triumph*, 1–13. Austin: University of Texas Press, 1995.

Woolfolk, George R. *The Free Negro in Texas, 1800–1860: A Study in Cultural Compromise*. Ann Arbor: University Microfilms, 1976.

_______. "The Free Negro and Texas, 1836–1860." *Journal of Mexican-American History* 3 (1973): 49–75.

_______. "Turner's Safety Valve and Free Negro Westward Migration." *Pacific Northwest Quarterly* 56 (1965): 125–130.

4. Slavery to 1865

Bruce A. Glasrud and Sheron Smith-Savage

Picking cotton.

The UT Institute of Texan Cultures, No. 68-1296
Library of Congress, Prints and Photo Division

Addington, Wendell C. "Slave Insurrections in Texas." *Journal of Negro History* 35 (1950): 408–434.

Anderson, John Q. "Old John and the Master." *Southern Folklore Quarterly* 25 (1961): 195–197.

Ashburn, Karl E. "Slavery and Cotton Production in Texas." *Southwestern Social Science Quarterly* 14 (1933): 257–271.

Atkinson, Lillie E. "Slavery in the Economy of Colorado County, 1822–1863." Master's thesis, Prairie View Agricultural and Mechanical College, 1954.

Baker, T. Lindsay. "More Than Just 'Possum'n Taters: Texas African-American Foodways in the WPA Slave Narratives." In *Juneteenth Texas: Essays in African-American Folklore*, edited by Francis E. Abernethy, Carolyn Fiedler Satterwhite, Patrick B. Mullen, and Alan B. Govenar, 95–128. Publications of the Texas Folklore Society No. 54. Denton: University of North Texas Press, 1996.

Baker, T. Lindsay, and Julie P. Baker, eds. *Till Freedom Cried Out: Memories of Texas Slave Life*. College Station: Texas A&M University Press, 1997.

Barker, Eugene C. "The African Slave Trade in Texas." *Texas Historical Association Quarterly* 6 (1902): 145–158.

_______. "The Influence of Slavery in the Colonization of Texas." *Mississippi Valley Historical Review* 11 (June 1924): 3–36.

_______. "The Influence of Slavery in the Colonization of Texas." *Southwestern Historical Quarterly* 28 (1924): 1–33.

Barrett, Faydell Lomma. "Slavery in the Economy of San Augustine County, 1822–1863." Master's thesis, Prairie View Agricultural and Mechanical College, 1963.

Barriffe, Eugene Jr. "Some Aspects of Slavery and Anti-Slavery Movements in Texas, 1830–1860." Master's thesis, University of Southwestern Louisiana, 1968.

Blassingame, John W., ed. "Lavinia Bell." In *Slave Testimony: Two Centuries of Letters, Speeches, Interviews, and Autobiographies,* 341–345. Baton Rouge: Louisiana State University Press, 1977.

Brown, Kenneth L. "Material Culture and Community Structure: The Slave and Tenant Community at Levi Jordan's Plantation, 1848–1892." In *Working Toward Freedom: Slave Society and Domestic Economy in the American South,* edited by Larry E. Hudson Jr., 95–118. Rochester, N.Y.: University of Rochester Press, 1994.

Brown, Kenneth L., and Doreen C. Cooper. "Structural Continuity in an African-American Slave and Tenant Community." *Historical Archeology* 24.4 (1990): 7–19.

Bugbee, Lester E. "Slavery in Early Texas." *Political Science Quarterly* 13 (September-December 1898): 398–412, 648–688.

Bullock, Henry Allen. "A Hidden Passage in the Slave Regime." *The Black Experience in America: Selected Essays*, edited by James C. Curtis and Lewis L. Gould, 3–32. Austin: University of Texas Press, 1970.

Campbell, Randolph B. *An Empire for Slavery: The Peculiar Institution in Texas, 1821–1865.* Baton Rouge: Louisiana State University Press, 1989.

_______. "The End of Slavery in Texas: A Research Note." *Southwestern Historical Quarterly* 88 (1984): 71–80.

_______. "Harrison County: A Study of Plantation Economics." In *Texana II: Cultural Heritage of the Plantation South*, edited by Candace Volz, 13–18. Austin: Texas Historical Commission, 1982.

_______. "Human Property: The Negro Slave in Harrison County, 1850–1860." *Southwestern Historical Quarterly* 76 (1973): 384–396.

_______. "Intermittent Slave Ownership: Texas as a Test Case." *Journal of Southern History* 51 (1985): 15–30.

_______. "Local Archives as a Source of Slave Prices: Harrison County, Texas, as a Test Case." *The Historian* 36 (1974): 660–669.

_______. "Planters and Plain Folk: Harrison County, Texas, as a Test Case, 1850–1860." *Journal of Southern History* 40 (1974): 369–398.

_______. "The Productivity of Slave Labor in East Texas, 1850–1860." *Louisiana Studies* 13 (Summer 1974): 154–172.

_______. "The Slave Family in Antebellum Texas." In *The American Family*, 1–28. Victoria, Tex.: Victoria College Press, 1988.

_______. "The Slave Hire System in Texas." *American Historical Review* 93 (1988): 107–114.

_______. "Slaveholding in Harrison County, 1850–1860: A Statistical Profile." *East Texas Historical Journal* 11 (Spring 1973): 18–27.

_______. "Slavery." In *The New Handbook of Texas*, edited by Ron Tyler, Douglas E. Barnett, Roy R. Barkley, Penelope C. Anderson, and Mark F. Odintz, vol. 5, 1081–1083. Austin: Texas State Historical Association, 1996.

Campbell, Randolph B., and Richard G. Lowe. "The Slave-Breeding Hypothesis: A Demographic Comment on the 'Buying' and 'Selling' States." *Journal of Southern History* 42 (1976): 401–412.

_______. "Slave Property and the Distribution of Wealth in Texas, 1860." *Journal of American History* 63 (1976): 316–324.

Campbell, Randolph B., and Donald K. Pickens. "'My Dearest Husband': A Texas Slave's Love Letter, 1862." *Journal of Negro History* 65 (Fall 1980): 361–364.

Carlson, Shawn Bonath, ed. *The Anson Jones Plantation: Archaeological and Historical Investigations at 41WT5 and 41WT6, Washington County, Texas.* Reports of Investigations No. 2. College Station: Center for Environmental Archaeology, Texas A&M University, 1995.

Carnathan, W. J. "The Attempt to Re-Open the African Slave Trade in Texas, 1857–1858." *Proceedings of the Sixth Annual Convention of the Southwestern Political and Social Science Association* (1925): 134–144.

Carrigan, William Dean. "Between South and West: Race, Class, and Power in Central Texas, 1836–1916." Ph.D. dissertation, Emory University, 1999.

_______. "Slavery on the Frontier: The Peculiar Institution in Central Texas." *Slavery and Abolition* 20 (August 1999): 63–86.

Cravens, John N. "Felix 'Zero' Ervin: Louisiana Negro Slave and East Texas Freeman." *East Texas Historical Journal* 10 (Fall 1972): 125–130.

Curlee, Abigail Scott (Holbrook). "The History of a Texas Slave Plantation, 1831–1863." Master's thesis, University of Texas, 1922.

_______. "A Study of Texas Slave Plantations, 1822–1865." Ph.D. dissertation, University of Texas, 1932.

_______. "A Glimpse of Life on Antebellum Slave Plantations in Texas." *Southwestern Historical Quarterly* 76 (1973): 361–383.

_______. "The History of a Texas Slave Plantation, 1831–1863." *Southwestern Historical Quarterly* 26 (1922): 79–127.

Dodgen, Mary. "The Slave Plantations as an Educational Institution." Master's thesis, University of Texas, 1932.

Eighmy, John Lee. "The Baptists and Slavery: An Examination of the Origins and Benefits of Segregation." *Social Science Quarterly* 49 (1968): 666–673.

Elam, Richard Lee. "Behold the Fields: Texas Baptists and the Problem of Slavery." Ph.D. dissertation, University of North Texas, 1993.

Engelking, Johanna Rosa. "Slavery in Texas." Master's thesis, Baylor University, 1933.

Foler, Karen Bigelow. "The Slave Question in Anglo-Texan Relations, 1836–1845: An Analysis of British Policy." Master's thesis, University of Wisconsin, 1966.

Fornell, Earl W. "The Abduction of Free Negroes and Slaves in Texas." *Southwestern Historical Quarterly* 60 (1957): 369–380.

_______. "Agitation in Texas for Reopening the Slave Trade." *Southwestern Historical Quarterly* 60 (1956): 245–259.

_______. "Texas and Filibusters in the 1850s." *Southwestern Historical Quarterly* 59 (1956): 411–428.

Freeman, Marcus A. "Taxes and Slavery in Texas, 1845–1860." Master's thesis, Prairie View Agricultural and Mechanical College, 1956.

Fuller, John D. P. "Slavery Propaganda During the Mexican War." *Southwestern Historical Quarterly* 38 (1935): 235–245.

Hamilton, Jeff, and Lenoir Hunt. *My Master: The Inside Story of Sam Houston and His Times*. Dallas: Manfred, Van Nort, and Company, 1940.

Harper, Cecil Jr. "Slavery without Cotton: Hunt County, Texas, 1846–1864." *Southwestern Historical Quarterly* 88 (1985): 387–405.

Hatch, James. "Negro Mother Murders Her Own Child." *Frontier Times* 1 (1924): 1–2.

Hawkins, Marjorie Brown. "Runaway Slaves in Texas." Master's thesis, Prairie View Agricultural and Mechanical College, 1952.

Haygood, Tamara Miner. "Use and Distribution of Slave Labor in Harris County, Texas, 1830–60." In *Black Dixie: Afro-Texan History and Culture in Houston*, edited by Howard Beeth and Cary D. Wintz, 32–53. College Station: Texas A&M University Press, 1992.

Henry, Willie Ray. "Slavery in the Economy of Brazos County, 1821–1860." Master's thesis, Prairie View Agricultural and Mechanical College, 1954.

Henson, Margaret Swett. "Development of Slave Codes in Texas, 1821–1845." Master's thesis, University of Houston, 1969.

Holbrook, Abigail Curlee. "A Glimpse of Life on Antebellum Slave Plantations in Texas." *Southwestern Historical Quarterly* 76 (1973): 361–383.

Howren, Alleine. "Causes and Origins of the Decree of April 6, 1830." *Southwestern Historical Quarterly* 16 (1913): 378–422.

Hunter, Irene P. "Slavery in the Economy of Cherokee County, Texas, 1846–1860." Master's thesis, Prairie View Agricultural and Mechanical College, 1956.

Hunter, J. Marvin. "Negro Slave [Tom Sullivan] Recalled Frontier History." *Frontier Times* 28 (1950): 47–54.

_______. "Runaway Slaves in Texas." *Frontier Times* 26 (1948): 40–43.

Hutchinson, Janis. "The Age-Sex Structure of the Slave Population in Harris County, Texas: 1850 and 1860." *American Journal of Physical Anthropology* 74 (October 1987): 231–238.

Jackson, Jack M. "Archaeological Investigations of Slave Plantations." In *Texana II: Cultural Heritage of the Plantation South,* edited by Candace Volz, 51–57. Austin: Texas Historical Commission, 1982.

Jackson, Susan. "Slavery in Houston: The 1850's." *The Houston Review* 2 (Summer 1980): 66–82.

Junkins, Enda. "Slave Plots, Insurrections, and Acts of Violence in the State of Texas, 1828–1865." Master's thesis, Baylor University, 1969.

Kahn, Joan M. "Slave Labor on an Ante-Bellum Texas Plantation as Revealed in The Ashbel Smith Papers." Master's thesis, Columbia University, 1951.

Kerrigan, William T. "Race, Expansion, and Slavery in Eagle Pass, Texas, 1852." *Southwestern Historical Quarterly* 101 (1998): 275–301.

Lack, Paul D. "The Black Texans and Slavery in Revolution and War." In *The Texas Revolutionary Experience: A Political and Social History, 1835–1836,* 238–252, 309–311. College Station: Texas A&M University Press, 1992.

_______. "Dave: A Rebellious Slave." In *Black Leaders: Texans for Their Times*, edited by Alwyn Barr and Robert A. Calvert, 1–18. Austin: Texas State Historical Association, 1981.

_______. "Slavery and the Texas Revolution." *Southwestern Historical Quarterly* 89 (1985): 181–202.

_______. "Slavery and Vigilantism in Austin, Texas, 1840–1860." *Southwestern Historical Quarterly* 85 (1981): 1–20.

_______. "Slavery, Urban." In *The New Handbook of Texas*, edited by Ron Tyler, Douglas E. Barnett, Roy R. Barkley, Penelope C. Anderson, and Mark F. Odintz, vol. 5, 1083–1084. Austin: Texas State Historical Association, 1996.

_______. "Urban Slavery in the Southwest." Ph.D. dissertation, Texas Tech University, 1973.

_______. "Urban Slavery in the Southwest." *Red River Valley Historical Review* 6 (Spring 1981): 8–27.

Ledbetter, Barbara A. "Black and Mexican Slaves in Young County, Texas, 1856–1865." *West Texas Historical Association Year Book* 56 (1980): 100–102.

Ledbetter, Billy D. "Slavery, Fear, and Disunion in the Lone Star State: Texas' Attitude Toward Secession and the Union, 1846–1861. Ph.D. dissertation, North Texas State University, 1972.

_______. "Slave Unrest and White Panic: The Impact of Black Republicanism in Ante-Bellum Texas." *Texana* 10 (1972): 335–350.

Lockhart, W. E. "The Slave Code of Texas." Master's thesis, Baylor University, 1929.

Lowe, Richard G., and Randolph B. Campbell. "The Slave-Breeding Hypothesis: A Demographic Comment on the 'Buying' and 'Selling' States." *Journal of Southern History* 42 (1976): 401–412.

Lyon, Annie Laurie Kurtz. "Slavery as an Economic and Political Factor in the Texas Gubernatorial Elections of 1857 and 1859." Master's thesis, University of Houston, 1964.

Maddox, Joleene. "Slavery in Texas, 1836–1860." Master's thesis, Southwest Texas State University, 1969.

Marks, Paula Mitchell. *Hands to the Spindle: Texas Women and Home Textile Production, 1822–1880.* College Station: Texas A&M University Press, 1996.

Marten, James Alan. "Slaves and Rebels: The Peculiar Institution in Texas, 1861–1865." *East Texas Historical Journal* 28.1 (1990): 29–36.

Mattison, Reverend H. "Louisa Picquet, the Octoroon: A Tale of Southern Slave Life." In *Black Women in Nineteenth Century American Life: Their Words, Their Thoughts, Their Feelings*, edited by Bert James Loewenberg and Ruth Bogin, 54–69. University Park: Pennsylvania State University Press, 1976.

McPherson, Hallie M. "Slavery in Texas." Master's thesis, University of Chicago, 1924.

Meier, Frederick L. "A Study of Slavery in Microcosm: Lamar County, Texas, 1850–1860." Master's thesis, Fort Hays State University, 1971.

Merk, Frederick. *Slavery and the Annexation of Texas*. New York: A. A. Knopf, 1972.

Moretta, John. "The Censoring of Lorenzo Sherwood: The Politics of Railroads, Slavery and Southernism in Antebellum Texas." *East Texas Historical Journal* 35.2 (1997): 39–52.

Nash, A. E. Keir. "Texas Justice in the Age of Slavery: Appeals Concerning Blacks and the Antebellum State Supreme Court." *Houston Law Review* 8 (January 1971): 438–456.

Palm, Reba W. "Protestant Churches and Slavery in Matagorda County." *East Texas Historical Journal* 14 (Spring 1976): 3–8.

_______. "Slavery in Microcosm: Matagorda County, Texas." Master's thesis, Texas A&I University, 1971.

Passmore, Leonard. "Heroism of a Negro Slave [Albert Chandler]." *Frontier Times* 6 (1928): 102–103.

Purcell, Linda Myers. "Slavery in the Republic of Texas." Master's thesis, North Texas State University, 1982.

Ragsdale, Crystal Sasse. "The South-Central Texas Slavery Research Project." In *Texana II: Cultural Heritage of the Plantation South,* edited by Candace Volz, 45–49. Austin: Texas Historical Commission, 1982.

Ramsdell, Charles W. "The Natural Limits of Slavery Expansion." *Mississippi Valley Historical Review* 16 (September 1929): 151–171.

Reynolds, Donald E. "Reluctant Martyr: Anthony Bewley and the Texas Slave Insurrection Panic of 1860." *Southwestern Historical Quarterly* 96 (1993): 344–361.

_______. "Smith County and Its Neighbors during the Slave Insurrection Panic of 1860." *Chronicles of Smith County* 10 (Fall 1971): 1–8.

_______. "Vigilante Law During the Texas Slave Panic of 1860." *Locus: An Historical Journal of Regional Perspectives* 2 (Spring 1990): 172–186.

Robbins, Fred. "The Origin and Development of the African Slave Trade in Galveston, Texas, and Surrounding Areas from 1816 to 1836." *East Texas Historical Journal* 9 (October 1971): 153–161.

_______. "The Origins and Development of the African Slave Trade into Texas, 1816–1860." Master's thesis, University of Houston, 1972.

Robbins, Hal. "Slavery in the Economy of Matagorda County, Texas, 1839–1860." Master's thesis, Prairie View Agricultural and Mechanical College, 1952.

Robertson, Robert J. "Slavery and the Coming of the Civil War as Seen in *The Beaumont Banner*." *East Texas Historical Journal* 34.1 (1996): 14–29.

Rogers, Marjorie. "Aunt Nellie Smith, Slave Mammy." *Frontier Times* 10 (1932): 98–100.

Sauer, Sandra R. "African American Spirituality at Fanthorp Inn." In *Fanthorp Inn State Historical Park (41GM79), Grimes County, Texas: Archeological Excavations, 1983–1989*, 79–86. Reports of Investigations No. 116. Austin: Prewitt and Associates and Texas Parks and Wildlife Department, 1998.

Smallwood, James M. "Slave Insurrections." In *The New Handbook of Texas*, edited by Ron Tyler, Douglas E. Barnett, Roy R. Barkley, Penelope C. Anderson, and Mark F. Odintz, vol. 5, 1080–1081. Austin: Texas State Historical Association, 1996.

Smith, Thomas H. "African Americans in Dallas: From Slavery to Freedom." In *Dallas Reconsidered: Essays in Local History*, edited by Michael V. Hazel, 122–133. Dallas: Three Forks Press, 1995.

Sowell, A. J. "The Heroism of a Faithful Negro Slave." *Frontier Times* 1 (1924): 4–9.

Stein, Bill, ed. "The Slave Narratives of Colorado County." *Nesbitt Memorial Library Journal: A Journal of Colorado County History* 3 (January 1993): 3–32.

Telford, Margaret J. A. "Slave Resistance in Texas." Master's thesis, Southern Methodist University, 1975.

Tyler, Ronnie C. "Fugitive Slaves in Mexico." *Journal of Negro History* 57 (1972): 1–12.

_______. "Slave Owners and Runaway Slaves in Texas." Master's thesis, Texas Christian University, 1966.

Tyler, Ronnie C., and Lawrence R. Murphy, eds. *The Slave Narratives of Texas*. Austin: Encino Press, 1974.

White, William W. "The Texas Slave Insurrection of 1860." *Southwestern Historical Quarterly* 52 (1949): 259–285.

Winegarten, Ruthe. "Slavery." In *Black Texas Women: 150 Years of Trial and Triumph*, 15–37. Austin: University of Texas Press, 1995.

_______. "Texas Slave Families." *Texas Humanist* 7 (March-April 1985): 29–30, 33.

Winningham, Mrs. David. "Sam Houston and Slavery." *Texana* 3 (1965): 93–104.

Wofford, Emma L. "A Glimpse of the Plantation Life." *Frontier Times* 12 (1935): 146–148.

Woolfolk, George R. "Cotton Capitalism and Slave Labor in Texas." *Southwestern Social Science Quarterly* 37 (1956): 43–52.

_______. "Sources of the History of the Negro in Texas, With Special Reference to Their Implications for Research in Slavery." *Journal of Negro History* 42 (1957): 38–47.

Wooster, Ralph A. "Notes on Texas' Largest Slaveholders, 1860." *Southwestern Historical Quarterly* 65 (1961): 72–79.

Yanez, Aaron Mahr. "The UGRR on the Rio Grande." *Cultural Resource Management* 21.4 (1998): 41–44.

5. Civil War and Reconstruction, 1861–1874

Negro woman spinning cotton, ca. 1880s.

The UT Institute of Texan Cultures, No. 72-60
Texas State Archives, Texas State Library

Albrecht, Winnell. "The Black Codes of Texas." Master's thesis, Southwest Texas State University, 1969.

Ashcraft, Allan Coleman. "Texas, 1860–1866: The Lone Star State in the Civil War." Ph.D. dissertation, Columbia University, 1960.

Austerman, Wayne Randolph. "Black Regulars: The 41st Infantry in Texas, 1867–1869." Master's thesis, Louisiana State University, 1971.

Baenziger, Ann Patton (Malone). "Bold Beginnings: The Radical Program in Texas, 1870–1873." Master's thesis, Southwest Texas State University, 1970.

_______. "Matt Gaines: Reconstruction Politician." In *Black Leaders: Texans for Their Times*, edited by Alwyn Barr and Robert A. Calvert, 49–81. Austin: Texas State Historical Association, 1981.

_______. "The Texas State Police During Reconstruction: A Reexamination." *Southwestern Historical Quarterly* 72 (1969): 470–491.

Baggett, James Alex. "The Rise and Fall of the Texas Radicals, 1867–1883." Ph.D. dissertation, North Texas State University, 1972.

Bailey, Anne J. "A Texas Cavalry Raid: Reaction to Black Soldiers and Contrabands." *Civil War History* 35 (1989): 138–152.

_______. "Was There a Massacre at Poison Spring?" *Military History of the Southwest* 20 (Fall 1990): 157–168.

Bain, Kenneth Ray. "The Changing Basis of the Republican Party, 1865–1877." Master's thesis, North Texas State University, 1970.

Baker, T. Lindsay. "The First Juneteenth." *Traveling Historic Texas* (June/July 1992): 3.

Barr, Alwyn. "Black Legislators of Reconstruction Texas." *Civil War History* 32 (1986): 340–352.

Boggess, George. "Political Activities of Negroes in the Reconstruction of Texas." Master's thesis, Howard University, 1938.

Brewer, J. Mason. *Negro Legislators of Texas and Their Descendants: A History of the Negro in Texas Politics from Reconstruction to Disfranchisement*. Dallas: Mathis Publishing, 1935.

Brock, Euline Williams. "Black Political Leadership during Reconstruction." Ph.D. dissertation, North Texas State University, 1974.

Brown, Arthur Z. "The Participation of Negroes in the Reconstruction Legislatures of Texas." *Negro History Bulletin* 20 (January 1957): 87–88.

Calvert, Robert A., ed. "The Freedmen and Agricultural Prosperity." *Southwestern Historical Quarterly* 76 (1973): 461–472.

Campbell, Randolph B. "The Burden of Local Black Leadership during Reconstruction: A Research Note." *Civil War History* 39 (1993): 148–153.

_______. "Carpetbagger Rule in Reconstruction Texas: An Enduring Myth." *Southwestern Historical Quarterly* 97 (1994): 587–596.

_______. "The End of Slavery in Texas: A Research Note." *Southwestern Historical Quarterly* 88 (1984): 71–80.

_______. *Grass-Roots Reconstruction in Texas, 1865–1880*. Baton Rouge: Louisiana State University Press, 1997.

_______. "Grass Roots Reconstruction: The Personnel of County Government in Texas, 1865–1876." *Legacies: A History Journal for Dallas and North Central Texas* 5 (1993): 4–12.

_______. *A Southern Community in Crisis: Harrison County, Texas, 1850–1880*. Austin: Texas State Historical Association, 1983.

_______. "Statehood, Civil War, and Reconstruction, 1846–76." In *Texas through Time: Evolving Interpretations*, edited by Walter L. Buenger and Robert A. Calvert, 163–196. College Station: Texas A&M University Press, 1991.

Cantrell, Gregg. "Racial Violence and Reconstruction Politics in Texas, 1867–1868." *Southwestern Historical Quarterly* 93 (1990): 333–355.

Carlson, Paul H. "William R. Shafter, Black Troops, and the Opening of the Llano Estacado, 1870–1875." *Panhandle-Plains Historical Review* 47 (1974): 1–18.

Carrier, John Pressley. "A Political History of Texas during the Reconstruction, 1865–1874." Ph.D. dissertation, Vanderbilt University, 1971.

Chunn, Prentis Walter. "Education and Politics, a Study of the Negro in Reconstruction Texas." Master's thesis, Southwest Texas State College, 1957.

Cohen-Lack, Nancy. "A Struggle for Sovereignty: National Consolidation, Emancipation, and Free Labor in Texas, 1865." *Journal of Southern History* 58 (1992): 57–98.

Colby, Ira Christopher. "The Freedmen's Bureau in Texas and Its Impact on the Emerging Social Welfare System and Black-White Social Relations, 1865–1885." Sw.D. dissertation, University of Pennsylvania, 1984.

Crews, John Robert. "Reconstruction in Brownsville, Texas." Master's thesis, Texas Tech University, 1969.

Crouch, Barry A. "'All the Vile Passions': The Texas Black Code of 1866." *Southwestern Historical Quarterly* 97 (1993): 13–34.

_______. "Black Dreams and White Justice [Texas, 1865–1868]." *Prologue* 6 (1974): 255–265.

_______. "The 'Cords of Love': Legalizing Black Marital and Family Rights in Postwar Texas." *Journal of Negro History* 79 (1994): 334–351.

_______. *The Freedman's Bureau and Black Texans*. Austin: University of Texas Press, 1992.

_______. "The Freedmen's Bureau and the 30th Sub-District of Texas: Smith County and Its Environs during Reconstruction." *Chronicles of Smith County, Texas* 11 (Spring 1972): 15–30.

_______. "The Freedmen's Bureau in Beaumont." *Texas Gulf Historical and Biographical Record* 28 (1992): 8–27.

_______. "Freedmen's Bureau Records: Texas, A Case Study." In *Afro-American History: Sources for Research*, edited by Robert L. Clarke, 74–94. Washington, D.C.: Howard University Press, 1981.

_______. "Guardian of the Freedpeople: Texas Freedmen's Bureau Agents and the Black Community." *Southern Studies* 31 (1992): 185–201.

_______. "Hesitant Recognition: Texas Black Politicians, 1865–1900." *East Texas Historical Journal* 31.1 (1993): 41–59.

_______. "Hidden Sources of Black History: The Texas Freedmen's Bureau Records as a Case Study." *Southwestern Historical Quarterly* 83 (1980): 211–226.

_______. "Seeking Equality: Houston Black Women during Reconstruction." In *Black Dixie: Afro-Texan History and Culture in Houston*, edited by Howard Beeth and Cary D. Wintz, 54–73. College Station: Texas A&M University Press, 1992.

_______. "Self-Determination and Local Black Leaders in Texas." *Phylon* 39 (1978): 344–355.

_______. "A Spirit of Lawlessness: White Violence; Texas Blacks, 1865–1868." *Journal of Social History* 18 (1984): 217–232.

_______. "'Unmanacling' Texas Reconstruction: A Twenty-Year Perspective." *Southwestern Historical Quarterly* 93 (1989): 275–302.

_______, ed. "View from Within: Letters of Gregory Barrett, Freedmen's Bureau Agent." *Chronicles of Smith County, Texas* 12 (Winter 1973): 13–28.

Crouch, Barry A., and Larry Madaras. "Reconstructing Black Families: Perspectives from the Texas Freedmen's Bureau Records." *Prologue* 18 (1986): 109–122.

Crouch, Barry A., and L. J. Schultz. "Crisis in Color: Racial Separation in Texas during Reconstruction." *Civil War History* 16 (1970): 37–49.

Dorsett, Jesse. "Blacks in Reconstruction Texas, 1865–1877." Ph.D. dissertation, Texas Christian University, 1981.

Douglas, LaNelle S. "Religious Work Done by the Texas Baptists among the Negroes in Texas from 1836 to 1873." Master's thesis, Sam Houston State University, 1967.

Dudney, Ross N. Jr. "Texas Reconstruction: The Role of the Bureau of Refugees, Freedmen and Abandoned Lands, 1865–1870, Smith County (Tyler), Texas." Master's thesis, Texas A&I University, 1986.

Elliott, Claude. "The Freedmen's Bureau in Texas." *Southwestern Historical Quarterly* 56 (1952): 1–24.

Faust, Drew Gilpin. "Trying to do a Man's Business: Gender Violence and Slave Management in Civil War Texas." In *Southern Stories in Peace and War*, edited by Drew Gilpin Faust, 174–192. Columbia: University of Missouri Press, 1992.

Fennell, Romey Jr. "The Negro in Texas Politics, 1865–1874." Master's thesis, North Texas State University, 1963.

Field, William T. Jr. "The Texas State Police, 1870–1873." *Texas Military History* 5 (Fall 1965): 131–141.

Gauss, John. "Give the Blacks Texas." *Civil War Times Illustrated* 29 (May 1990): 54–56.

Goodwyn, Lawrence C. "Populist Dreams and Negro Rights: East Texas as a Case Study." *American Historical Review* 76 (1971): 1435–1456.

Greene, A. C. "The Durable Society: Austin in the Reconstruction." *Southwestern Historical Quarterly* 72 (1969): 492–519.

Hagood, Louise Wimberley. "Negroes in Northeast Texas, 1850–1875." Master's thesis, East Texas State College, 1966.

Hall, Martin Hardwick. "Negroes with Confederate Troops in West Texas and New Mexico." *Password* 13 (1968): 11–12.

Hayman, Bettie. "A Short History of the Negro of Walker County, 1860–1942." Master's thesis, Sam Houston State Teachers College, 1942.

Hill, John Thomas. "The Negro in Texas during Reconstruction." Master's thesis, Texas Christian University, 1965.

Holland, J. K. "Freedmen in the Legislature." *Southwestern Historical Quarterly* 1 (1897): 125–126.

Hornsby, Alton Jr. "The Freedmen's Bureau Schools in Texas, 1865–1870." *Southwestern Historical Quarterly* 76 (1973): 397–417.

Houston, Darrell. "A Political History of Black Politicians of Ft. Bend County, Texas, during the Reconstruction Era." Master's thesis, Texas Southern University, 1979.

Keener, Charles V. "Racial Turmoil in Texas, 1865–1874." Master's thesis, North Texas State University, 1971.

Kinsey, Winston Lee. "The Immigrant in Texas Agriculture during Reconstruction." *Agricultural History* 53 (1979): 125–141.

_______. "Negro Labor in Texas, 1865–1876." Master's thesis, Baylor University, 1965.

Kremm, Thomas Wesley. "Race Relations in Texas, 1865 to 1870." Master's thesis, University of Houston, 1970.

LaPlante, Christopher. "Reconstruction in Dallas County, 1865–1873." Master's thesis, University of Texas at Arlington, 1974.

Ledbetter, Billy D. "White Texans' Attitudes toward the Political Equality of Negroes, 1865–1870." *Phylon* 40 (1979): 255–263.

Malone, Ann Patton. "Matt Gaines: Reconstruction Politician." In *Black Leaders: Texans For Their Times*, edited by Alwyn Barr and Robert A. Calvert, 49–81. Austin: Texas State Historical Association, 1981.

Marten, James Alan. "Drawing the Line: Dissent and Disloyalty in Texas, 1856–1874." Ph.D. dissertation, University of Texas at Austin, 1986.

_______. "Slaves and Rebels: The Peculiar Institution in Texas, 1861–1865." *East Texas Historical Journal* 28.1 (1990): 29–36.

Maxwell, Louise Passey. "Freedmantown: The Evolution of a Black Neighborhood in Houston, 1865–1880." Master's thesis, Rice University, 1993.

_______. "Freedmantown: The Origins of a Black Neighborhood in Houston, 1865–1880." In *Bricks Without Straw: A Comprehensive History of African Americans in Texas*, edited by David A. Williams, 125–152. Austin: Eakin Press, 1997.

Merseburger, Marion. "A Political History of Houston, Texas, during the Reconstruction Period as Recorded by the Press: 1868–1873." Master's thesis, Rice University, 1950.

Moneyhon, Carl H. "George T. Ruby and the Politics of Expediency in Texas." In *Southern Black Leaders in the Reconstruction Era*, edited by Howard N. Rabinowitz, 363–392. Urbana: University of Illinois Press, 1982.

_______. "Public Education and Texas Reconstruction Politics, 1871–1874." *Southwestern Historical Quarterly* 92 (1989): 393–416.

_______. *Republicanism in Reconstruction Texas*. Austin: University of Texas Press, 1980.

Moore, Richard R. "Radical Reconstruction: The Texas Choice." *East Texas Historical Journal* 16 (Spring 1978): 15–23.

Moring, Margaret Carol. "Brave Nigger Brit." Master's thesis, University of Texas at Austin, 1972. [Fiction]

Neal, Diane, and Thomas W. Kremm. "'What Shall We Do with the Negro?': The Freedmen's Bureau in Texas." *East Texas Historical Journal* 26 (Spring 1988): 36–45.

Nieman, Donald G. "African Americans and the Meaning of Freedom: Washington County, Texas, as a Case Study, 1865–1886." *Chicago Kent Law Review* 70 (1994): 541–579.

_______. "Black Political Power and Criminal Justice: Washington County, Texas, 1868–1884." *Journal of Southern History* 55 (1989): 391–420.

Nunn, William C. *Texas Under the Carpetbaggers*. Austin: University of Texas Press, 1962.

Owens, Nora Estelle. "Presidential Reconstruction in Texas: A Case Study." Ph.D. dissertation, Auburn University, 1983.

Passey, M. Louise. "Freedmantown: The Evolution of a Black Neighborhood in Houston, 1865–1880." Master's thesis, Rice University, 1993.

Pitre, Merline. "The Evolution of Black Political Participation in Reconstruction Texas." *East Texas Historical Journal* 26.1 (1988): 36–45.

_______. A Note on the Historiography of Blacks in the Reconstruction of Texas." *Journal of Negro History* 66 (1981): 340–348.

_______. "Richard Allen: The Chequered Career of Houston's First Black State Legislator." In *Black Dixie: Afro-Texan History and Culture in Houston,* edited by Howard Beeth and Cary D. Wintz, 74–83. College Station: Texas A&M University Press, 1992.

_______. *Through Many Dangers, Toils, and Snares: Black Leadership in Texas, 1868–1900.* Austin: Eakin Press, 1985.

Ramsdell, Charles William. "Presidential Reconstruction in Texas." *Quarterly of the Texas State Historical Association* 11 (April 1908): 288–294.

_______. *Reconstruction in Texas*. New York: Columbia University Press, 1910.

Rankin, Dan F. "The Role of the Negro Officeholder in the Reconstruction of the Southwest." Master's thesis, North Texas State University, 1954.

Richter, William L. "The Army and the Negro During Reconstruction, 1865–1875." *East Texas Historical Journal* 10 (Spring 1972): 7–13.

_______. *The Army in Texas during Reconstruction*. College Station: Texas A&M University Press, 1987.

_______. "'Devil Take Them All': Military Rule in Texas, 1862–1870." *Southern Studies* 25 (Spring 1986): 5–30.

_______. "'It Is Best to Go in Strong Handed': Army Occupations of Texas, 1865–1866." *Arizona and the West* 27 (Summer 1985): 113–142.

_______. "Outside . . . My Profession: The Army and Civil Affairs in Texas Reconstruction." *Military History of Texas and the Southwest* 9 (1971): 5–21.

_______. *Overreached on All Sides: The Freedmen's Bureau Administrators in Texas, 1865–1868.* College Station: Texas A&M University Press, 1991.

_______. "'The Revolver Rules the Day!': Colonel DeWitt C. Brown and the Freedman's Bureau in Paris, Texas, 1867–1868." *Southwestern Historical Quarterly* 93 (1990): 303–332.

_______. "Spread-Eagle Eccentricities: Military-Civilian Relations in Reconstruction Texas." *Texana* 8 (1970): 311–327.

_______. "Texas Politics and the United States Army, 1866–1867." *Military History of Texas and the Southwest* 10 (1972): 159–186.

_______. "Tyrant and Reformer: General Griffin Reconstructs Texas, 1865–1866." *Prologue* 10 (1978): 225–241.

_______. "'We Must Rubb Out and Begin Anew': The Army and the Republican Party in Texas Reconstruction, 1867–1870." *Civil War History* 19 (1973): 334–352.

_______. "Who Was the Real Head of the Texas Freedmen's Bureau? The Role of Brevet Colonel William H. Sinclair as Acting Assistant Inspector General." *Military History of the Southwest* 20 (Fall 1990): 121–156.

Russ, William A. Jr. "Radical Disfranchisement in Texas, 1867–1870." *Southwestern Historical Quarterly* 38 (1934): 40–52.

Shook, Robert W. "Federal Occupation and Administration of Texas, 1865–1870." Ph.D. dissertation, North Texas State University, 1970.

_______. "Federal Occupation and Administration of Texas, 1865–1870." *Texas Military History* 6 (Spring 1967): 3–45.

_______. "Toward a List of Reconstruction Loyalists." *Southwestern Historical Quarterly* 76 (1973): 315–320.

Smallwood, James M. "The Black Community in Reconstruction Texas: Readjustments in Religion and the Evolution of the Negro Church." *East Texas Historical Journal* 16 (Fall 1978): 16–28.

_______. "Black Education in Reconstruction Texas: The Contributions of the Freedmen's Bureau and Benevolent Societies." *East Texas Historical Journal* 19.1 (1981): 17–40.

_______. "Black Freedwomen after Emancipation: The Texas Experience." *Prologue* 27 (1995): 303–317.

_______. "Black Texans during Reconstruction, 1865–1874." Ph.D. dissertation, Texas Tech University, 1974.

_______. "Black Texans during Reconstruction: First Freedom." *East Texas Historical Journal* 14 (Spring 1976): 9–23.

_______. "Charles E. Culver: A Reconstruction Agent in Texas: The Work of Local Freedman's Bureau Agents and the Black Community." *Civil War History* 27 (1981): 350–361.

_______. "Early 'Freedom Schools': Black Self-Help and Education in Reconstruction Texas: A Case Study." *Negro History Bulletin* 41 (1978): 790–793.

_______. "Emancipation and the Black Family: A Case Study in Texas." *Social Science Quarterly* 57 (1977): 849–857.

_______. "The Freedman's Bureau Reconsidered: Local Agents and the Black Community." *Texana* 11 (1973): 309–320.

_______. "From Slavery to Freedom: Smith County's Black Community in 1870; a Statistical Overview." *Chronicles of Smith County, Texas* 18 (Summer 1979): 58–61.

_______. "G. T. Ruby: Galveston's Black Carpetbagger in Reconstruction Texas." *The Houston Review* 5 (Winter 1983): 24–33.

_______. "Perpetuation of Caste: Black Agricultural Workers in Reconstruction Texas." *Mid-America* 61 (1979): 5–23.

_______. *Time of Hope, Time of Despair: Black Texas during Reconstruction.* Port Washington, N.Y.: Kennikat Press, 1981.

_______. "When the Klan Rode: White Terror in Reconstruction Texas." *Journal of the West* 25 (October 1986): 4–13.

_______. "The Woodward Thesis Revisited: The Origins of Social Segregation in Texas." *Negro History Bulletin* (1984): 6–9.

Smith, Thomas H. "Conflict and Corruption: The Dallas Establishment vs. the Freedmen's Bureau Agent." *Legacies* 1 (Fall 1989): 24–30.

Sneed, Edgar P. "A Historiography of Reconstruction in Texas." *Southwestern Historical Quarterly* 72 (1969): 435–448.

Stripling, Paul Wayne. "The Negro Excision from Baptist Churches in Texas (1861–1870)." Ph.D. dissertation, Southwest Baptist Theological Seminary, 1967.

Thompson, Ester Lane. "The Influence of the Freedmen's Bureau on the Education of the Negro in Texas." Master's thesis, Texas Southern University, 1972.

Wade, Melvin. "The Independent Black Farmer in East Texas, 1865–1885." In *Texana II: Cultural Heritage of the Plantation South,* edited by Candace Volz, 89–92. Austin: Texas Historical Commission, 1982.

Wallace, Ernest. *Texas in Turmoil: The Saga of Texas, 1849–1875.* Austin: Steck-Vaughn, 1965.

Woods, Randall B. "George T. Ruby: A Black Militant in the White Business Community." *Red River Valley Historical Review* 1 (1974): 269–280.

Wooster, Ralph A. "The Civil War and Reconstruction in Texas." In *A Guide to the History of Texas,* edited by Light Townsend Cummins and Alvin R. Bailey Jr., 37–50. Westport, Conn.: Greenwood Press, 1988.

Work, Monroe N., comp. "Some Negro Members of Reconstruction Legislatures: Texas." *Journal of Negro History* 5 (1920): 111–113.

6. Cowboys

Unidentified cowboy on horseback, Rio Grande Plain of Texas, 1900s.

The UT Institute of Texan Cultures, No. 88-77
Courtesy of John Wildenthal Family

Acosta, Teresa Palomo. "Black Cowboys." In *The New Handbook of Texas*, edited by Ron Tyler, Douglas E. Barnett, Roy R. Barkley, Penelope C. Anderson, and Mark F. Odintz, vol. 1, 565–566. Austin: Texas State Historical Association, 1996.

Beverly, Bob. "The Negro Ranch Hand." *The Cattleman* 40 (May 1954): 56–64.

Baker, T. Lindsay. "Remembrances: Black Cowboy Life in Texas." In *Black Cowboys of Texas*, edited by Sara R. Massey, 23–38. College Station: Texas A&M University Press, 2000.

Brady, Marilyn Dell. "The Paynes of Texas: Black Seminole Cowboys of the Big Bend." In *African American Cowboys in Texas,* edited by Sara Massey, 255–272. College Station: Texas A&M University Press, 2000.

Branch, Hettye Wallace. *The Story of "80 John": A Biography of One of the Most Respected Negro Ranchmen in the Old West.* New York: Greenwich Book Publishers, 1960.

Brand, Donald D. "The Early History of the Range Cattle Industry in Northern Mexico." *Agricultural History* 35 (1961): 132–139.

Burroughs, Jean M. "Black Cowboys on the Open Range." *The Greater Llano Estacado Southwest Heritage* (Summer 1977): 13–14.

Carlson, Paul. "The Texas Background—Spanish or American?" *West Texas Historical Association Year Book* 52 (1976): 61–70.

Clayton, Lawrence. "Bill 'Tige' Avery." In *Cowboys Who Rode Proudly*, edited by J. Evetts Haley, 7–14. Midland, Tex.: Nita Stewart Haley Memorial Library, 1992.

Crane, R. C. "D. W. Wallace ('80 John'): A Negro Cattleman on the Texas Frontier." *West Texas Historical Association Year Book* 28 (1952): 113–118.

Davis, Alvin G. "Black Cowboys and Ranchers in Texas." *Heritage* (Winter 1994): 1–12.

Downey, Bill. *Tom Bass, Black Horseman.* St. Louis: Saddle and Bridle, 1975.

Durham, Philip. "The Lost Cowboy." *Midwest Journal* 7 (1955): 176–182.

_______. "The Negro Cowboy." *American Quarterly* 7 (1955): 291-302.

Durham, Philip, and Everett L. Jones. *The Adventures of the Negro Cowboys.* New York: Bantam Books, 1969.

_______. "Negro Cowboys." *American West* 1 (Fall 1964): 26–31, 87.

_______. *The Negro Cowboys.* Dodd: Mead, 1965. Lincoln: University of Nebraska Press, 1983.

_______. "Slaves on Horseback." *Pacific Historical Review* 33 (1964): 405–409.

Ehly, Jean. "'Bones' Hooks of the Panhandle." *Frontier Times* 37 (1963): 20–23.

Fuller, John H. "Ben Kinchlow: A Trail Driver on the Chisholm Trail." In *Black Cowboys of Texas*, edited by Sara R. Massey, 99–116. College Station: Texas A&M University Press, 2000.

Gale, Gill. "Texas Trail Ride, Negro Cowboys." *Ebony* 18 (May 1963): 115–122, 124.

Gillespie, A. S. "More About Negro Cowmen." *Cattleman* 23 (June 1936): 32.

Govenar, Alan. "Musical Traditions of Twentieth-Century African-American Cowboys." In *Juneteenth Texas: Essays in African-American Folklore,* edited by Francis Edward Abernethy, Carolyn Fiedler Satterwhite, Patrick B. Mullen, and Alan G. Govenar, 195–206. Publications of the Texas Folklore Society No. 54. Denton: University of North Texas Press, 1996.

Guice, John D. W. "Cattle Raisers of the Old Southwest: A Reinterpretation." *Western Historical Quarterly* 8 (April 1977): 167–189.

Hancock, Sibyl. *Bill Pickett: First Black Rodeo Star.* New York: Harcourt, Brace, Jovanovich, 1977.

Hanes, Colonel Bailey C. *Bill Pickett, Bulldogger: The Biography of a Black Cowboy.* Norman: University of Oklahoma Press, 1977.

Hendrix, John M. "Tribute Paid to Negro Cowmen." *Cattleman* 22 (February 1936): 24–26.

Johnson, Cecil. *Guts: Legendary Black Rodeo Cowboy Bill Pickett.* Fort Worth: Summit Group, 1994.

Jordan, Terry G. *Trails to Texas: Southern Roots of Western Cattle Ranching.* Lincoln: University of Nebraska Press, 1981.

Kelton, Elmer. "Man on the Wagontongue." In *They Won Their Spurs*, edited by Nelson Nye, 129–143. New York: Avon Books, 1962. [Fiction]

LeComte, Mary Lou. "Pickett, William." In *The New Handbook of Texas*, edited by Ron Tyler, Douglas E. Barnett, Roy R. Barkley, Penelope C. Anderson, and Mark F. Odintz, vol. 5, 191. Austin: Texas State Historical Association, 1996.

Lowry, Jack. "The Forgotten Cowboys." *Texas Highways* 38 (August 1991): 4–11.

Massey, Sara R., ed. *Black Cowboys of Texas.* College Station: Texas A&M University Press, 2000.

Morrisey, Richard J. "The Northward Expansion of Cattle Ranching in New Spain, 1550–1600." *Agricultural History* 25 (1951): 115–121.

Mundis, Jerrold J. "He Took the Bull by the Horns." *American Heritage* 19 (December 1967): 50–55.

Myres, Sandra L. "The Ranching Frontier: Spanish Institutional Backgrounds of the Plains Cattle Industry." In *Essays on the American West*, edited by Harold M. Hollingsworth and Sandra L. Myres, 19–39. Austin: University of Texas Press, 1969.

_______. "The Spanish Cattle Kingdom in the Province of Texas." *Texana* 4 (1966): 233–246.

Porter, Kenneth Wiggins. "Negro Labor in the Western Cattle Industry, 1866–1900." *Labor History* 10 (Summer 1969): 346–374.

Richardson, Barbara J. "Black Cowboys Also Rode." *Password* 31 (1986): 29–34, 41.

Savage, W. Sherman. "The Negro Cowboys on the Texas Plains." *Negro History Bulletin* 24 (April 1961): 157–158, 163.

_______. "Negroes on the Cattlemen's Frontier." *Midwest Journal* 6 (1954–1955): 35–48.

Searles, Michael N. "Addison Jones: The Most Noted Negro Cowboy That Ever 'Topped Off' A Horse." In *Black Cowboys of Texas*, edited by Sara R. Massey, 193–206. College Station: Texas A&M University Press, 2000.

_______. "The Black Cowboy—Yesterday and Today: A Hard Won Reputation." *Augusta Today Magazine* 4 (January/February 1997): 20–24.

_______. "The Black Cowboy—Yesterday and Today: A Hard Won Reputation." *Texas Illustrated: A Magazine of History and Folklore* 1 (February 1997): 5, 8–10.

_______. "Nigger Add-Addison Jones: Black, West Texas Cowboy." In *American National Biography*, edited by John A. Garraty and Mark C. Carnes. vol. 16, 429–431. 24 volumes. New York: Oxford University Press, 1998.

Shange, Ntozake. "Ridin' the Moon in Texas." In *Ridin' the Moon in Texas: Word Paintings*, 5–11. New York: St. Martin's Press, 1987.

Slatta, Richard W. "African-American Cowboys." In *The Cowboy Encyclopedia*, 5–8. Santa Barbara, Calif.: ABC-CLIO, 1994.

_______. *Cowboys of the Americas*. New Haven: Yale University Press, 1990.

Smallwood, James M. "James Kelly: The Ebony Gun." In *Black Cowboys of Texas*, edited by Sara R. Massey, 143–153. College Station: Texas A&M University Press, 2000.

Tyler, Ronnie C. "The Greatest Show in Mexico: A Wild West Spectacular in the Bull Ring." *American West* 9.3 (1972): 38–43.

Webb, Hertha Auburn. "D. W. '80 John' Wallace: Black Cattleman, 1875–1939." Master's thesis, Prairie View Agricultural and Mechanical College, 1957.

7. Black Seminoles

Black Seminole scouts at Fort Clark, Texas, ca. 1885.

The UT Institute of Texan Cultures, No. 74-1111
Courtesy of Charles G. Downing

Adams, Mischa B. "Naming Practices among the Black Seminole of the Texas-Mexico Border Region." *Journal of Big Bend Studies* 11 (1999): 119–144.

Brady, Marilyn Dell. "The Paynes of Texas: Black Seminole Cowboys of the Big Bend." *Black Cowboys of Texas*, edited by Sara R. Massey, 255–272. College Station: Texas A&M University Press, 2000.

Britten, Thomas A. *A Brief History of the Seminole-Negro Indian Scouts*. Lewiston, N.Y.: Mellen Press, 1999.

_______. "The Dismissal of the Seminole-Negro Indian Scouts, 1880–1914." *Fort Concho and the South Plains Journal* 24 (1992): 54–77.

_______. "The History of the Seminole-Negro Indian Scouts." Master's thesis, Hardin-Simmons University, 1990.

_______. "The Seminole-Negro Indian Scouts in Texas." In *Bricks Without Straw: A Comprehensive History of African Americans in Texas*, edited by David A. Williams, 95–104. Austin: Eakin Press, 1997.

_______. "The Seminole-Negro Indian Scouts in the Big Bend." *Journal of Big Bend Studies* 5 (1993): 67–77.

Callan, Austin. "The End of the 'Seminoles'." *Frontier Times* 8 (1930): 9–11.

Dickerson, W. E. S. "Seminole Indians." In *Handbook of Texas*, edited by Walter Prescott Webb, H. Bailey Carroll, Llerena B. Friend, Mary Jane Carroll, and Louise Nolen, vol. 2, 592. Austin: Texas State Historical Association, 1952.

Goggin, John M. "The Mexican Kickapoo Indians." *Southwestern Journal of Anthropology* 7 (1951): 314–327.

Gray, Trace Etienne. "Black Seminole Indians." In *The New Handbook of Texas*, edited by Ron Tyler, Douglas E. Barnett, Roy R. Barkley, Penelope C. Anderson, and Mark F. Odintz, vol. 1, 571–572. Austin: Texas State Historical Association, 1996.

Gwaltney, William W. "The Story of the Seminole-Negro Indian Scouts." *Lest We Forget* 4 (October 1996): 9, 12, 14.

Hancock, Ian F. "Texas Gullah: The Creole English of the Bracketville Afro-Seminoles." In *Perspectives on American English*, edited by Joseph L. Dillard, 305–333. The Hague: Mouton, 1980.

_______. *The Texas Seminoles and Their Language*. Austin: University of Texas African and Afro-American Studies and Research Center, 1980.

Heard, Joseph Norman. "Luis Pacheco—Traitor, Scapegoat, or Patriot?" In *The Black Frontiersmen: Adventures of Negroes among American Indians, 1528–1918*, 95–107. New York: John Day, 1969.

Jones, H. Conger. "Old Seminole Scouts Still Thrive on Border." *Frontier Times* 11 (1934): 327–332.

Katz, William Loren. "That You Know Who We Are." In *Black Indians: A Hidden Heritage*, 76–88. New York: Atheneum, 1986.

Krapf, Kellie A., and Floyd B. Largent Jr. "The Black Seminole Scouts: Soldiers Who Deserve High Praise." *Persimmon Hill* 24 (Winter 1996): 73–75.

Lancaster, Jane F. *Removal Aftershock: The Seminoles' Struggle to Survive in the West, 1836–1866*. Knoxville: University of Tennessee Press, 1994.

LaTorre, Felipe A., and Dolores L. LaTorre. *The Mexican Kickapoo Indians*. Austin: University of Texas Press, 1976.

Lawuyi, Olatunde Bayo. "Why I am Afro-Seminole: The Search for Identity among a Bracketville Ethnic Group." Master's thesis, University of Illinois at Urbana-Champaign, 1985.

Miller, Susan A. "Wild Cat and the Origins of the Seminole Migration to Mexico." Master's thesis, University of Oklahoma, 1988.

Moseley, Edward H. "Indians from the Eastern United States and the Defense of Northeastern Mexico, 1855–1864." *Southwestern Social Science Quarterly* 46 (1965): 273–280.

Mulroy, Kevin. *Freedom on the Border: The Seminole Maroons in Florida, the Indian Territory, Coahuila, and Texas*. Lubbock: Texas Tech University Press, 1993.

Nance, Carol Conley. "United States Army Scouts: The Southwestern Experience, 1866–1890." Master's thesis, North Texas State University, 1975.

Opala, Joseph A. *A Brief History of the Seminole Freedmen*. Austin: University of Texas at Austin, 1980.

Porter, Kenneth W. *The Black Seminoles: History of a Freedom-Seeking People*, edited by Alcione M. Amos and Thomas P. Senter. Gainesville, Fla.: University Press of Florida, 1996.

_______. "Farewell to John Horse: An Episode of Seminole Negro Folk History." *Phylon* 8 (1947): 265–273.

_______. "The Hawkins Negroes Go To Mexico." *Chronicles of Oklahoma* 24 (1946): 55–58.

_______. "Seminole in Mexico, 1850–1861." *Chronicles of Oklahoma* 29 (1951): 153–168.

_______. "The Seminole [and Seminole-Negroes] in Mexico, 1850–1861." *Hispanic American Historical Review* 31 (1951): 1–36.

_______. "The Seminole Negro-Indian Scouts, 1870–1881." *Southwestern Historical Quarterly* 55 (1952): 358–377.

_______. "Wild Cat's Death and Burial." *Chronicles of Oklahoma* 21 (1943): 41–43.

Rogers, B. Ann, and Linda Schott. "'My Mother Was a Mover': African American Seminole Women in Bracketville, Texas, 1914–1964." In *Writing the Range: Race, Class, and Culture in the Women's West*, edited by Elizabeth Jameson and Susan Armitage, 585–599. Norman: University of Oklahoma Press, 1997.

Root, George A., ed. "No-ko-aht's Talk: A Kickapoo Chief's Account of a Tribal Journey from Kansas to Mexico and Return in the Sixties." *Kansas Historical Quarterly* 1 (1932): 153–159.

Schubert, Frank N. "The Seminole Negro Scouts." In *Black Valor: Buffalo Soldiers and the Medal of Honor, 1870–1898*, 27–40. Wilmington, Del.: Scholarly Resources, 1997.

Sivad, Doug. *The Black Seminole Indians of Texas*. Boston: American Press, 1984.

Strong, Eric Emmerson. "The Lost Treaty of the Black Seminoles." *West Texas Historical Association Year Book* 75 (1999): 120–130.

Swisher, C. Kevin. "Frontier Heroes [Seminole-Negro Indian Scouts]." *Texas Highways* 39 (July 1992): 48–51.

Tate, Michael L. "Black Seminole Scouts." In *The New Handbook of Texas*, edited by Ron Tyler, Douglas E. Barnett, Roy R. Barkley, Penelope C. Anderson, and Mark F. Odintz, vol. 1, 572–573. Austin: Texas State Historical Association, 1996.

Thybony, Scott. "Against All Odds, Black Seminoles Won Their Freedom." *Smithsonian* 22 (August 1991): 90–101. Also referred to as "The Black Seminole: A Tradition of Courage."

Wallace, Ernest, and Adrian N. Anderson. "R. S. Mackenzie and the Kickapoos: The Raid into Mexico in 1873." *Arizona and the West* 7 (1965): 105–126.

Woodhull, Frost. "The Seminole Indian Scouts on the Border." *Frontier Times* 15 (1937): 118–127.

Woolley, Bryan. "Freedom Fighters." *Dallas Life Magazine* (February 2, 1992): 8, 10–12, 15.

8. Soldiers

Photo of Tenth Cavalrymen, Troop C and K, who were captured by Mexicans at the Battle of Corrizal, June 21, 1916, and taken to the Mexican Penitentiary of Chihuahua, and released to U.S. Army at El Paso, Texas.

The UT Institute of Texan Cultures, No. 68-1097
National Archives

Adams, Thomas Richard. "The Houston Riot of 1917." Master's thesis, Texas A & M University, 1972.

Austerman, Wayne Randolph. "Black Regulars: The 41st Infantry in Texas, 1867–1869." Master's thesis, Louisiana State University, 1971.

Baenziger, Ann Patton (Malone). "The Texas State Police during Reconstruction: A Reexamination." *Southwestern Historical Quarterly* 72 (1969): 470–491.

Bailey, Anne J. "A Texas Cavalry Raid: Reaction to Black Soldiers and Contrabands." *Civil War History* 35 (1989): 138–152.

_______. "Was There a Massacre at Poison Spring?" *Military History of the Southwest* 20 (Fall 1990): 157–168.

Barr, Alwyn. "The Black Militia of the New South: Texas as a Case Study." *Journal of Negro History* 63 (1978): 209–219.

Black, Lowell D., and Sara H. Black. *An Officer and a Gentleman: The Military Career of Lieutenant Henry O. Flipper*. Dayton: The Lora Company, 1985.

Boggess, George. "Political Activities of Negroes in the Reconstruction of Texas." Master's thesis, Howard University, 1938.

Braddy, Haldeen. *Pershing's Mission in Mexico*. El Paso: Texas Western Press, 1966.

Britten, Thomas A. "The Dismissal of the Seminole-Negro Indian Scouts, 1880–1914." *Fort Concho and the South Plains Journal* 24 (1992): 54–77.

_______. "The Seminole-Negro Indian Scouts in the Big Bend." *Journal of Big Bend Studies* 5 (1993): 67–77.

Buecker, Thomas R. "Prelude to Brownsville: The Twenty-fifth Infantry at Fort Niobrara, Nebraska, 1902–06." *Great Plains Quarterly* 16 (1996): 95–106.

Cage, James C., and James M. Day. *The Court Martial of Henry Ossian Flipper: West Point's First Black Graduate*. El Paso: El Paso Corral of the Westerners, 1981.

Carlson, Paul H. *"Pecos Bill": A Military Biography of William R. Shafter*. College Station: Texas A&M University Press, 1989.

_______. "William R. Shafter, Black Troops, and the Opening of the Llano Estacado, 1870–1875." *Panhandle-Plains Historical Review* 47 (1974): 1–18.

_______. "William R. Shafter, Black Troops, and the Finale to the Red River War." *Red River Valley Historical Review* 3 (1978): 247–258.

_______. "William R. Shafter Commanding Black Troops in West Texas." *West Texas Historical Association Year Book* 50 (1974): 104–116.

Carroll, John M. "Lieutenant Henry Ossian Flipper." In *The Black Military Experience in the American West*, edited by John M. Carroll, 347–352. New York: Liveright, 1971.

Christian, Garna L. "Adding on Fort Bliss to Black Military Historiography." *West Texas Historical Association Year Book* 54 (1978): 41–54.

_______. *Black Soldiers in Jim Crow Texas, 1899–1917.* College Station: Texas A&M University Press, 1995.

_______. "The Brownsville Raid's 168th Man: The Court-Martial of Corporal Knowles." *Southwestern Historical Quarterly* 93 (1989): 45–59.

_______. "The El Paso Racial Crisis of 1900." *Red River Valley Historical Review* 6 (Spring 1981): 28–41.

_______. "The Ordeal and the Prize: The 24th Infantry and Camp MacArthur." *Military Affairs* 50 (1986): 65–70.

_______. "Rio Grande City: Prelude to the Brownsville Raid." *West Texas Historical Association Year Book* 57 (1981): 118–132.

_______. "The Twenty-fifth Regiment at Fort McIntosh: Precursor to Retaliatory Racial Violence." *West Texas Historical Association Year Book* 55 (1979): 149–161.

_______. "The Violent Possibility: The Tenth Cavalry at Texarkana." *East Texas Historical Journal* 23.1 (1985): 3–15.

Clendenen, Clarence Clemens. *Blood on the Border: The United States Army and the Mexican Irregulars*. New York: Macmillan, 1969.

_______. "The Punitive Expedition of 1916: A Re-evaluation." *Arizona and the West* 3 (Winter 1961): 311–320.

Cook, Lawrence Hugh. "The Brownsville Affray of 1906." Master's thesis, University of Colorado, 1942.

Cox, Clinton. "The Hawk Moon." In *The Forgotten Heroes: The Story of the Buffalo Soldiers*, 112–136. New York: Scholastic Books, 1993.

Crimmins, Colonel Martin L. "Captain Nolan's Lost Troop on the Staked Plains." *West Texas Historical Association Year Book* 10 (1934): 68–73.

______. "Colonel Buell's Expedition into Mexico in 1880." *New Mexico Historical Review* 10 (1935): 133–142.

_______, ed. "Shafter's Explorations in Western Texas, 1875." *West Texas Historical Association Year Book* 9 (1933): 82–96.

Daniel, Wayne. "The 10th at Fort Concho, 1875–1882." *Fort Concho Report* 14 (Spring 1982): 7–14.

Dinges, Bruce J. "Colonel Grierson Invests on the West Texas Frontier." *Fort Concho Report* 16 (Fall 1984): 2–14.

_______. "The Court-Martial of Lieutenant Henry O. Flipper: An Example of Black-White Relationships in the Army." *American West* 9 (January 1972): 12–17, 59–61.

Dobak, William A. "Black Regulars Speak." *Panhandle-Plains Historical Review* 47 (1974): 19–27.

Dobie, J. Frank. "Eight Days towards the Sunset." In *Apache Gold and Yaqui Silver*, 203–209. Boston: Little, Brown, 1939.

East, Brenda K. "Henry Ossian Flipper: Lieutenant of the Buffalo Soldiers." *Persimmon Hill* 23 (Summer 1995): 68–69.

Eppinga, Jane. *Henry Ossian Flipper: West Point's First Black Graduate.* Plano, Tex.: Republic of Texas Press, 1996.

Fain, Samuel S. "The Pershing Punitive Expedition and Its Diplomatic Battleground." Master's thesis, University of Arizona, 1951.

Fleming, Elvis Eugene. "Captain Nicholas Nolan: Lost on the Staked Plains." *Texana* 4 (1966): 1–13.

Foraker, Joseph Benson. "A Review of the Testimony in the Brownsville Investigation." *North American Review* 187 (April 1908): 550–558.

Fowler, Arlen L. *The Black Infantry in the West, 1869-1891.* Westport, Conn.: Greenwich Publishing, 1971.

_______. "The Texas Years." In *The Black Infantry in the West, 1869–1891*, 16–46. Norman: University of Oklahoma Press, 1996.

Fuller, Charles. "The Brownsville Raid." *Literary Cavalcade* 30 (January 1978): 9–23, 28–39. [Fiction]

Glasrud, Bruce A. "Western Black Soldiers Since *The Buffalo Soldiers*: A Review of the Literature." *Social Science Journal* 36 (1999): 251–270.

Glasrud, Bruce A., and William H. Leckie. "Buffalo Soldiers." In *African Americans in the West: A Bibliography of Secondary Sources*, comp. by Bruce A. Glasrud, 32–53. Occasional Papers No. 2. Alpine, Tex.: Center for Big Bend Studies, Sul Ross State University, 1998.

Gwaltney, William W. "The Story of the Seminole-Negro Indian Scouts." *Lest We Forget* 4 (October 1996): 9, 12, 14.

Hall, Martin Hardwick. "Negroes with Confederate Troops in West Texas and New Mexico." *Password* 13 (1968): 11–12.

Harris, Theodore D., ed. *Black Frontiersman: The Western Memoirs of Henry O. Flipper*. Fort Worth: Texas Christian University Press, 1997.

_______. "Henry Flipper and Pancho Villa." *Password* 6 (1961): 39–46.

_______. "Henry Ossian Flipper: The First Negro Graduate of West Point." Ph.D. dissertation, University of Minnesota, 1971.

_______, ed. *Negro Frontiersman: The Western Memoirs of Henry O. Flipper, First Negro Graduate of West Point*. El Paso: Texas Western College Press, 1963.

Haynes, Robert V. "The Houston Mutiny and Riot of 1917." *Southwestern Historical Quarterly* 76 (1973): 418–439.

_______. *A Night of Violence: The Houston Riot of 1917*. Baton Rouge: Louisiana State University Press, 1976.

_______. "Unrest at Home: Racial Conflict between White Civilians and Black Soldiers in 1917." *Journal of the American Studies Association of Texas* 6 (1975): 43–54.

Hilton, David Edmond. *Lieutenant Henry O. Flipper: "Buffalo Soldier."* Odessa, Tex.: Kwik Kopy Printing, 1992. [Children's book]

Hunter, John W. "A Trooper of the Ninth Cavalry." *Frontier Times* 4 (1927): 9–11.

_______. "Mutiny of Negro Soldiers at Fort Concho, 1882." *Hunter's Magazine* (December 1911): 4–5, 13.

Jackson, Sara Dunlap, ed. *Henry O. Flipper, The Colored Cadet at West Point*. New York: Arno Press Reprint, 1968.

Johnson, Barry C. *Flipper's Dismissal: The Ruin of Lt. Henry O. Flipper, U.S.A., First Coloured Graduate of West Point*. London: Privately printed, 1980.

Johnson, Robert B. "The Punitive Expedition: A Military, Diplomatic, and Political History of Pershing's Chase after Pancho Villa, 1916–1917." Ph.D. dissertation, University of Southern California, 1964.

Jones, H. Conger. "Old Seminole Scouts Still Thrive on Border." *Frontier Times* 11 (1934): 327–332.

Joseph, Harriett Denise. *The Brownsville Raid*. Brownsville, Tex.: Texas Southmost College, 1976.

Kelton, Elmer. *The Wolf and the Buffalo*. Fort Worth: Texas Christian University Press, 1986. [Fiction]

Kenner, Charles L. *Buffalo Soldiers and Officers of the Ninth Cavalry, 1867–1898*. Norman: University of Oklahoma Press, 1999.

Kinevan, Marcos E. *Frontier Cavalryman: Lieutenant John Bigelow and the Buffalo Soldiers in Texas.* El Paso: Texas Western Press, 1998.

Krapf, Kellie A., and Floyd B. Largent Jr. "The Black Seminole Scouts: Soldiers Who Deserve High Praise." *Persimmon Hill* 24 (Winter 1996): 73–75.

Lamkin, Patricia E. "Blacks in San Angelo: Relations between Fort Concho and the City, 1875–1889." *West Texas Historical Association Year Book* 66 (1990): 26–37.

Lane, Ann J. *The Brownsville Affair: National Crisis and Black Reaction.* Port Washington, N.Y.: Kennikat Press, 1971.

Leckie, William H. "Black Regulars on the Texas Frontier, 1866–1885." In *The Texas Military Experience: From the Texas Revolution through World War II*, edited by Joseph G. Dawson III, 86–96, 219–221. College Station: Texas A&M University Press, 1995.

_______. *The Buffalo Soldiers: A Narrative of the Negro Cavalry in the West.* Norman: University of Oklahoma Press, 1967.

Ledbetter, Barbara A. Neal. *Fort Belknap Frontier Saga: Indians, Negroes, and Anglo-Americans on the Texas Frontier.* Burnet, Tex.: Eakin Press, 1982.

Lowry, Jack. "Buffalo Soldiers." *Texas Highways* 36 (February 1989): 40–47.

Martinal, Doris. "The Negro Raid." *Texas History Teachers Bulletin* 14 (December 1927): 129–133.

Matthews, James T. "Always in the Vanguard: Patrolling the Texas Frontier with Captain Louis Carpenter and Company H of the Tenth Cavalry." *West Texas Historical Association Year Book* 75 (1999): 110–119.

McChristian, Douglas C., ed. *Garrison Tangles in the Friendless Tenth: The Journal of First Lieutenant John Bigelow, Jr., Fort Davis, Texas.* Bryan, Tex.: J. M. Carroll, 1985.

_______. "Grierson's Fight at Tinaja de las Palmas: An Episode in the Victorio Campaign." *Red River Valley Historical Review* 7 (Winter 1982): 45–63.

McClung, Donald R. "Henry O. Flipper: The First Negro Officer in the United States Army, 1878–1882." Master's thesis, East Texas State University, 1970.

_______. "Second Lieutenant Henry O. Flipper: A Negro Officer on the West Texas Frontier." *West Texas History Association Year Book* 47 (1971): 20–31.

Meltzer, Richard. "On Villa's Trail in Mexico: The Experiences of a Black Cavalryman and a White Infantry Officer, 1916–1917." *Military History of the Southwest* 20 (Fall 1990): 23–42; 21(1991): 173–190.

Miles, Susan. "The Soldiers' Riot." *Fort Concho Report* 3 (Spring 1981): 1–20.

Mulroy, Kevin. "The Seminole Negro Indian Scouts." In *Freedom on the Border: The Seminole Maroons in Florida, the Indian Territory, Coahuila, and Texas*, 107–132. Lubbock: Texas Tech University Press, 1993.

Nance, Carol Conley. "United States Army Scouts: The Southwestern Experience, 1866–1890." Master's thesis, North Texas State University, 1975.

Nunn, W. Curtis. "Eighty-Six Hours without Water on the Texas Plains." *Southwestern Historical Quarterly* 43 (1940): 356–364.

Odintz, Mark. "Buffalo Soldiers." In *The New Handbook of Texas*, edited by Ron Tyler, Douglas E. Barnett, Roy R. Barkley, Penelope C. Anderson, and Mark F. Odintz, vol. 1, 815. Austin: Texas State Historical Association, 1996.

Park, Phocion Samuel Jr. "The Twenty-Fourth Infantry Regiment and the Houston Riot of 1917." Master's thesis, University of Houston, 1971.

Pickens, William. "Death Detail: Trial and Execution of Thirteen Negro Soldiers at Fort Sam Houston, Texas, December, 1917." *World Tomorrow* 13 (April 1930): 162–165.

Porter, Kenneth Wiggins. "Negroes and Indians on the Texas Frontier, 1834–1874." *Southwestern Historical Quarterly* 53 (1949): 151–163.

_______. "Negroes and Indians on the Texas Frontier, 1831–1876, A Study in Race and Culture I." *Journal of Negro History* 41 (1956): 185–214.

_______. "Negroes and Indians on the Texas Frontier, 1831–1876, A Study in Race and Culture II." *Journal of Negro History* 41 (1956): 285–310.

_______. "The Seminole-Negro Indian Scouts, 1870–1881." *Southwestern Historical Quarterly* 55 (1952): 358–377.

_______. "The Seminole Negro Indian Scouts, Texas, 1870–1914." In *The Black Seminoles: History of a Freedom-Seeking People*, edited by Alcione M. Amos and Thomas P. Senter, 173–214. Gainesville, Fla.: University Press of Florida, 1996.

Porter, Kenneth W., and Edward S. Wallace. "Thunderbolt of the Frontier." *Westerners New York Posse Brand Book* 8 (1961): 73–75, 82–86.

Richter, William L. *The Army in Texas during Reconstruction*. College Station: Texas A&M University Press, 1987.

Robinson, Charles M. III. *The Court-Martial of Lieutenant Henry Flipper*. El Paso: Texas Western Press, 1994.

Savage, W. Sherman. "Blacks in the Military." In *Blacks in the West*, 48–64. Westport, Conn.: Greenwood Press, 1976.

Sayre, Harold Ray. *Warriors of Color*. Fort Davis, Tex.: Privately printed, 1995.

Schubert, Frank N. *Black Valor: Buffalo Soldiers and the Medal of Honor, 1870–1898.* Wilmington, Del.: Scholarly Resources, 1997.

_______. *On the Trail of the Buffalo Soldier: Biographies of African-Americans in the U.S. Army, 1866–1917.* Wilmington, Del.: Scholarly Resources, 1995.

Schuler, Edgar A. "The Houston Race Riot, 1917." *Journal of Negro History* 29 (1944): 300–338.

Siler, Benjamin T. "The Brownsville, Texas, Affray of August 13–14, 1906, and Subsequent Proceedings (A Historical Interpretation)." Master's thesis, North Carolina College of Durham, 1963.

Singletary, Otis A. *Negro Militia and Reconstruction.* Austin: University of Texas Press, 1957.

_______. "The Texas Militia during Reconstruction." *Southwestern Historical Quarterly* 60 (1956): 23–35.

Smith, C. Calvin. "The Houston Riot of 1917, Revisited." *The Houston Review* 13 (1991): 84–102.

_______. "On the Edge: The Houston Riot of 1917 Revisited." *The Griot* 10 (Spring 1991): 3–12.

Stallard, Patricia Y. *Glittering Misery: Dependents of the Indian Fighting Army.* Fort Collins, Colo.: The Old Army Press, 1979.

Stout, Joseph A. Jr. *Border Conflict: Villistas, Arrancistas and the Punitive Expedition, 1915–1920.* Fort Wort: Texas Christian University Press, 1999.

Swisher, C. Kevin. "Frontier Heroes [Seminole-Negro Indian Scouts]." *Texas Highways* 39 (July 1992): 48–51.

Taylor, Quintard. "Comrades of Color: Buffalo Soldiers in the West, 1866–1917." *Colorado Heritage* (Spring 1996): 3–27.

Temple, Frank M. "Colonel B. H. Grierson's Administration of the District of the Pecos." *West Texas Historical Association Year Book* 38 (1962): 85–96.

_______. "Colonel B. H. Grierson's Texas Commands." Master's thesis, Texas Tech University, 1956.

_______. "Colonel B. H. Grierson's Victorio Campaign." *West Texas Historical Association Year Book* 35 (1959): 99–111.

_______. "Colonel Grierson in the Southwest." *Panhandle-Plains Historical Review* 30 (1957): 27–54.

_______. "Discipline and Turmoil in the Tenth U.S. Cavalry." *West Texas Historical Association Year Book* 58 (1982): 103–118.

_______. "The Tenth United States Cavalry in Texas." *Fort Concho Report* 17 (Winter 1985): 11–17.

Terrell, Mary Church. "Taft and the Negro Soldiers." *Independent* 65 (July 23, 1908).

Thiesen, Lee Scott, ed. "The Fight in Lincoln, N.M., 1878: The Testimony of Two Negro Participants." *Arizona and the West* 12 (Summer 1970): 173–198.

Thompson, Erwin N. "The Negro Soldiers on the Frontier: A Fort Davis Case Study." *Journal of the West* 7 (1968): 217–235.

Thompson, Jerry. *Sabers on the Rio Grande.* Austin: Presidial Press, 1974.

Thornbrough, Emma Lou. "The Brownsville Episode and the Negro Vote." *Mississippi Valley Historical Review* 44 (December 1957): 469–493.

Thybony, Scott. "Against All Odds, Black Seminoles Won Their Freedom." *Smithsonian* 22 (August 1991): 90–101.

Tinsley, James A. "The Brownsville Affray." Master's thesis, University of North Carolina, 1948.

_______. "Roosevelt, Foraker, and the Brownsville Affray." *Journal of Negro History* 41 (1956): 43–65.

Troxel, Orlando C. "The Tenth Cavalry in Mexico." *Journal of the United States Cavalry Association* 18 (October 1917): 197–205.

Utley, Robert M. "'Pecos Bill' on the Texas Frontier." *American West* 6 (January 1969): 4–13, 61–62.

Waide, C. D. "When Psychology Failed: An Unbiased Fact-Story of the Houston Race Riot of 1917." *Houston Gargoyle* May 15, 22, 29, 1928; June 5, 12, 1928.

Wallace, Andrew. "The Sabre Retires: Pershing's Cavalry Campaign in Mexico, 1916." *The Smoke Signal* 9 (Spring 1964): 1–24.

Wallace, Edward S. "General John Lapham Bullis, The Thunderbolt of the Texas Frontier, I." *Southwestern Historical Quarterly* 54 (1951): 452–461.

_______. "General John Lapham Bullis, Thunderbolt of the Texas Frontier, II." *Southwestern Historical Quarterly* 55 (1951): 77–85.

Warner, Ezra J. "A Black Man in the Long Gray Line." *American History Illustrated* 4 (January 1970): 30–38.

Weaver, John D. *The Brownsville Raid.* New York: W. W. Norton, 1970.

_______. *The Senator and the Sharecropper's Son: Exoneration of the Brownsville Soldiers.* College Station: Texas A&M University Press, 1997.

Wharfield, Colonel H. B. "The Affair at Carrizal: Pershing's Punitive Expedition." *Montana: The Magazine of Western History* 18 (October 1968): 24–39.

_______. *Tenth Cavalry and Border Fights*. El Cajon, Calif.: Privately printed, 1964.

Williams, Clayton W. "A Threatened Mutiny of Soldiers at Fort Stockton in 1873 Resulted in Penitentiary Sentences of Five to Fifteen Years." *West Texas Historical Association Year Book* 52 (1976): 78–83.

Williams, Mary L. "Empire Building: Colonel Benjamin H. Grierson at Fort Davis, 1882–1885." *West Texas Historical Association Year Book* 61 (1985): 58–73.

_______. "Fort Davis, Texas: Key Defense Post on the San Antonio–El Paso Road." *Password* 31 (1986): 205–210.

_______. "Servants at Frontier Military Posts: A Glimpse at 'Domesticity' through the Letters of Alice Kirk Grierson." *Journal of Big Bend Studies* 11 (1999): 145–157.

Wilson, Steve. "A Black Lieutenant in the Ranks." *American History Illustrated* 18 (December 1983): 30–39.

Woodhull, Frost. "The Seminole Indian Scouts on the Border." *Frontier Times* 15 (1937): 118–127.

Woolley, Bryan. "Freedom Fighters." *Dallas Life Magazine* (February 2, 1992): 8, 10–12, 15.

Wooster, Robert. *Fort Davis: Outpost on Texas Frontier*. Austin: Texas State Historical Association, 1994.

_______. *History of Fort Davis, Texas*. Santa Fe: Southwest Cultural Resources Center, National Park Service, 1990.

_______. *Soldiers, Sutlers, and Settlers: Garrison Life on the Texas Frontier*. College Station: Texas A&M University Press, 1987.

Wynne, Lewis N. "Brownsville—The Reaction of the Negro Press." *Phylon* 33 (1972): 153–160.

Young, Karl. "A Fight that could have meant War." *American West* 3 (Spring 1966): 16–23.

Young, Richard. "The Brownsville Affray." *American History Illustrated* 21 (October 1986): 10–17.

9. Late Nineteenth Century, 1874–1900

U.S. Army, Tenth Cavalry on the Punitive Expedition in Colonia Dublan, Mexico, April 17, 1916.

The UT Institute of Texan Cultures, No. 68-1096 National Archives

Abramowitz, Jack. "John B. Rayner—A Grass-Roots Leader." *Journal of Negro History* 36 (1951): 160–193.

Barr, Alwyn. "Black Migration into Southwestern Cities, 1865–1900." In *Essays on Southern History: Written in Honor of Barnes F. Lathrop*, edited by Gary W. Gallagher, 15–38. Austin: General Libraries of University of Texas, 1980.

_______. "Black State Conventions." In *The New Handbook of Texas*, edited by Ron Tyler, Douglas E. Barnett, Roy R. Barkley, Penelope C. Anderson, and Mark F. Odintz, vol. 1, 575–576. Austin: Texas State Historical Association, 1996.

_______. "Black Urban Churches on the Southern Frontier, 1865–1900." *Journal of Negro History* 82 (1997): 368–383.

_______. "Occupational and Geographic Mobility in San Antonio, 1870–1900." *Social Science Quarterly* 51 (1970): 396–403.

_______."The Right to Vote." In *Reconstruction to Reform: Texas Politics, 1876–1906*, 193–208. Austin: University of Texas Press, 1971.

_______. "The Texas 'Black Uprising' Scare of 1883." *Phylon* 41 (1980): 179–186.

Behrends, Carey F. "Historic Tour of Historic Fort Stockton, Texas: A Milestone in Black History." *Heritage* 11 (Winter 1993): 24–25.

Brandon, Ida. "The Tax Payers Union in Brazoria County." *Texas History Teacher's Bulletin* 14 (1926): 86–92.

Brewer, J. Mason. *Negro Legislators of Texas and Their Descendants: A History of the Negro in Texas Politics from Reconstruction to Disfranchisement.* Dallas: Mathis Publishing, 1935.

Budd, Harrel. "The Negro in Politics in Texas, 1867–1898." Master's thesis, University of Texas, 1925.

Cain, Jerry Berlyn. "The Thought and Action of Nineteenth-Century Texas Baptists Concerning the Negro." Master's thesis, Baylor University, 1971.

_______. "The Thought and Action of Some Early Texas Baptists Concerning the Negro." *East Texas Historical Journal* 13 (Spring 1975): 3–12.

Cantrell, Gregg. "'Dark Tactics': Black Politics in the 1887 Texas Prohibition Campaign." *Journal of American Studies* 25 (April 1991): 85–93.

_______. "John B. Rayner: A Study in Black Populist Leadership." *Southern Studies* 24 (Winter 1985): 432–443.

_______. *Kenneth and John B. Rayner and the Limits of Southern Dissent.* Urbana: University of Illinois Press, 1993.

Cantrell, Gregg, and D. Scott Barton. "Texas Populists and the Failure of Biracial Politics." *Journal of Southern History* 55 (1989): 659–692.

Carroll, Robert. "Robert Lloyd Smith and the Farmers' Improvement Society of Texas." Master's thesis, Baylor University, 1974.

Carter, Purvis M. "Robert Lloyd Smith and the Farmer's Improvement Society, a Self-Help Movement in Texas." *Negro History Bulletin* 29 (1966): 175–176, 190–191.

Casdorph, Paul Douglas. "Norris Wright Cuney and Texas Republican Politics, 1883–1896." *Southwestern Historical Quarterly* 68 (1965): 455–464.

Christopher, Nehemiah McKinley. "The History of Negro Public Education in Texas, 1865–1900." Ed.D. dissertation, University of Pittsburgh, 1948.

Chumley, Leo Bertice. "Negro Labor and Property Holdings in Shelby County, Texas, 1870–1945." Master's thesis, Prairie View Agricultural and Mechanical College, 1948.

Crouch, Barry A. "Hesitant Recognition: Texas Black Politicians, 1865–1900." *East Texas Historical Journal* 31.1 (1993): 41–58.

Cuthbertson, Gilbert. "The Jaybird Woodpecker War." *Texana* 10 (1972): 297–309.

Daniel, Wayne. "The 10th at Fort Concho, 1875–1882." *Fort Concho Report* 14 (Spring 1982): 7–14.

Dann, Martin. "Black Populism: A Study of Colored Farmers' Alliance through 1891." *Journal of Ethnic Studies* 2 (Fall 1974): 58–71.

Davidson, James M. "Freedman's Cemetery (1869–1907): Establishing a Chronology for Exhumed Burials from an African-American Burial Ground, Dallas, Texas." *African-American Archaeology, Newsletter of the African-American Archeology Network* 26 (Early Winter 1999): 4–5.

DeVany, Mrs. S.V. "A Ghost in West Texas." *Frontier Times* 7 (1930): 287–289.

Engerand, Steven W. "Black and Mulatto Mobility and Stability in Dallas, Texas, 1880–1910." *Phylon* 39 (1978): 203–215.

Findley, James Lee Jr. "Lynching and the Texas Anti-Lynch Law of 1897." Master's thesis, Baylor University, 1974.

Fine, Bernice Rash. "Agrarian Reform and the Negro Farmer in Texas, 1886–1896." Master's thesis, North Texas State University, 1971.

Foley, Neil Francis. "The New South in the Southwest: Anglos, Blacks and Mexicans in Central Texas, 1880–1930." Ph.D. dissertation, University of Michigan, 1990.

Gauss, John. "Give the Blacks Texas." *Civil War Times Illustrated* 29 (May 1990): 54–56.

Ginn, Duane E. "Racial Violence in Texas, 1884–1900." Master's thesis, Prairie View Agricultural and Mechanical College, 1954.

Glasrud, Bruce A. "Early Black Nationalist Movements in Texas." *Journal of Big Bend Studies* 11 (1999): 159–169.

Goodwyn, Lawrence C. "Populist Dreams and Negro Rights: East Texas as a Case Study." *American Historical Review* 76 (1971): 1435–1456.

Gulley, Steve D. "M. M. Rodgers, the Politician, 1877–1909." Master's thesis, Prairie View Agricultural and Mechanical College, 1955.

Hare, Maud Cuney. *Norris Wright Cuney: A Tribune of the Black People*. New York: Crisis, 1913.

Hinze, Virginia Neal. "Norris Wright Cuney." Master's thesis, Rice University, 1965.

Keeling, Hightower T. *History of African Methodism in Texas*. Waco: C. F. Blanks Publisher, 1885.

Kirven, Lamar L. "A Century of Warfare: Black Texans." Ph.D. dissertation, Indiana University, 1974.

Kochan, Millie Longtin. "The Jaybird-Woodpecker Feud: A Study in Social Conflict." Master's thesis, University of Texas, 1929.

Lamkin, Patricia E. "Blacks in San Angelo: Relations between Fort Concho and the City, 1875–1889." *West Texas Historical Association Year Book* 66 (1990): 26–37.

_______. "A History of Blacks in San Angelo, 1869–1930." Master's thesis, Angelo State University, 1990.

Lewis, J. Vance. *Out of the Ditch: A True Story of an Ex-Slave*. Houston: Rein and Sons, 1910.

Lightfoot, Billy Bob. "The Negro Exodus from Comanche County, Texas." *Southwestern Historical Quarterly* 56 (1953): 407–416.

Long, Christopher. "White Man's Union Associations." In *The New Handbook of Texas*, edited by Ron Tyler, Douglas E. Barnett, Roy R. Barkley, Penelope C. Anderson, and Mark F. Odintz, vol. 6, 938. Austin: Texas State Historical Association, 1996.

Margraves, Nina Benware. "The Jaybird Democratic Association of Fort Bend County—A White Man's Union." Master's thesis, University of Houston, 1955.

Miller, Worth Robert. "Harrison County Methods: Election Fraud in Late Nineteenth-Century Texas." *Locus: Regional and Local History of the Americas* 7 (1995): 111–128.

Moseley, J. A. R. "The Citizens White Primary of Marion County." *Southwestern Historical Quarterly* 49 (1940): 524–526.

Nolen, Oran Warder. "Darkey [Tom Sullivan] of Old School Passes Century Mark." *Frontier Times* 7 (1930): 247–251.

Perry, Douglas Geraldyne. "Black Populism: The Negro in the People's Party in Texas." Master's thesis, Prairie View University, 1945.

Pitre, Merline. "Robert Lloyd Smith: A Black Lawmaker in the Shadow of Booker T. Washington." *Phylon* 46 (1985): 262–268.

_______. *Through Many Dangers, Toils, and Snares: Black Leadership in Texas, 1868–1900.* Austin: Eakin Press, 1985.

Rice, Lawrence D. *The Negro n Texas, 1874-1900.* Baton Rouge: Louisiana State University Press, 1971.

_______. "The Negro in Texas, 1874–1900." Ph.D. dissertation, Texas Technological College, 1967.

Rippy, J. Fred. "A Negro Colonization Project in Mexico, 1895." *Journal of Negro History* 6 (1921): 66–73.

_______. "Some Precedents of the Pershing Expedition into Mexico." *Southwestern Historical Quarterly* 24 (1921): 292–316.

Scott, Janelle DuPont. "Married Women at Work: Dallas, Texas 1880–1900." Master's thesis, University of Texas at San Antonio, 1979.

Smith, Robert Lloyd. "Elevation of Negro Farm Life." *Independent* 1 (August 30, 1900): 2103–2106.

_______. "The Farmers' Improvement Society of Texas." *AME Review* (January 1909): 289–296.

_______. "An Uplifting Negro Cooperative Society in Texas." *The World's Work* 16 (July 1908): 10462–10466.

_______. "Village Improvement Among the Negroes." *Outlook* 64 (March 31, 1900): 733–736.

Spindler, Frank MacD. "Concerning Hempstead and Waller County." *Southwestern Historical Quarterly* 59 (1956): 455–472.

Wilson, Leonard Jr. "Texas and the Kansas Fever, 1879–1888." Master's thesis, University of Houston, 1973.

Woodson, Carter G. "The Cuney Family." *Negro History Bulletin* 11 (1948): 123–125, 143.

Xie, Jingjing. "The Black Community in Waco, Texas: A Study of Place, Family, and Work, 1880–1900." Master's thesis, Baylor University, 1988.

Yates, Rutherford B. H., and Paul L. Yates. *The Life and Efforts of Jack Yates*. Houston: Texas Southern University Press, 1985.

Yelderman, Pauline. "The Jaybird Democratic Association of Fort Bend County." Master's thesis, University of Texas, 1938.

_______. *The Jay Bird Democratic Association of Fort Bend County*. Waco: Texian Press, 1979.

10. Twentieth Century Experience, 1900–1954

Calvin Bluitt in his Studebaker with his children, Leroy and Horace, in Dallas, Texas.

The UT Institute of Texan Cultures, No. 68-2005
Courtesy of Leroy Bluitt

Aden, Alonzo J. "Educational Tour through the Hall of Negro Life." *Southern Workman* 65 (November 1936): 331–341.

Ahlfield, Danny Lee. "Fraternalism Gone Awry: The Ku Klux Klan in Houston, 1920–1925." Master's thesis, University of Texas at Austin, 1984.

Akers, Monte. *Flames after Midnight: Murder, Vengeance, and the Desolation of a Texas Community*. Austin: University of Texas Press, 1999.

Alexander, Charles C. *Crusade for Conformity: The Ku Klux Klan in Texas, 1920–1930.* Houston: Texas Gulf Coast Historical Association, 1962.

_______. "Secrecy Bids for Power: The Ku Klux Klan in Texas Politics in the 1920's." *Mid-America* 46 (1964): 3–28.

Armstrong, Ira E. "A Historical Study of Public Elementary Schools in San Antonio, Texas with Special Emphasis on Elementary Schools for Negroes from 1910 to 1940." Master's thesis, Prairie View State Normal and Industrial College, 1941.

Asbury, Doris T. "Negro Participation in the Primary and General Elections in Texas." Master's thesis, Boston University, 1951.

Atkins, J. Alton. *The Texas Negro and His Political Rights: A History of the Fight of the Negro to Enter the Democratic Primaries of Texas*. Houston: Webster Publishing Company, 1932.

Baeza, Abelardo. "*La Escuela Escondida*: History of the Morgan School in Alpine, Texas, 1929–1954." *Journal of Big Bend Studies* 6 (1994): 85–98.

Bailey, Herbert J. "Charles Bellinger and Jim Crow in San Antonio, Texas, 1905–1937." *South Texas Studies* (1993): 75–88.

Baker, Margaret Bouland. "The Texas Negro and the World War." Master's thesis, University of Texas, 1938.

Baker, Paul E. "Negroes Secure the Franchise in the Texas Primary." In *Negro-White Adjustment: An Investigation and Analysis of Methods in the Interracial Movement in the United States,*" 80–83. New York: Association Press, 1934.

Banks, Melvin James. *The History of the New Hope Baptist Church: A Century of Faith*. Dallas: New Hope Baptist Church, 1967.

_______. "The Pursuit of Equality: The Movement for First Class Citizenship among Negroes in Texas, 1920–1950." Ss.D. dissertation, Syracuse University, 1962.

Barchus, Gale Leslie. "The Dynamics of Black Demands and White Responses for Negro Higher ducation in Texas, 1945–1950." Master's thesis, University of Texas at Austin, 1970.

Barnes, Glynell Shakelford. "A History of Public Library Service to Negroes in Galveston, Texas 1904–1955." Master's thesis, Atlanta University, 1957.

Barth, Shell Jr. "A History of the Negro Presbyterian Church U.S. in Texas." Master's thesis, University of Texas, 1965.

Beeth, Howard. "A Black Elite Agenda in the Urban South: The Call for Political and Racial Economic Solidarity in Houston during the 1920s." *Essays in Economic and Business History* 10 (June 1992): 41–55.

_______. "Houston and History, Past and Present: A Look at Black Houston in the 1920's." *Southern Studies* 25 (Summer 1986): 172–186.

_______. "How to Resist? Reformism vs. Communism in Houston's Black Press during the 1920s." *Bringing the World Together: Proceedings of the National Association of African American Studies* (1996): 62–84.

Bell, Gail K. "James Leonard Farmer: Texas' First African American Ph.D." *East Texas Historical Journal* 36.1 (1998): 18–25.

Bentley, Max. "The Ku Klux Klan in Texas." *McClure's* 57 (May 1924): 11–21.

Bessent, Nancy Echols. "The Publisher: A Biography of Carter Wesley." Master's thesis, University of Texas at Austin, 1981.

Billington, Monroe Lee. "Lyndon B. Johnson and Blacks: The Early Years." *Journal of Negro History* 62 (1977): 26–42.

Blackshear, E. L. "Industrial Training and the Race Question." *Southern Workman* 35 (1906): 396–401.

Board, Edna Theresa. "The Historical Development of the Public Schools for Negroes in Liberty County, Texas from 1918 to 1948." Master's thesis, Prairie View Agricultural and Mechanical College, 1949.

Boone, Theodore Sylvester. *Feet Like Polished Brass.* Fort Worth: Masonic Printing Department, 1933.

_______. *"Old Chief", Alexander Lorenza Boone, D.D., LL.D.; A Biography by his Son.* Houston: Western Star Publishing Company, 1927.

Boswell, John David. "Negro Participation in the 1936 Texas Centennial Exposition." Master's thesis, University of Texas at Austin, 1969.

Botson, Michael. "Jim Crow Wearing Steel-Toed Shoes and Safety Glasses: Duel Unionism at the Hughes Tool Company, 1918–1942." *The Houston Review* 16.2 (1994): 101–116.

Bourgeois, Christie L. "Stepping over Lines: Lyndon Johnson, Black Texans, and the National Youth Administration, 1935–1937." *Southwestern Historical Quarterly* 91 (1987): 149–172.

Brandenstein, Sherilyn. "Prominent Roles of Black Womanhood in *Sepia Record*, 1952–1954." Master's thesis, University of Texas at Austin, 1989.

_______. "*Sepia Record* as a Forum for Negotiating Women's Roles." In *Women and Texas History: Selected Essay,* edited by Fane Downs and Nancy Baker Jones, 143–157. Austin: Texas State Historical Association, 1993.

Brophy, William Joseph. "Black Business Development in Texas Cities, 1900–1950." *Red River Valley Historical Review* 6 (Spring 1981): 42–55.

_______. "The Black Texan, 1900–1950: A Quantitative History." Ph.D. dissertation, Vanderbilt University, 1974.

_______. "Black Texans and the New Deal." In *The Depression in the Southwest*, edited by Donald W. Whisenhunt, 117–133, 153–154. Port Washington, N.Y.: Kennikat, 1980.

Brown, Norman D. "The Ku Klux Klan in Texas." In *Hood, Bonnet, and Little Brown Jug: Texas Politics, 1921–1928*, 49–87, 446–453. College Station: Texas A&M University Press, 1984.

Brown, Olive D., and Michael R. Heintze. "Mary Branch: Private College Educator." In *Black Leaders: Texans for Their Times*, edited by Alwyn Barr and Robert A. Calvert, 112–127. Austin: Texas State Historical Association, 1981.

Bryant, Ira B. Jr. "News Items about Negroes in White Urban and Rural Newspapers." *Journal of Negro Education* 4 (1935): 169–178.

Bryson, Conrey. *Dr. Lawrence A. Nixon and the White Primary*. Southwestern Studies Monograph no. 42. El Paso: Texas Western Press, 1974.

_______. "El Paso and the Poll Tax." *Password* 4 (1959): 46–52.

Bullock, Henry Allen. "The Availability of Education in the Texas Negro Separate School." *The Journal of Negro Education* 16 (1947): 425–432.

_______. "Racial Attitudes and the Employment of Negroes." *American Journal of Sociology* 56 (March 1951): 448–457.

_______. "Some Readjustments of the Texas Negro Family to the Emergency of the War." *Southwestern Social Science Quarterly* 25 (1944): 100–117.

Bundy, William Oliver. *Life of William Madison McDonald*. Fort Worth: Bunker Printing and Book Company, 1925.

Burran, James A. "Violence in an 'Arsenal of Democracy': The Beaumont Race Riot, 1943." *East Texas Historical Review* 14.1 (1976): 39–51.

Chalmers, David M. "The Eyes of Texas." In *Hooded Americanism: The History of the Ku Klux Klan*, 39–48, 401. Chicago: Quadrangle Books, 1968.

Chambers, Bill. "The History of the Texas Negro and His Development Since 1900." Master's thesis, North Texas State College, 1940.

Chapman, David L. "Lynching in Texas." Master's thesis, Texas Tech University, 1973.

Christian, Garna L. *Black Soldiers in Jim Crow Texas, 1899–1917*. Centennial Series of the Association of Former Students No. 57. College Station: Texas A&M University Press, 1995.

_______. "The El Paso Racial Crisis of 1900." *Red River Valley Historical Review* 6 (Spring 1981): 28–41.

_______. "The Twenty-Fifth Regiment at Fort McIntosh: Precursor to Retaliatory Racial Violence." *West Texas Historical Association Year Book* 55 (1979): 149–161.

Chumley, Leo Bertice. "Negro Labor and Property Holdings in Shelby County, Texas, 1870–1945." Master's thesis, Prairie View Agricultural and Mechanical College, 1948.

Cotton, Walter, comp. *History of Negroes of Limestone County from 1860 to 1939*. Mexia, Tex.: J. A. Chatman and S. M. Merriwether, 1939.

Cox, Patrick. "'Nearly a Statesman': LBJ and Texas Blacks in the 1948 Election." *Social Science Quarterly* 74 (June 1993): 241–263.

Crabb, Beth. "May 1930: White Man's Justice for a Black Man's Crime." *Journal of Negro History* 75 (1990): 29–40.

Dailey, Nancy. "History of the Beaumont, Texas, Chapter of the National Association for the Advancement of Colored People, 1918–1970." Master's thesis, Lamar University, 1971.

Davis, Lucille. "Negro Voting in the Democratic Primaries in Texas, 1901–1945." Master's thesis, Texas Southern University, 1976.

Davis, Marilyn B. "Local Approach to the Sweatt Case." *Negro History Bulletin* 23 (March 1960): 133–137.

Davis, Patricia Lefforge. "*Sweatt v. Painter*: Integration in Texas Higher Education." Master's thesis, University of Texas at Austin, 1971.

Davis, William R. *The Development and Present Status of Negro Education in East Texas*. New York: Columbia Teachers College Press, 1934.

Dickens, Edwin Larry. "The Poll Tax in Texas." Master's thesis, Texas College of Arts and Industries, 1963.

Dickerman, George S. "The Negroes of San Antonio." *Southern Workman* 43 (April 1914): 246–248.

Dixon, Thomas Jr. "The Famous Ku Klux Klan." *Frontier Times* 7 (1930): 493–500.

Doyle, Judith Kaaz. "Maury Maverick and Racial Politics in San Antonio, Texas, 1938–1941." *Journal of Southern History* 53 (1987): 194–224.

Dressman, Frances. "'Yes We Have No Jitneys!': Transportation Issues in Houston's Black Community, 1914–1924." *The Houston Review* 9.2 (1987): 69–81.

Du Bois, W. E. B. "A Journey to Texas and New Orleans." *The Crisis* 41 (April 1934): 97–98.

Dulaney, W. Marvin. "The Progressive Voters League: A Political Voice for African Americans." In *Dallas Reconsidered: Essays in Local History*, edited by Michael V. Hazel, 169–183. Dallas: Three Forks Press, 1995.

_______. "The Texas Negro Peace Officers' Association: The Origins of Black Police Unionism." *The Houston Review* 12 (1990): 59–78.

Durham, Kenneth R. "The Longview Race Riot of 1919." *East Texas Historical Journal* 18 (Fall 1980): 13–24.

Dyer, Stanford Phillips. "Lyndon B. Johnson and the Politics of Civil Rights, 1935–1960: The Art of Moderate Leadership." Ph.D. dissertation, Texas A&M University, 1978.

Edwards, George Milton. "White Justice in Dallas." *The Nation* 161 (September 15, 1945): 253–255.

Edwards, Mildred. "The History of Racial Integration in the Amarillo, Texas, Public Schools, 1915–1973." Master's thesis, West Texas State University, 1974.

Ellison, William M. Jr. "Negro Suffrage in Texas and Its Exercise." Master's thesis, Colorado State College of Education, 1943.

Emmons, Martha. *Deep Like the Rivers: Stories of My Negro Friends*. Austin: Encino Press, 1969.

Estes, Mary Elizabeth. "An Historical Survey of Lynchings in Oklahoma and Texas." Master's thesis, University of Oklahoma, 1942.

Evans, Eola Adeline. "Activity of Black Women in the Woman Suffrage Movement, 1900–1920." Master's thesis, Lamar University, 1987.

Evans, Hiram Wesley. "The Klan: Defender of Americanism." *Forum* 74 (December 1925): 801–814.

Fleming, Robert E. "Sutton E. Griggs: Militant Black Novelist." *Phylon* 34 (1973): 73–77.

Foley, Neil Francis. "The New South in the Southwest: Anglos, Blacks, and Mexicans in Central Texas, 1880–1930." Ph.D. dissertation, University of Michigan, 1990.

_______. *The White Scourge: Mexicans, Blacks, and Poor Whites in Texas Cotton Culture.* Berkeley: University of California Press, 1997.

Fontaine, Jacob III, and Gene Burd. *Jacob Fontaine: From Slavery to the Greatness of the Pulpit, the Press, and Public Service.* Austin: University of Texas Press, 1983.

Foster, Robert L. "Black Lubbock: A History of Negroes in Lubbock, Texas, to 1940." Master's thesis, Texas Tech University, 1974.

Freydberg, Elizabeth A. H. *Bessie Coleman: The Brownskin Lady Bird.* New York: Garland Publishing, 1994.

Gee, Ruth Ella. "The History and Development of the Prairie View Training School, 1916–1946." Master's thesis, Prairie View University, 1946.

Gillette, Michael L. "Blacks Challenge the White University." *Southwestern Historical Quarterly* 86 (1982): 321–344.

_______. "Heman Marion Sweatt: Civil Rights Plaintiff." In *Black Leaders: Texans for Their Times*, edited by Alwyn Barr and Robert A. Calvert, 157–188. Austin: Texas State Historical Association, 1981.

_______. "The NAACP in Texas, 1937–1957." Ph.D. dissertation, University of Texas at Austin, 1984.

_______. "National Association for the Advancement of Colored People." In *The New Handbook of Texas*, edited by Ron Tyler, Douglas E. Barnett, Roy R. Barkley, Penelope C. Anderson, and Mark F. Odintz, vol. 4, 941–942. Austin: Texas State Historical Association, 1996.

_______. "The Rise of the NAACP in Texas." *Southwestern Historical Quarterly* 81 (1978): 393–416.

Glasrud, Bruce A. "Blacks and Texas Politics during the Twenties." *Red River Valley Historical Review* 7 (Spring 1982): 39–53.

_______. "Black Texans, 1900–1930: A History." Ph.D. dissertation, Texas Tech University, 1969.

_______. "Child or Beast? White Texas' View of Blacks, 1900–1910." *East Texas Historical Journal* 15.2 (1977): 38–44.

_______. "Early Black Nationalist Movements in Texas." *Journal of Big Bend Studies* 11 (1999): 159–169.

_______. "Enforcing White Supremacy in Texas, 1900–1910." *Red River Valley Historical Review* 4 (Fall 1979): 65–74.

_______. "Nixon *vs.* Condon, 286 US 73 (1932)." In *Encyclopedia of African-American Civil Rights: From Emancipation to the Present*, edited by Charles D. Lowery and John F. Marszalak, 405. Westport, Conn.: Greenwood Press, 1992.

_______. "William M. McDonald: Business and Fraternal Leader." In *Black Leaders: Texans for Their Times*, edited by Alwyn Barr and Robert A. Calvert, 83–111. Austin: Texas State Historical Association, 1981.

Gloster, Hugh M. "Sutton E. Griggs: Novelist of the New Negro." *Phylon* 34 (1973): 335–345.

Gooch, Jane P. "Barbara C. Jordan: Her First Forty Years; A Rhetorical Analysis." Master's thesis, Baylor University, 1977.

Gooden, Burnice R. "The Development of Negro Life in Madisonville, Texas, since 1900." Master's thesis, Prairie View Agricultural and Mechanical College, 1949.

Gooden, John Eddie. "Negro Participation in Civil Government with Emphasis on Public Education in Texas." Ph.D. dissertation, University of Southern California, 1950.

Gordon, John Ramsey. "The Negro in McLennan County, Texas." Master's thesis, Baylor University, 1932.

Green, Casey. "Guardians Against Change: The Ku Klux Klan in Houston and Harris County, 1920–1925." *The Houston Review* 10 (1988): 3–20.

Green, Lorenzo. "Sidelights on Houston Negroes, as Seen by an Associate of Dr. Carter G. Woodson in 1930." In *Black Dixie: Afro-Texan History and Culture in Houston*, edited by Howard Beeth and Cary D. Wintz, 134–154. College Station: Texas A&M University Press, 1992.

Greenberg, Sanford N. "White Primary." In *The New Handbook of Texas*, edited by Ron Tyler, Douglas E. Barnett, Roy R. Barkley, Penelope C. Anderson, and Mark F. Odintz, vol. 6, 940–941. Austin: Texas State Historical Association, 1996.

Greene, Carrie Etta. "The History of Education Provided for Negroes in San Angelo, Texas, from Inception to Integration, September, 1955." Master's thesis, Texas Southern University, 1956.

Griggs, Sutton E. *The Story of My Struggle*. Memphis: n.p., 1914.

Gruening, Martha. "Houston: An NAACP Investigation." *The Crisis* 15 (November 1917): 14–18.

Hainsworth, Robert W. "The Negro and the Texas Primaries." *Journal of Negro History* 18 (1933): 426–451.

Hall, Jacquelyn Dowd. *Revolt Against Chivalry: Jessie Daniel Ames and the Women's Campaign Against Lynching*. Revised edition. New York: Columbia University Press, 1993.

Hardman, Peggy. "The Anti-tuberculosis Crusade and the Texas African American Community, 1900–1950." Ph.D. dissertation, Texas Tech University, 1997.

Haynes, Robert V. "Black Houstonians and the White Democratic Primary, 1920–45." In *Black Dixie: Afro-Texan History and Culture in Houston* edited by Howard Beeth and Cary D. Wintz, 192–210. College Station: Texas A&M University Press, 1992.

Hedgepath, Donald R. "The Plan of San Diego: A Border Conspiracy." Master's thesis, Southwest Texas State College, 1969.

Hill, Artis. "'Jim Crow-ism' in Several Areas of Twentieth-Century Texas Life Relative to the Negro: Transportation, Eating and Lodging Places, Public Parks, and Movie Theaters." Master's thesis, Abilene Christian College, 1969.

Hill, Forest Garrett. "The Negro in the Texas Labor Supply." Master's thesis, University of Texas, 1946.

Hilliard, Roby Waldo. "Juvenile Delinquency Among Negroes in Houston, Texas." Master's thesis, University of Wisconsin, 1936.

Hine, Darlene Clark. "Blacks and the Destruction of the Democratic White Primary, 1932–1944." *Journal of Negro History* 62 (1977): 43–59.

_______. *Black Victory: The Rise and Fall of the White Primary in Texas*. Millwood, N.Y.: KTO Press, 1979.

_______. "The Elusive Ballot: The Black Struggle against the Texas Democratic White Primary, 1932–1945." *Southwestern Historical Quarterly* 81 (1978): 371–392.

Holloway, Harry. "The Negro and the Vote: The Case of Texas." *Journal of Politics* 23 (1961): 526–556.

Hornsby, Alton Jr. "The 'Colored Branch University' Issue in Texas—Prelude to *Sweatt v. Painter*." *Journal of Negro History* 61 (1976): 51–60.

Hunter, J. Marvin. "Bob Taylor's Tribute to the Old Family Darkey." *Frontier Times* 10 (1933): 528.

_______. "Negress [Caroline Wilson] 106 Dies." *Frontier Times* 11 (1934): 524.

_______. "Negress [Mary Ware Humphries] Died at Age of 125." *Frontier Times* 9 (1932): 200.

Jackson, A. W. *A Sure Foundation and a Sketch of Negro Life in Texas*. Houston: A. W. Jackson, 1940.

Jackson, Charles Christopher. "A Southern Black Community Comes of Age: Black San Antonio in the Great Depression, 1930–1941." Master's thesis, Texas A&M University, 1989.

Jackson, James Thomas. "The Burning of the Books." In *Waiting in Line at the Drugstore and Other Writings of James Thomas Jackson*, collected by June Acosta, 78–84. Denton: University of North Texas Press, 1993.

_______. "Of Roses and a Black Family's Unusual Visitor." In *Waiting in Line at the Drugstore and Other Writings of James Thomas Jackson*, collected by June Acosta, 11–14. Denton: University of North Texas Press, 1993.

_______. "Once Upon a Time in Houston." In *Waiting in Line at the Drugstore and Other Writings of James Thomas Jackson*, collected by June Acosta, 7–10. Denton: University of North Texas Press, 1993.

_______. "On Learning Values, and People." In *Waiting in Line at the Drugstore and Other Writings of James Thomas Jackson*, collected by June Acosta, 23–28. Denton: University of North Texas Press, 1993.

Jackson, Kenneth T. "Dallas: Dynamo of the Southwest." In *The Ku Klux Klan in the City, 1915–1930,* 66–80, 265–266. New York: Oxford University Press, 1967.

James, Allie Winifred. "The Homemaking Activities of a Selected Group of Negro Homemakers in East Texas." Master's thesis, Kansas State College, Manhattan, 1939.

Johnson, Basco. "Venereal Disease Health Education Project for Negroes in Texas." *Journal of Social Hygiene* 30 (February 1944): 72–75.

Johnson, S. W. *How I Got Through: Ten Years of Religious and Civic Activities in Houston.* Houston: Houston Labor Journal Publishing Company, [1928].

Johnson, William Decker. *Marching Orders: Annual Addresses Delivered to the Texas Conferences of the A.M.E. Church.* n.p.: n.p., [1922].

Johnson, W. L. D. "Organization of the Public Schools in Houston, Texas, 1905–1940." Master's thesis, Prairie View University, 1943.

Johnston, O. G. "A Sociological Study of Standards of Living of Families in the Waco Negro Housing Project." Master's thesis, Baylor University, 1951.

Jones, Walter Benson. "A Study of the Graduates of Douglas High School, Sulphur Springs, Texas, 1924 to 1937, with a View to Curricular Revision along Vocational Lines." Master's thesis, Hampton Institute, 1938.

Kaplan, Barry J. "Race, Income and Ethnicity: Residential Change in a Houston Community, 1920–1970." *The Houston Review* 3 (Winter 1981): 178–203.

Kilgore, Linda Elaine. "The Ku Klux Klan and the Press in Texas—1920–1927." Master's thesis, University of Texas, 1964.

Kirven, Lamar L. "A Century of Warfare: Black Texans." Ph.D. dissertation, Indiana University, 1974.

Kroutter, Thomas E. Jr. "The Ku Klux Klan in Jefferson County, Texas, 1921–1924." Master's thesis, Lamar University, 1972.

LaGrone, Cyrus Wilson. "A Sociological Study of the Negro Population of Marshall, Texas." Master's thesis, University of Texas, 1932.

Lamkin, Patricia E. "A History of Blacks in San Angelo, 1869–1930." Master's thesis, Angelo State University, 1990.

Lanier, Raphael O. "The History of Higher Education for Negroes in Texas, 1930–1955, with Particular Reference to Texas Southern University." Ph.D. dissertation, New York University, 1957.

Lay, Shawn. "Imperial Outpost on the Border: El Paso's Frontier Klan No. 100." In *The Invisible Empire in the West: Toward a New Appraisal of the Ku Klux Klan of the 1920s*, edited by Shawn Lay, 67–95. Urbana: University of Illinois Press, 1992.

_______. *Revolution and the Ku Klux Klan: A Study of Intolerance in a Border City*. El Paso: Texas Western Press, 1985.

Lindsey, Walter. "Black Houstonians Challenge the White Democratic Primary, 1921–1944." Master's thesis, University of Houston, 1969.

Linsley, Judith W. "Main House, Carriage House: African-American Domestic Employees at the McFaddin-Ward House in Beaumont, Texas, 1900–1950." *Southwestern Historical Quarterly* 103 (1999): 17–51.

Livingston, David W. "The Lynching of Negroes in Texas, 1900–1925." Master's thesis, East Texas State University, 1972.

Logan, Rayford W., ed. "Texas." In *The Attitude of the Southern White Press Toward Negro Suffrage, 1932–1940*, 94–107. Washington, D.C.: The Foundation Publishers, 1940.

Lomax, John A., and Alan Lomax, eds. *Negro Folk Songs as Sung by Leadbelly*. New York: Macmillan, 1936.

Loud, I. B. "Methodism and the Negroes." In *History of Texas Methodism, 1900–1960*, edited by Olin W. Nail, 87–112. Austin: Capital Print, 1961.

Lowrey, Flora. "The Dallas Negro Players." *Southwest Review* 16 (1931): 373–382.

Luter, Buckner Sythias. "A Historical and Educational Analysis of the Administration and Curriculum of the Hempstead Negro School from 1867 to 1938: Inclusive." Master's thesis, Prairie View State Normal and Industrial College, 1939.

Marshall, Thurgood. "The Rise and Collapse of the White Democratic Party." *Columbia Law Review* 42 (1943): 1022–1077.

Mays, Fayrene Neuman. "A History of Public Library Service to Negroes in Houston, Texas, 1907–1962." Master's thesis, Atlanta University, 1964.

McDonald, Roy W. "Negro Voters in Democratic Primaries." *Texas Law Review* 5 (June 1927): 393–400.

McGowan-Johnson, Cernoria. "A Study in the History and Development of the Urban League Program in Fort Worth, Texas, 1944–1945." Master's thesis, Atlanta University, 1946.

Middagh, John. "A Newspaper Fights the Klan." In *Frontier Newspaper: The El Paso Times*, 185–213. El Paso: Texas Western Press, 1958.

Miller, Dale. "AAA Aggravates Negro Problem in the South." *Texas Weekly* 10 (December 1, 1934): 8–9.

Miller, Vickie Gail. *Doris Miller: A Silent Medal of Honor Winner*. Austin: Eakin Press, 1997.

Milton, Kenneth E. "The Drive for Civil Rights among Dallas Negroes during the 1930's." *North Texas Historian* 1 (November 1977): 95–102.

Montgomery, Ellie Walls. *Juvenile Delinquency among Negroes in Houston, Texas*. Houston: Houston College for Negroes, 1936.

_______. *Possibilities of Improving Negro Business through Better Business Methods*. Houston: Webster Printing, 1935.

_______. *A Survey of Negro Youths not in School—Houston, Texas*. Houston: Houston College for Negroes, 1936.

Morris, Mark Noland. "Saving Society Through Politics: The Ku Klux Klan in Dallas, Texas, in the 1920s." Ph.D. dissertation, University of North Texas, 1997.

Moten, D. S. *An Open Letter: Resolutions, Editorials, Comments, etc., in* The Texas Recorder. Dallas: Texas Recorder Printing, 1904.

Moye, Arnette. 'Longview.' In "Major Race Riots in the Red Summer of 1919," 22–27. Master's thesis, Texas Southern University, 1971.

Nelum, Junior Nathaniel. "A Study of the First Seventy Years of the Colored Teachers State Association of Texas." Ed.D. dissertation, University of Texas, 1955.

Nolen, Oran Warder. "Darkey [Tom Sullivan] of Old School Passes Century Mark." *Frontier Times* 7 (1930): 247–251.

Obadele-Starks, Ernest M. B. "Black Labor, the Black Middle Class, and Organized Protest along the Upper Texas Gulf Coast, 1883–1945." *Southwestern Historical Quarterly* 103 (1999): 53–65.

_______. *Black Unionism in the Industrial South*. College Station: Texas A&M University Press, 2000.

_______. "The Road to Jericho: Black Workers, The Fair Employment Practice Commission, and the Struggle for Racial Equality on the Upper Texas Gulf Coast, 1941–1947." Ph.D. dissertation, University of Houston, 1996.

O'Brien, Florence Bradshaw. "Adequacy of Texas History Texts in Reporting Negro Achievements." Master's thesis, Stephen F. Austin State Teachers College, 1939.

Ohler, George. "Background Causes of the Longview Race Riot of July 10, 1919." *Journal of the American Studies Association of Texas* 12 (1981): 46–54.

Olien, Roger M., and Diana Davids Olien. "Black and Mexican Americans." In *Oil Booms: Social Change in Five Texas Towns*, 109–126. Lincoln: University of Nebraska Press, 1982.

Olson, James S., and Sharon Phair. "The Anatomy of a Race Riot: Beaumont, Texas, 1943." *Texana* 11 (1973): 64–72.

Paley, Lillie M. "The Education and Responsibilities of Negro Home Demonstration Agents in Texas." Master's thesis, Kansas State College of Agriculture and Applied Science, 1941.

Pate, James E. "The Texas White Primary Law." *National Municipal Review* 16 (1927): 617–619.

Payne, Marcello. "The Monroe Payne Family." In *The Marvelous Marathon Basin: A History of Marathon, Texas, Its People, and Events*, 449–450. Austin: Nortex Press, 1989.

Perry, George Sessions. "Hayneses of Milam County, Texas." *Saturday Evening Post* 221 (October 23, 1948): 32–33, 93, 100, 103–104.

_______. "A Negro Doctor Wins-Over a Southern Town." *Saturday Evening Post* 226 (October 24, 1953): 36–37, 74, 77, 80.

Phillips, Edward Hake. "The Sherman Courthouse Riot of 1930." *East Texas Historical Journal* 25.2 (1987): 12–19.

Pickens, William. "Death Detail: Trial and Execution of Thirteen Negro Soldiers at Fort Sam Houston, Texas, December, 1917." *World Tomorrow* 13 (April 1930): 162–165.

_______. "Jim Crow in Texas." *The Nation* 117 (August 15, 1923): 155–156.

Pitre, Merline. *In Struggle against Jim Crow: Lulu B. White and the NAACP, 1900–1957*. College Station: Texas A&M University Press, 1999.

Price, Granville. "A Sociological Study of a Segregated District." Master's thesis, University of Texas, 1930.

Pruden, Durward. "A Sociological Study of a Texas Lynching." Master's thesis, Southern Methodist University, 1935.

Raper, Arthur Franklin. "Burning down the Courthouse: Sherman, Grayson County, Texas." *The Tragedy of Lynching*, 319–355. Chapel Hill: University of North Carolina Press, 1933.

Reich, Steven A. "Soldiers of Democracy: Black Texans and the Fight for Citizenship, 1917–1921." *Journal of American History* 82 (1996): 1478–1504.

Richardson, Clifton F. "Houston's Colored Citizens: Activities and Conditions among the Negro Population in the 1920s." In *Black Dixie: Afro-Texan History and Culture in Houston*, edited by Howard Beeth and Cary D. Wintz, 128–133. College Station: Texas A&M University Press, 1992.

Rich, Doris L. *Queen Bess: Daredevil Aviator*. Washington, D.C.: Smithsonian Institution Press, 1993.

Roberts, Randy. "Galveston's Jack Johnson: Flourishing in the Dark." *Southern Historical Quarterly* 87 (1983): 37–56.

_______. *Papa Jack: Jack Johnson and the Era of White Hope*. New York: Free Press, 1983.

Rudoff, Judith Kidd. "The Poll Tax in Texas: Political Panacea." Master's thesis, East Texas State University, 1968.

Santos, R. Chris. "Doris 'Dorie' Miller." *Texas Historian* 37 (May 1977): 10–13.

Sapper, Neil G. "Aboard the Wrong Ship in the Right Books: Doris Miller and Historical Accuracy." *East Texas Historical Journal* 18 (January 1980): 3–11.

_______. "Black Culture in Urban Texas: A Lone Star Renaissance." *Red River Valley Historical Review* 6 (Spring 1981): 56–77.

_______. "A Survey of the History of the Black People of Texas, 1930–1954." Ph.D. dissertation, Texas Tech University, 1972.

Scott, Emmett J. *The Red Book of Houston: A Compendium of Social, Professional, Religious, Educational and Industrial Interests of Houston's Colored Population*. Houston: Sotex Publishing, [1915].

Sharpless, Rebecca. *Fertile Ground, Narrow Choices: Women on Texas Cotton Farms, 1900–1940*. Chapel Hill: University of North Carolina Press, 1998.

Siler, Benjamin T. "The Brownsville, Texas, Affray of August 13–14, 1906, and Subsequent Proceedings." Master's thesis, North Carolina College at Durham, 1963.

Simpson, Julie. *The Clever Leader: Dr. L. H. Simpson, D.D.* Houston: Privately printed, 1963.

Smead, Howard. "Solely on Account of Race: The Defeat of the Texas White Primary." Master's thesis, University of Maryland, 1972.

Smith, Dick. "Texas and the Poll Tax." *Southwestern Social Science Quarterly* 35 (1955): 167–173.

Smith, Rogers Melton. "The Waco Lynching of 1916: Perspective and Analysis." Master's thesis, Baylor University, 1971.

Snow, Laura. "The Poll Tax in Texas: Its Historical, Legal, and Fiscal Aspects." Master's thesis, University of Texas, 1936.

SoRelle, James M. "The Darker Side of 'Heaven': The Black Community in Houston, Texas, 1917–1945." Ph.D. dissertation, Kent State University, 1980.

_______. "'An de Po Culled Man is In de Wuss Fix uv Awl': Black Occupational Status in Houston, Texas, 1920–1940." *The Houston Review* 1 (Spring 1979): 15–26.

_______. "Race Relations in 'Heavenly Houston', 1919–1945." In *Black Dixie: Afro-Texan History and Culture in Houston*, edited by Howard Beeth and Cary D. Wintz, 175–191. College Station: Texas A&M University Press, 1992.

_______. "The 'Waco Horror': The Lynching of Jesse Washington." *Southwestern Historical Quarterly* 86 (1983): 517–536.

Stiles, Jo Ann P. "The Changing Economic and Educational Status of Texas Negroes, 1940–1960." Master's thesis, University of Texas, 1966.

Stimpson, Eddie Jr. *My Remembers: A Black Sharecropper's Recollections of the Depression*, edited by James W. Byrd. Denton: University of North Texas Press, 1996.

Stone, Pearle Pippen. "An Analysis of the Changes and the Development of Negro Education in Rural Harrison County, 1940–1950." Master's thesis, North Texas State College, 1950.

Strong, Donald S. "The Poll Tax: The Case of Texas." *The American Political Science Review* 38 (August 1944): 693–709.

_______. "The Rise of Negro Voting in Texas." *The American Political Science Review* 42 (June 1948): 510–522.

Sullivan, Frederick B. "A Study of Home and Community Conditions of Negroes in Cass County, Texas." Master's thesis, Agricultural and Mechanical College of Texas, 1936.

Terrell, Mary Church. "Taft and the Negro Soldiers." *Independent* 65 (July 23, 1908): 189–190.

Terrell, Wendell Phillips. "A Short History of the Negro Longshoreman." Bachelor's essay, Houston College for Negroes, 1936.

Thomas, W. H. *Some Current Folk-Songs of the Negro*. n.p.: Folk-lore Society of Texas, 1912.

Thompson, Charles H. "Separate but not Equal: The Sweatt Case." *Southwest Review* 33 (1948): 105–112.

Timmons, Donnal M. "The Texas Commission on Interracial Cooperation." Master's thesis, Sam Houston State University, 1971.

Torrance, Lois E. "The Ku Klux Klan in Dallas, 1915–1928: An American Paradox." Master's thesis, Southern Methodist University, 1948.

Turner, Douglas. "The *Dallas Express* as a Forum on Lynching, 1919–1921." Master's thesis, Southern Methodist University, 1974.

Tuttle, William. "Violence in a 'Heathen' Land: The Longview Race Riot of 1919." *Phylon* 33 (1972): 324–333.

Ulrich, Ora Emma. "A Study of the Expenditure of Urban Negro Work Relief Families in Travis County, Texas as compared to an Adequate Diet." Master's thesis, University of Texas, 1935.

Vest, Deed L. "Watterson, A Texas Rural Community." Master's thesis, St. Mary's University, 1946.

Ware, Ural F. "The History of the Church of the Living God from 1906 to 1971." Master's thesis, Texas Southern University, 1972.

Wassenich, Paul Green. "A Social Study of the Negro Population of Austin, Texas, 1928–1935." Master's thesis, University of Texas, 1936.

Weaver, John D. *The Senator and the Sharecropper's Son: Exoneration of the Brownsville Soldiers*. College Station: Texas A&M University Press, 1997.

Webber, Carolyn Cott. "The Negro in the Texas Industrial Labor Market, 1940–1947." Master's thesis, University of Texas, 1948.

Weeks, O. Douglas. "The White Primary, 1944–1948." *The American Political Science Review* 42 (June 1948): 500–510.

Wesley, Carter W. "Texans Seek Right to Vote." *The Crisis* 47 (1940): 312–313, 322.

Wilson, Samuel Paschal Jr. "The White Primary Laws in Texas from 1923 to 1953." Master's thesis, Southwest Texas State University, 1971.

Wilson, William H. "Growing Up Black in East Texas: Some Twentieth-Century Experiences." *East Texas Historical Journal* 32.1 (1994): 49–54.

_______. "Private Planning for Black Housing in Dallas, Texas, 1945–1955." In *Proceedings of the Second National Conference on American Planning History*, 67–84. Columbus, Ohio: Society for American City and Regional Planning History, 1988.

_______. "'This Negro Housing Matter:' The Search for a Viable African-American Residential Subdivision in Dallas, 1945–1950." *Legacies* 4 (Fall 1994): 28–40.

Wood, Dale Brown. "The Poll Tax as a Voting Prerequisite." Master's thesis, University of Texas, 1942.

Woods, Sister Frances Jerome. "Negro Suffrage under the Texas Direct Primary System." Master's thesis, Catholic University, 1945.

Woolfolk, George R. "W. R. Banks: Public College Educator." In *Black Leaders: Texans for Their Times*, edited by Alwyn Barr and Robert A. Calvert, 129–158. Austin: Texas State Historical Association, 1981.

Yancy, C. D. "Negro Participation in the Agricultural Adjustment Agency Program in Texas." Master's thesis, Colorado A&M College, Fort Collins, 1946.

11. Civil Rights Revolution

Barbara Jordan, 1966, the first Afro-American woman to serve in the Texas Senate.

The UT Institute of Texan Cultures, No. 68-971

Barchus, Gale Leslie. "The Dynamics of Black Demands and White Responses for Negro Higher Education in Texas, 1945–1950." Master's thesis, University of Texas at Austin, 1970.

Breed, Warren. *Beaumont, Texas: College Desegregation without Popular Support.* New York: Anti-Defamation League of B'nai B'rith, 1957.

Brophy, William Joseph. "Active Acceptance—Active Containment: The Dallas Story." In *Southern Businessmen and Desegregation*, edited by Elizabeth Jacoway and David R. Colburn, 137–150. Baton Rouge: Louisiana State University Press, 1982.

Bruton, Frederic A. "Desegregation in San Antonio." Master's thesis, Trinity University, 1971.

Burrow, Rachel Northington. "Juanita Craft." Master's thesis, Southern Methodist University, 1994.

Calvert, Robert. "The Civil Rights Movement in Texas." In *The Texas Heritage*, edited by Ben Proctor and Archie P. McDonald, 147–164. Arlington Heights, Ill.: Forum Press, 1980.

Cole, Thomas. *No Color is my Kind: The Life of Eldrewey Stearns and the Integration of Houston.* Austin: University of Texas Press, 1997.

Craft, Juanita. *A Child, the Earth, and a Tree of Many Seasons: The Voice of Juanita Craft.* Dallas: Halifax Publishing, 1982.

Curtis, Gregory. "The First Protester." *Texas Monthly* 25 (June 1997): 7–8, 10.

Dailey, Nancy. "History of the Beaumont, Texas, Chapter of the National Association for the Advancement of Colored People, 1918–1970." Master's thesis, Lamar University, 1971.

Davidson, Chandler. "Negro Politics and the Rise of the Civil Rights Movement in Houston, Texas." Ph.D. dissertation, Princeton University, 1968.

De Shazo, Elmer Anthony. "An Equal Opportunities Committee at Work in Texas." *Social Science* 41 (1966): 99–106.

Dulaney, W. Marvin. "Whatever Happened to the Civil Rights Movement in Dallas, Texas?" In *Essays on the American Civil Rights Movement*, edited by W. Marvin Dulaney and Kathleen Underwood, 66–95. College Station: Texas A&M University Press, 1993.

Duren, Almetris Marsh, and Louise Iscoe. *Overcoming: A History of Black Integration at the University of Texas at Austin.* Austin: University of Texas at Austin, 1979.

Dyer, Stanford Phillips. "Lyndon B. Johnson and the Politics of Civil Rights, 1935–1960: The Art of Moderate Leadership." Ph.D. dissertation, Texas A&M University, 1978.

Edwards, Mildred. "The History of Racial Integration in the Amarillo, Texas, Public Schools, 1915–1973." Master's thesis, West Texas State University, 1974.

Gillespie, Dair Lindsay. "The Texas Southern University Incident: A Case Study of Local Newspaper Coverage of Racial Conflict." Master's thesis, University of Houston, 1968.

Gillette, Michael L. "Blacks Challenge the White University." *Southwestern Historical Quarterly* 86 (1982): 321–344.

_______. "Heman Marion Sweatt: Civil Rights Plaintiff." In *Black Leaders: Texans for Their Times*, edited by Alwyn Barr and Robert A. Calvert, 157–188. Austin: Texas State Historical Association, 1981.

Goldberg, Robert A. "Racial Change on the Southern Periphery: The Case of San Antonio, Texas, 1960–1965." *Journal of Southern History* 49 (1983): 349–374.

Griffin, John Howard. *Black Like Me*. New York: Houghton Mifflin, 1960.

Griffin, John Howard, and Theodore Freedman. *Mansfield, Texas: A Report of the Crisis Situation Resulting from Efforts to Desegregate the School System*. New York: Anti-Defamation League of B'nai B'rith, 1957.

Grunbaum, Werner F. "Desegregation in Texas: Voting and Action Patterns." *Public Opinion Quarterly* 28 (Winter 1964): 604–614.

Halsell, Grace. *Soul Sister*. New York: World, 1969.

Hart, Norris. "You Must Go Home Again." *Center Magazine* 2 (July 1969): 15–20.

Jensen, F. Kenneth. "The Houston Sit-in Movement of 1960–61." In *Black Dixie: Afro-Texan History and Culture in Houston*, edited by Howard Beeth and Cary D. Wintz, 211–222. College Station: Texas A&M University Press, 1992.

Jones, Carolyn. *Volma. . .My Journey: One Man's Impact on the Civil Rights Movement in Austin, Texas*. Austin: Eakin Press, 1998.

Jones, Douglas L. "The Sweatt Case and the Development of Legal Education for Negroes in Texas." *Texas Law Review* 47 (March 1969): 677–693.

Kellar, William Henry. "Make Haste Slowly: A History of School Desegregation in Houston, Texas." Ph.D. dissertation, University of Houston, 1994.

_______. *Make Haste Slowly: Moderates, Conservatives, and School Desegregation in Houston*. College Station: Texas A&M University Press, 1999.

King, Larry L. *Confessions of a White Racist*. New York: Viking Press, 1971.

Kirk, W. Aston, and John T. Q. King. "Desegregation of Higher Education in Texas." *Journal of Negro Education* 27 (1958): 318–323.

Kuhlman, Martin. "The Civil Rights March on Austin, Texas, 1963." In *Bricks Without Straw: A Comprehensive History of African Americans in Texas*, edited by David A. Williams, 153–166. Austin: Eakin Press, 1997.

_______. "The Civil Rights Movement in Texas: Desegregation of Public Accommodations, 1950–1964." Ph.D. dissertation, Texas Tech University, 1994.

_______. "Direct Action at the University of Texas During the Civil Rights Movement, 1960–1965." *Southwestern Historical Quarterly* 98 (1995): 550–566.

Ladino, Robyn Duff. *Desegregating Texas Schools: Eisenhower, Shivers, and the Crisis at Mansfield High*. Austin: University of Texas Press, 1996.

Linden, Glenn. *Desegregating Schools in Dallas*. Dallas: Three Forks Press, 1995.

Marcello, Ronald E. "The Integration of Intercollegiate Athletics in Texas: North Texas State College as a Test Case, 1956." *Journal of Sport History* 14 (Winter 1987): 286–316.

_______. "Reluctance versus Reality: The Desegregation of North Texas State College, 1954–1956." *Southwestern Historical Quarterly* 100 (1996): 153–185.

McCaslin, Richard B. "Steadfast in His Intent: John W. Hargis and the Integration of the University of Texas at Austin." *Southwestern Historical Quarterly* 95 (1991): 21–41.

Meltzer, Mildred Huber. "Chapters in the Struggle for Negro Rights in Houston, 1944–1962." Master's thesis, University of Houston, 1963.

Milton, Kenneth E. "The Drive for Civil Rights among Dallas Negroes during the 1930's." *North Texas Historian* 1 (November 1977): 95–102.

Montejano, David. "The Demise of 'Jim Crow' for Texas Mexicans, 1940–1970." *Aztlan* 16 (1985): 27–69.

Moreland, J. Kenneth. *Lunch-Counter Desegregation in Corpus Christi, Galveston, and San Antonio, Texas.* Atlanta: Randolph-Macon Woman's College, 1960.

Morse, Arthur D. "When Negroes Entered a Texas School: Del Mar College." *Harper's* 209 (September 1954): 47–49.

Obadele-Starks, Ernest M. B. "Ralph Yarborough of Texas and the Road to Civil Rights." *East Texas Historical Journal* 32.1 (1994): 39–48.

Pennington, Richard. *Breaking the Ice: The Racial Integration of Southwest Conference Football.* Jefferson, N.C.: McFarland, 1987.

Peters, William. "Houston's Quiet Victory." *Negro History Bulletin* 23 (January 1960): 75–79.

Pitre, Merline. "Black Houstonians and the 'Separate but Equal' Doctrine: Carter W. Wesley versus Lulu B. White." *The Houston Review* 12 (1990): 23–36.

_______. *In Struggle Against Jim Crow: Lulu B. White and the NAACP, 1900–1957.* College Station: Texas A&M University Press, 1999.

_______. "White, Lulu Belle Madison." In *The New Handbook of Texas*, edited by Ron Tyler, Douglas E. Barnett, Roy R. Barkley, Penelope C. Anderson, and Mark F. Odintz, vol. 6, 929. Austin: Texas State Historical Association, 1996.

Sapper, Neil G. "The Fall of the NAACP in Texas." *The Houston Review* 7 (Summer 1985): 53–68.

Scott, Alan. "Twenty-five Years of Opinion on Integration in Texas." *Southwestern Social Science Quarterly* 48 (1967): 155–163.

Shabazz, Amilcar. "The Desegregation of Lamar State College of Technology: An Analysis of Race and Education in Southeast Texas." Master's thesis, Lamar University, 1990.

Smith, Bryan L. "The Desegregation of the Ector County (Odessa) Independent School District, 1965–1985." Master's thesis, University of Texas-Permian Basin, 1992.

_______. "Desegregation in West Texas: The *United States v. Ector County ISD* Case." *West Texas Historical Association Year Book* 69 (1993): 59–73.

Stephens, Margene. "The Civil Rights Act of 1964 and Its Effects on the Black Vote in Harris County, Houston, Texas." Master's thesis, Texas Southern University, 1976.

Thompson, Charles H. "Separate But Not Equal: The Sweatt Case." *Southwest Review* 33 (1948): 105–112.

Werlin, Herbert H. "The Victory in Slaton." *Negro History Bulletin* 25 (February 1962): 112–113.

Westbrook, Johnnie Mae. "The Sweatt Case: A Study in Minority Strategy in Texas." Master's thesis, Prairie View A&M University, 1953.

Wilson, William H. "Desegregation of the Hamilton Park School, 1955–1975." *Southwestern Historical Quarterly* 95 (1991): 43–63.

Winegarten, Ruthe. "The Civil Rights Movement." In *Black Texas Women: 150 Years of Trial and Triumph*, 241–259. Austin: University of Texas Press, 1995.

12. Recent, 1954 to Present

June 13, 1984.

The UT Institute of Texan Cultures, No. L 7210.65
The San Antonio Light *Collection*

Amin, Julius. "Black Lubbock: 1955 to the Present." *West Texas Historical Association Year Book* 65 (1989): 24–35.

Aoyagi, Kiyotaka. "Kinship and Friendship in Black Los Angeles: A Study of Migrants from Texas." In *The Extended Family in Black Societies*, edited by Demitri B. Shimkin, Edith M. Shimkin, and Dennis A. Frate, 271–353. The Hague: Mouton Publishers, 1978.

Atkinson, M. Jourdan. "Familialism in Texas: A Texan View." In *The Extended Family in Black Societies*, edited by Demitri B. Shimkin, Edith M. Shimkin, and Dennis A. Frate, 355–362. The Hague: Mouton Publishers, 1978.

Biggers, John Thomas, Carroll Simms, and John Edward Weems. *Black Art in Houston: The Texas Southern University Experience.* College Station: Texas A&M University Press, 1978.

Bluiett, Calvin C. "The Political Potential of the Negro in Houston, Texas." Master's thesis, North Texas State University, 1968.

Botson, Michael. "No Gold Watch for Jim Crow's Retirement: The Abolition of Segregated Unionism at Houston's Hughes Tool Company." *Southwestern Historical Quarterly* 101 (1998): 497–521.

Bowman, Larry. "Breaking Barriers: David Hoskins and the Integration of the Texas League." In *Dallas Reconsidered: Essays in Local History*, edited by Michael V. Hazel, 184–193. Dallas: Three Forks Press, 1995.

Briley, Mary. "The T.S.U. Debate Team: Communicating with a City." *Texas Historian* 54.2 (November 1993): 1–4.

Broyles, William. "The Making of Barbara Jordan." *Texas Monthly* 4 (October 1976): 33–47.

Bryant, Ira B. Jr. *Barbara Charline Jordan: From the Ghetto to the Capitol.* Houston: D. Armstrong Company, 1977.

Bullard, Robert D. "The Black Family: Housing Alternatives in the 80s." *Journal of Black Studies* 14 (March 1984): 341–351.

_______. "Black Housing in the Golden Buckle of the Sunbelt." *Free Inquiry* 8 (November 1980): 169–172.

_______. "Dispute Resolution and Toxics: Case Studies." In *Dumping in Dixie: Race, Class, and Environmental Quality*, second edition 37–74. Boulder: Westview Press, 1994.

_______. "Endangered Environs: The Price of Unplanned Growth in Boomtown Houston." *California Sociologist* 7 (Summer 1984): 84–102.

_______. *Fear of Crime, Fear of Police and Black Residents' Endorsement of Crime-reduction Strategies.* Houston: Texas Southern University, 1981.

_______. "Housing Problems and Prospects in Contemporary Houston." In *Black Dixie: Afro-Texan History and Culture in Houston*, edited by Howard Beeth and Cary D. Wintz, 236–252. College Station: Texas A&M University Press, 1992.

_______. *Invisible Houston: The Black Experience in Boom and Bust*. College Station: Texas A&M University Press, 1987.

_______. "Solid Waste Sites and the Black Houston Community." *Sociological Inquiry* 53 (1983): 273–288.

Bullard, Robert D., and Odessa L. Pierce. "Black Housing in a Southern Metropolis: Competition for Housing in a Shrinking Market." *Black Scholar* 11 (November/December 1979): 60–67.

Bullard, Robert D., and Donald L. Tryman. "Competition for Decent Housing: A Focus on Housing Discrimination in a Sunbelt City." *Journal of Ethnic Studies* 7 (Winter 1980): 561–563.

Bullard, Robert D., and Beverly H. Wright. "Dumping Grounds in a Sunbelt City." *Urban Resources* 2 (Winter 1985): 37–39.

_______. "Environmentalism and the Politics of Equity: Emergent Trends in the Black Community." *Mid-American Review of Sociology* 14 (1987): 21–37.

Bullock, Henry Allen. "Expansion of Negro Suffrage in Texas." *Journal of Negro Education* 26 (1957): 369–374.

_______. "Significance of the Racial Factor in the Length of Prison Sentences." *Journal of Criminal Law, Criminology, and Police Science* 52 (1961): 411–417.

_______. "Urban Homicide in Theory and Fact." *Journal of Criminal Law, Criminology, and Police Science* 45 (1955): 565–575.

Burka, Paul. "Major Barbara [Jordan]." *Texas Monthly* 24 (March 1996): 88–89, 110–111.

Cohen, Carl. "Race, Lies, and 'Hopwood.'" *Commentary* 101 (June 1996): 39–45.

Crawford, Ann Fears, and Crystal Sasse Ragsdale. "Congresswoman from Texas [Barbara Jordan]." In *Women in Texas: Their Lives, Their Experiences, Their Accomplishments*, 296–307. Burnet, Tex.: Eakin Press, 1982.

Curtis, Tom. "Guilty until Proven Innocent." *Texas Monthly* 15 (September 1987): 94–97, 157–158, 160–163, 170–171.

Davidson, Chandler. *Race and Class in Texas Politics*. Princeton: Princeton University Press, 1990.

Davies, Nick. *White Lies: Rape, Murder and Justice, Texas Style*. New York: Avon Books, 1993.

Day, Barbara Thompson. "The Heart of Houston: The Early History of the Houston Council on Human Relations, 1958–1972." *The Houston Review* 8 (Spring 1986): 1–32.

De Shazo, Elmer Anthony. "An Equal Opportunities Committee at Work in Texas." *Social Science* 41 (1966): 99–106.

Dometrius, Nelson C., and Lee Sigelman. "The Cost of Quality: Teacher Testing and Racial-Ethnic Representativeness in Public Education." *Social Science Quarterly* 69 (1988): 70–82.

Dulaney, W. Marvin. "Long Ride to Blue." *Our Texas* (Summer 1992): 14–15.

_______. "The Progressive Voters League." *Legacies: A History Journal for Dallas and North Central Texas* 3 (1991): 27–35.

_______. "The Texas Negro Peace Officers' Association: The Origins of Black Police Unionism." *The Houston Review* 12 (1990): 59–78.

Duren, Almetris Marsh, and Louise Iscoe. *Overcoming: A History of Black Integration at the University of Texas at Austin.* Austin: University of Texas at Austin, 1979.

Dyer, James A., Arnold Vedlitz, and Stephen Worchel. "Social Distance among Racial and Ethnic Groups in Texas: Some Demographic Correlates." *Social Science Quarterly* 70 (1989): 607–616.

Ekland-Olson, Sheldon. "Structured Discretion, Racial Bias, and the Death Penalty: The First Decade after Furman in Texas." *Social Science Quarterly* 69 (1988): 853–873.

Frederickson, George M. "Jasper, Texas: A Historical Perspective on a Brutal Killing." *The Journal of Blacks in Higher Education* 23 (Spring 1999): 136–137.

Freeman, Janice Catherine. "The Effects of Relocation upon the Sense of Community Among Afro-Americans." Master's thesis, University of Texas at Austin, 1969.

Gite, Lloyd. "Affirmative Action Watch." *Black Enterprise* 20 (November 1989): 34.

_______. "Texas: Are There Bigger Opportunities for Blacks in Dallas and Houston?" *Black Enterprise* 24 (June 1994): 192–198.

Goode, Victor L. "The Blackest Dirt, the Whitest People: An East Texas Municipal Election Scheme." *Journal of Ethnic Studies* 11 (Winter 1984): 11–27.

Gotcher, Patrick Donald. "Attitudes of White Southern Baptist Ministers in Dallas-Tarrant Baptist Associations Toward Blacks." Master's thesis, University of Texas at Arlington, 1972.

Halsell, Grace. *In Their Shoes: A White Woman's Journey Living as a Black, Navajo, and Mexican Illegal.* Fort Worth: Texas Christian University Press, 1996.

Haggerty, Sue Irene. "A Historic District Designation in a Black Setting." Master's thesis, University of Texas at Arlington, 1976.

Hart, Norris. "You Must Go Home Again." *Center Magazine* 2 (July 1969): 15–20.

Henderson, Thomas (Hollywood). "Unsportsmanlike Conduct: A Fallen Dallas Cowboys' Star Tells How He Blew the Game of Life." *Texas Monthly* 15 (September 1987): 110–113, 126, 128.

Hickman, R. C. *Behold the People: R. C. Hickman's Photographs of Black Dallas, 1949–1961.* Austin: Texas State Historical Association, 1994.

Hollandsworth, Skip. "Does DaRoyce Mosley Deserve to Die?" *Texas Monthly* 24 (February 1996): 82–85, 108–109, 134–139.

Holloway, Harry. "The Negro and the Vote: The Case of Texas." *Journal of Politics* 23 (1961): 526–556.

_______. "The Texas Negro as a Voter." *Phylon* 24 (Summer 1963): 135–145.

Holloway, Harry, and David M. Olson. "Electoral Participation by White and Negro in a Southern City." *Midwest Journal of Political Science* 10 (February 1966): 99–122.

Hula, Richard C. "Housing Market Effects of Public School Desegregation: The Case of Dallas, Texas." *Urban Affairs Quarterly* 19 (1984): 409–423.

Hwang, Sean-Shong, and Steven H. Murdock. "Residential Segregation in Texas in 1980." *Social Science Quarterly* 63 (December 1982): 737–748.

Hwang, Sean-Shong, Steven H. Murdock, and Banoo Parpia. "The Effects of Race and Socioeconomic Status on Residential Segregation in Texas, 1970–1980." *Social Forces* 63 (1985): 732–747.

Jackson, Jerome E. "Race and Correctional Officers' Punitive Attitudes toward Treatment Programs for Inmates." *Journal of Criminal Justice* 24 (1996): 153–166.

Jackson, Vicki Diane. "Relationships of Harmful Health and Safety Misconceptions Among Selected Negro and Caucasian Ethnic Groups of Texas." Master's thesis, Texas Woman's University, 1973.

James, Jo Anne. "Lyndon Johnson and the Black American. "Master's thesis, Texas A&I University, 1971.

Jones, Nancy Baker, and Ruthe Winegarten. "Eddie Bernice Johnson." *Capitol Women: Texas Female Legislators, 1923–1999*, 169–173. Austin: University of Texas Press, 2000.

_______. "Senfronia Paige Thompson" *Capitol Women: Texas Female Legislators, 1923–1999*, 176–179. Austin: University of Texas Press, 2000.

_______. "Wilhelmina Ruth Fitzgerald Delco" *Capitol Women: Texas Female Legislators, 1923–1999*, 182–186. Austin: University of Texas Press, 2000.

Keeler, John Day. "Public Relations and the Black Community: Need for a New Approach." Master's thesis, University of Texas at Austin, 1973.

Kilmer, Rita Kathryn McCoulskey. "Residental Movement of Blacks in Austin, Texas, 1950–1970." Master's thesis, University of Texas at Austin, 1974.

Kirk, Rita G. "Barbara Jordan: The Rise of a Black Woman Politician." Master's thesis, University of Arkansas, 1978.

Lede, Naomi W. *Precious Memories of a Black Socialite: A Narrative of the Life and Times of Constance Houston Thompson*. Houston: D. Armstrong Company, 1991.

Lewis, Linda. "Young, Gifted and Black." In *No Apologies: Texas Radicals Celebrate the '60s*, edited by Daryl Janes, 62–71. Austin: Eakin Press, 1992.

Loewenstein, Gaither, and Lyttleton T. Sanders. "Bloc Voting, Rainbow Coalitions, and the Jackson Presidential Candidacy: A View from Southeast Texas." *Journal of Black Studies* 18 (September 1987): 86–96.

Lorentz, Robert L., and Carroll D. Aby Jr. "Enhancing Profits and Dispelling Misconceptions: A Refutation of Popular Views Concerning Black Welfare Recipients." *Midwestern Business and Economic Review* 16 (Fall 1992): 24–27.

Madison, Anna Marie. "Black Political Power in Dallas County, Texas." Master's thesis, University of Texas at Arlington, 1972.

Madla, Frank L. "The Political Impact of Latin Americans and Negroes in Texas Politics." Master's thesis, St. Mary's University, 1964.

Milligan, Alfred Ray. "A Study of Opinions of a Selected Group of Ministers Toward Race Relations." Master's thesis, North Texas State College, 1957.

Mindiola, Tatcho Jr. "The Cost of being Mexican American and Black in Texas, 1960–1970." Ph.D. dissertation, Brown University, 1978.

Mitchell, Joseph Clouis. "Community Education Advisory Councils: A Profile of Black Leadership Power in Selected Texas Communities." Ph.D. dissertation, Texas A&M University, 1983.

Nash, Sunny. *Bigmama Didn't Shop at Woolworth's*. College Station: Texas A&M University Press, 1996.

_______. "A Mission Completed for Doll." In *State Lines*, edited by Ken Hammond, 40–44. College Station: Texas A&M University Press, 1993.

Nimmo, Dan, and Clifton McCleskey. "Impact of the Poll Tax System on Voter Participation: The Houston Metropolitan Area in 1966." *Journal of Politics* 31 (1969): 682–699.

Powell-Griner, Eve. "Differences in Infant Mortality among Texas Anglos, Hispanics, and Blacks." *Social Science Quarterly* 69 (1988): 452–467.

Rankin, Jerry Lawrence. "An Exploration in Community Integration: The Houston Negro Press, 1960–1967." Master's thesis, University of Houston, 1967.

Richardson, Clifton F. "Houston's Colored Citizens: Activities and Conditions among the Negro Population in the 1920s. In *Black Dixie: Afro-Texan History and Culture in Houston*, edited by Howard Beeth and Cary D. Wintz, 128–133. College Station: Texas A&M University Press, 1992.

Ringheim, Karin. "Investigating the Structural Determinants of Homelessness: The Case of Houston." *Urban Affairs Quarterly* 28 (1993): 617–640.

Roberts, Guy Otha. "Knowledge and Attitudes Toward Welfare Laws in Texas of Low Income Negroes, Latins and Anglos in Austin, Texas." Master's thesis, University of Texas at Austin, 1967.

Roberts, Velma, and Ruby Williams. "Welfare is a Right." In *No Apologies: Texas Radicals Celebrate the '60s*, edited by Daryl Janes, 110–119. Austin: Eakin Press, 1992.

Rodriguez, Roberto. "Mamie McKnight: Promoting Education and Preserving Black Dallas History." *Black Issues in Higher Education* 10 (December 16, 1993): 24–25.

Rodriguez, Romeo. "Mortality Experiences of Chicanos, Blacks, and Anglos, Texas, 1970." Master's thesis, University of Texas at Austin, 1975.

Saenz, Rogelio, and John K. Thomas. "Minority Poverty in Nonmetropolitan Texas." *Rural Sociology* 56 (1991): 204–223.

Sanders, Charles L. "Barbara Jordan: Texan is a New Power on Capitol Hill." *Ebony* 30 (February 1975): 136–142.

Sapper, Neil G. "The Fall of the NAACP in Texas." *The Houston Review* 7 (Summer 1985): 53–68.

Scally, Billy F. "The Effect of Social Class on Racial Discrimination." Master's thesis, East Texas State University, 1966.

Shimkin, Demitri B. "Texas indeed is Different: Some Historical and Demographic Observations." In *The Extended Family in Black Societies*, edited by Demitri B. Shimkin, Edith M. Shimkin, and Dennis A. Frate, 363–378. The Hague: Mouton Publishers, 1978.

Stanley, William David. "Southern Black Women's Orientation toward Interracial Relations: Study of a Small Nonmetropolitan-Urban East Texas Town, 1970–1977." Master's thesis, Texas A&M University, 1982.

Storey, John W. "Texas Baptist Leadership, the Social Gospel, and Race, 1954–1968." *Southwestern Historical Quarterly* 83 (1979): 29–46.

Stowers, Kevin Ross. "Residential Segregation in Dallas County, Texas: A Comparison of Two Stratification Models." Master's thesis, Texas A&M University, 1973.

Taylor, Rives. "Fourth Ward and the Siege of Allen Parkway Village." *Cite* 25 (Fall 1990): 6–11, 31.

Tullis, David S. "A Comparative Study of Negro, Latin, and Anglo Children in a West Texas Community." Ed.D. dissertation, Texas Technological College, 1964.

Valdez, Avelardo, Zenong Yin, and Charles D. Kaplan. "A Comparison of Alcohol, Drugs, and Aggressive Crime among Mexican-American, Black, and White Male Arrestees in Texas." *American Journal of Drug and Alcohol Abuse* 23 (May 1997): 249–265.

Webeshete, Asefa. "Level of Education and Job Satisfaction: The Case of Ethiopian Refugees and Defacto Refugees in Houston, Texas." Ed.D. dissertation, Texas Southern University, 1985.

Wilheim, Gene Jr. "Dooryard Gardens and Gardening in the Black Community of Brushy, Texas." *Geographical Review* 65 (1975): 73–92.

Williams, J. Allen Jr., Nicholas Babchuk, and David R. Johnson. "Voluntary Associations and Minority Status: A Comparative Analysis of Anglo, Black, and Mexican Americans." *American Sociological Review* 38 (October 1973): 637–646.

Wilson, Anna Victoria. "Forgotten Voices: Remembered Experiences of Cross-over Teachers during Desegregation in Austin, Texas, 1964–1971." Ph.D. dissertation, University of Texas at Austin, 1997.

13. Culture

Lightnin' Hopkins in a recording studio.

The UT Institute of Texan Cultures, No. 77-417

Abernethy, Francis E. "African-American Folklore in Texas and in the Texas Folklore Society." In *Juneteenth Texas: Essays in African-American Folklore*, edited by Francis E. Abernethy, Carolyn Fiedler Satterwhite, Patrick B. Mullen, and Alan B. Govenar, 1–13. Publication of the Texas Folklore Society No. 54. Denton: University of North Texas Press, 1996.

Acosta, June, coll. *Waiting in Line at the Drugstore and Other Writings of James Thomas Jackson*. Denton: University of North Texas Press, 1993.

Adele, Lynne. "Frank Jones: The Psychological Belief System of a Black Folk Artist." Master's thesis, University of Texas at Austin, 1987.

Aden, Alonzo J. "Educational Tour through the Hall of Negro Life." *Southern Workman* 65 (November 1936): 331–341.

Alyn, Glen. *I Say Me for a Parable: The Oral Autobiography of Mance Lipscomb, Texas Bluesman*. New York: Da Capo Press, 1993.

_______. "Mance Lipscomb: Fight, Flight, or the Blues." In *Juneteenth Texas: Essays in African-American Folklore*, edited by Francis E. Abernethy, Carolyn Fiedler Satterwhite, Patrick B. Mullen, and Alan B. Govenar, 69–92. Publication of the Texas Folklore Society No. 54. Denton: University of North Texas Press, 1996.

Anderson, James S. *The Sunday School Talker*. Austin: Herald Press, 1904.

Anderson, John Q. "Old John and the Master." *Southern Folklore Quarterly* 25 (1961): 195–197.

Baker, Orestes Jeremiah. "A Study of Senior College Library Facilities for Negroes in Texas." Master's thesis, Columbia University, 1936.

Bales, Mary Virginia. "Negro Folk-Songs in Texas, Their Definition and Origin." Master's thesis, Texas Christian University, 1927.

_______. "Some Negro Folk-Songs of Texas." In *Follow de Drinkin' Gou'd*, edited by J. Frank Dobie, 85–112. Dallas: Southern Methodist University Press, 1965.

Balester, Valerie M. *Cultural Divide: A Study of African-American College-Level Writers*. Portsmouth, N.H.: Boynton/Cook, 1993.

Banks, Melvin James. *The History of the New Hope Baptist Church: A Century of Faith*. Dallas: New Hope Baptist Church, 1967.

Barnes, Glynell Shakelford. "A History of Public Library Service to Negroes in Galveston, Texas 1904–1955." Master's thesis, Atlanta University, 1957.

Barnes, Marian. "Ada DeBlanc Simond: Author, Community Leader, Storyteller." In *Black Texans: They Overcame*, 96–102. Austin: Eakin Press, 1996. [Children's book]

Barr, Alwyn. "Juneteenth." In *Encyclopedia of Southern Culture*, edited by Charles Reagan Wilson and William Ferris, 216. Chapel Hill: University of North Carolina Press, 1989.

Barrett, Anna Pearl. *Juneteenth: Celebrating Freedom in Texas*. Austin: Eakin Press, 1999.

Barth, Shell Jr. "A History of the Negro Presbyterian Church U.S. in Texas." Master's thesis, University of Texas, 1965.

Bennett, Patrick. "Elmer Kelton: Racial Friction Out West." In *Talking With Texas Writers: Twelve Interviews*, 179–203. College Station: Texas A&M University Press, 1980.

Berardi, Gayle K., and Thomas W. Segady. "Community Identification and Cultural Transformation: The Role of African-American Newspapers in Texas, 1868–1970." Ph.D. dissertation, University of Texas at Austin, 1972.

Bessent, Nancy Echols. "The Publisher: A Biography of Carter Wesley." Master's thesis, University of Texas at Austin, 1981.

Biggers, John Thomas, Carroll Simms, and John Edward Weems. *Black Art in Houston: The Texas Southern University Experience.* College Station: Texas A&M University Press, 1978.

Blesch, Rudi. "Scott Joplin." *American Heritage* 26 (June 1975): 26–32, 86–89.

Boone, Theodore Sylvester. *Feet Like Polished Brass.* Fort Worth: Masonic Printing Department, 1933.

_______. *"Old Chief", Alexander Lorenza Boone, D.D., LL.D.; A Biography by his Son.* Houston: Western Star Publishing Company, 1927.

Boswell, John David. "Negro Participation in the 1936 Texas Centennial Exposition." Master's thesis, University of Texas at Austin, 1969.

Bowman, Larry. "Breaking Barriers: David Hoskins and the Integration of the Texas League." In *Dallas Reconsidered: Essays in Local History*, edited by Michael V. Hazel, 184–193. Dallas: Three Forks Press, 1995.

Brackner, Elmer Joe Jr. "The Transition from Slave Potter to Free Potter: The Wilson Potteries of Guadalupe County, Texas." In *Texana II; Cultural Heritage of the Plantation South,* edited by Candace Volz, 39–43. Austin: Texas Historical Commission, 1982.

_______. "The Wilson Potteries." Master's thesis, University of Texas at Austin, 1981.

Brandenstein, Sherilyn. "*Sepia Record* as a Forum for Negotiating Women's Roles." In *Women and Texas History: Selected Essays*, edited by Fane Downs and Nancy Baker Jones, 143–157. Austin: Texas State Historical Association, 1993.

Brewer, J. Mason. *Aunt Dicy Tales: Snuff-Dipping Tales of the Texas Negro.* Austin: J. Mason Brewer, 1956.

_______. *Dog Ghosts and Other Texas Negro Folk Tales*. Austin: University of Texas Press, 1958.

_______, ed. *Heralding Dawn: An Anthology of Verse by Texas Negroes*. Dallas: June Thomason Printing, 1936.

_______. "Juneteenth." In *Tone the Bell Down*, edited by J. Frank Dobie, 9–54. Austin: Texas Folklore Society, 1932.

_______. *Negrito*. San Antonio: Naylor, 1933.

_______. "Old Time Negro Proverbs." In *Spur-of-the-Cock*, edited by J. Frank Dobie, 101–105. Austin: Texas Folklore Society, 1933.

_______. "Tales from *Juneteenth*." In *The Folklore of Texan Cultures*, edited by Francis Edward Abernethy and Dan Beaty, 115–118. Austin: Encino Press, 1974.

_______. *The Word on the Brazos: Negro Preacher Tales from the Brazos Bottoms of Texas*. Austin: University of Texas Press, 1953.

Briscoe, Dorothy Lee. "A Survey of the Materials Collection of the Texas Southern University Library, Houston, Texas." Master's thesis, Atlanta University, 1957.

Bryan, Frank. "On the Jefferson Road." In *Texian Stomping Grounds*, edited by J. Frank Dobie, Mody C. Boatright, and Harry H. Ranson, 1–25. Austin: Texas Folk-Lore Society, 1941.

Buchholz, Michael. "Racial References in the Texas Press, 1813–1836." *Journalism Quarterly* 67 (1990): 586–591.

Burns, Richard Allen. "African-American Blacksmithing in East Texas." In *Juneteenth Texas: Essays in African-American Folklore*, edited by Francis E. Abernethy, Carolyn Fiedler Satterwhite, Patrick B. Mullen, and Alan B. Govenar, 167–193. Publication of the Texas Folklore Society No. 54. Denton: University of North Texas Press, 1996.

_______. "Afro-American Blacksmithing in East Texas." Master's report, University of Texas at Austin, 1984.

Byrd, James W. "Afro-American Writers in the American West." In *A Literary History of the West*, 1139–1147. Sponsored by the Western Literature Association. Fort Worth: Texas Christian University Press, 1987.

_______. "Aunt Dicy: Legendary Black Lady." In *Legendary Ladies of Texas*, edited by Francis Edward Abernethy, 123–131. Dallas: E-Heart Press, 1981.

_______. "Brewer, John Mason." In *The New Handbook of Texas*, edited by Ron Tyler, Douglas E. Barnett, Roy R. Barkley, Penelope C. Anderson, and Mark F. Odintz, vol. 1, 724–725. Austin: Texas State Historical Association, 1996.

_______. "Folk Anecdote Survives in Black Fiction." In *The Folklore of Texan Cultures*, edited by Francis Edward Abernethy and Dan Beaty, 139–140. Austin: Encino Press, 1974.

_______. *J. Mason Brewer: Negro Folklorist.* Austin: Steck-Vaughn, 1967.

Campbell, Jeff H. "Negro." In *Southwestern American Literature: A Bibliography,* edited by John Q. Anderson, Edwin W. Gaston Jr., and James W. Lee, 48–50. Chicago: Swallow Press, 1980.

Carlisle, Natalie Taylor. "Old Time Darky Plantation Melodies." *Rainbow in the Morning*, edited by J. Frank Dobie, 137–143. Hatboro, Pa.: Folklore Association, 1965.

Carstarphen, Meta G. "Rare Films: The Tyler, Texas Treasure Trove." *American Visions* 4 (1989): 36–38.

Cartwright, Gary. "Spur of the Moment [David Robinson]." *Texas Monthly* 15 (November 1987): 146, 148.

Cartwright, Marguerita. "Etta Moten: Glamorous Grandmother." *Negro History Bulletin* 18 (March 1955): 137–138.

Center Magazine. "You Must Go Home Again: An Interview with Norris Hart." *The Center Magazine* 2 (July 1969): 15–20.

Christian, Garna L. "Texas Beginnings: Houston in the World of Jazz." *The Houston Review* 12.3 (1990): 144–156.

_______. "They Brightened the Corner: The Era of Gulf Coast Western Swing." *The Houston Review* 9.1 (1987): 25–38.

Cobb, Lucy M., and Mary A. Hicks. "Negro Folk Tales." *Texian Stomping Grounds*, edited by J. Frank Dobie, Mody C. Boatright, and Harry H. Ranson, 108–112. Austin: Texas Folk-Lore Society, 1941.

Condon, Cynthia G., Joy L. Becker, Heather Edgar, James Davidson, Juerena Hoffman, Patricia Kalima, Daniel Kysar, Susan Moorehead, Victoria Owens, and Keith Condon. *Freedman's Cemetery: Site 41DL316, Dallas, Texas, Assessments of Sex, Age-at Death, Stature and Date of Interment.* Report No. 9. Austin: Archaeological Studies Program, Environmental Affairs Division, Texas Department of Transportation, 1998.

Craft, Juanita. *A Child, the Earth, and a Tree of Many Seasons: The Voice of Juanita Craft.* Dallas: Halifax Publishing, 1982.

Cripps, Thomas R. "*The Birth of a Race*: A Lost Film Rediscovered in Texas." *Texas Humanist* 5 (March-April 1983): 10–11.

Damora, Robert. "Houston Zydeco: From Churches to Clubs." *Living Blues* 116 (July/August 1994): 44–47.

Dance, Helen Oakley. *Stormy Monday: The T-Bone Walker Story.* Baton Rouge: Louisiana State University Press, 1987.

Davidson, James M. "Freedman's Cemetery: A Chronological Reconstruction of an Excavated African-American Burial Ground, Dallas, Texas." Master's thesis, University of Arkansas, 1999.

_______. The Old Dallas Burial Ground: A Forgotten Cemetery. *Southwestern Historical Quarterly* 102.2 (1998):162–184.

Davis, Charles Gilbert. "Turning the Tune in Texas: A Survey of Printed Texas Music from Plain Chant to Ragtime." Master's thesis, Stephen F. Austin State University, 1984.

Delta Sigma Theta Sorority. *The Black Heritage Exhibit: A Pictorial History of Austin, Travis County, Texas' Black Community, 1839–1920.* Austin: Delta Sigma Theta Sorority, c.1973.

Dobie, J. Frank. "Eight Days towards the Sunset." In *Apache Gold and Yaqui Silver*, 203–209. Boston: Little, Brown, 1939.

Dulaney, W. Marvin. "The Black Church: An Agent of Social and Political Change." *Texas Journal of Ideas, History and Culture* 10 (Fall/Winter 1988): 8–10.

Eddins, A.W. "Brazos Bottom Philosophy." In *Coffee in the Gourd*, edited by J. Frank Dobie, 50–51. Dallas: Southern Methodist University Press, 1979.

Emmons, Martha. *Deep Like the Rivers: Stories of My Negro Friends.* Austin: Encino Press, 1969.

Ennis, Michael. "Long Shot." *Texas Monthly* 20 (February 1992): 42, 44–45.

_______. "Shock Therapy: Austin Painter Michael Ray Charles." *Texas Monthly* 25 (June 1997): 88–93.

Evans, Roxanne J. "Black Catholics." In *The New Handbook of Texas*, edited by Ron Tyler, Douglas E. Barnett, Roy R. Barkley, Penelope C. Anderson, and Mark F. Odintz, vol. 1, 561–562. Austin: Texas State Historical Association, 1996.

Fleming, Robert E. "Sutton E. Griggs: Militant Black Novelist." *Phylon* 34 (1973): 73–77.

Fly, LaBarbara Wigfall, and Everett L. Fly. "Black Vernacular Resources in Texas." *Heritage* 5 (Fall 1987): 24–27.

Fontaine, Jacob III, and Gene Burd. *Jacob Fontaine: From Slavery to the Greatness of the Pulpit, the Press, and Public Service.* Austin: University of Texas Press, 1983.

Fowler, Manet Harrison. "History of the Texas Association of Negro Musicians." *The Negro Musician* (August 1929): 114–116.

Franklin, J. E. *"Black Girl": From Genesis to Revelations*. Washington, D.C.: Howard University Press, 1973.

Fuller, Charles. "The Brownsville Raid." *Literary Cavalcade* 30 (January 1978): 9–23, 28–39. [Drama]

Garvin, Richard M. *The Midnight Special: The Legend of Leadbelly*. New York: B. Geis, 1971.

Gay, Willie Lee Washington, comp. *Rufus F. Hardin Homecoming and Juneteenth Celebration, June 18–20, 1999*. Brownwood, Tex.: Rufus F. Hardin Museum, Inc., 1999.

Gee, Sadye, comp., and Darnell Williams, ed. *Black Presence in Dallas, Historic Black Dallasites*. Dallas: Museum of African-American Life and Culture, 1986.

Glasrud, Bruce A., and Laurie Champion. "African Americans in the West: A Short Story Tradition." *Journal of Big Bend Studies* 10 (1998): 221–242.

_______. *The African American West: A Century of Short Stories*. Niwot, Colo.: University Press of Colorado, 2000.

_______. "Fiction." In *African Americans in the West: A Bibliography of Secondary Sources*, comp. Bruce A. Glasrud, 155–174. Occassional Papers No. 2. Alpine, Tex.: Center for Big Bend Studies, Sul Ross State University, 1998.

Gloster, Hugh M. "Sutton E. Griggs: Novelist of the New Negro." *Phylon* 34 (1973): 335–345.

Govenar, Alan B. "The Blues and Jives of Dr. Hepcat." In *Corners of Texas: Publication of the Texas Folklore Society*, edited by Francis Edward Abernethy, 239–245. Denton: University of North Texas Press, 1993.

_______. "Buster Smith: Dallas Jazz Patriarch." *Parkway* (April 1983): 34–35.

_______. *Living the Blues*. Dallas: Dallas Museum of Art, 1985.

_______. *Meeting the Blues*. Dallas: Taylor, 1988.

_______. *Portraits of Community: African American Photography in Texas*. Austin: Texas State Historical Association, 1996.

_______. "That Black Snake Moan: The Music and Mystery of Blind Lemon Jefferson." In *Bluesland: Portraits of Twelve Major American Blues Masters*, edited by Pete Welding and Toby Bryon, 16–37. New York: Penguin Books, 1991.

_______. "Them Deep Ellum Blues: A Street, a Sound, and a Time." *Legacies* 2 (Spring 1990): 4–9.

Govenar, Alan B., and Jay E. Brakefield. *Deep Ellum and Central Track: Where the Black and White Worlds of Dallas Converged*. Denton: University of North Texas Press, 1998.

Govenar, Alan B., and Benny Joseph. *The Early Years of Rhythm and Blues: Focus on Houston.* Houston: Rice University Press, 1990.

Green, Ely. *Ely: Too Black, Too White.* Amherst: University of Massachusetts Press, 1970.

Griffin, Marvin C. *Texas African-American Baptists: The Story of the Baptist General Convention of Texas.* Austin: Publisher's Marketing House, 1994.

Grose, Charles William. "Black Newspapers in Texas, 1868–1970." Ph.D. dissertation, University of Texas, 1972.

Hall, Frank. *The Burning Walls.* Amarillo: Russell Stationery, 1934.

Harris, Trudier. "'The Yellow Rose of Texas': A Different Cultural View." In *Juneteenth Texas: Essays in African-American Folklore*, edited by Francis Edward Abernethy, Carolyn Fiedler Satterwhite, Patrick B. Mullen, and Alan B. Govenar, 315–333. Publications of the Texas Foklore Society No. 54. Denton: University of North Texas Press, 1996.

Harrison, R. C. "The Negro as Interpreter of His Own Folk-Songs." *Rainbow in the Morning*, edited by J. Frank Dobie, 144–153. Hatboro, Pa.: Folklore Association, 1965.

Head, Dorothy Womack. "Survey of Library Use of the Memorial Library for Negroes, Sherman, Texas." Master's thesis, Texas State College for Women, 1952.

Hickman, R. C. *Behold the People: R. C. Hickman's Photographs of Black Dallas, 1949–1961.* Austin: Texas State Historical Association, 1994.

Hicks, Doris A. "Career Opportunities for Negroes in Texas Libraries, 1957." Master's thesis, University of Texas, 1959.

Hines, Carrie P. *The Surmounters.* Amarillo: Shepherd Printing Company, 1959.

Iglehart, Alfreda. "Waco Jive." In *The Folklore of Texan Cultures*, edited by Francis Edward Abernethy and Dan Beaty, 129–139. Austin: Encino Press, 1974.

Jackson, A. W. *A Sure Foundation and A Sketch of Negro Life in Texas.* Houston: A. W. Jackson, 1940.

Jackson, Bruce, ed. *Wake Up Dead Man: Afro-American Worksongs from Texas Prisons.* Cambridge: Harvard University Press, 1972.

Jackson, James Thomas. "The Burning of the Books." In *Waiting in Line at the Drugstore and Other Writings of James Thomas Jackson*, collected by June Acosta, 78–84. Denton: University of North Texas Press, 1993.

_______. "Houston's Fourth Ward." In *Juneteenth Texas: Essays in African-American Folklore*, edited by Francis E. Abernethy, Carolyn Fiedler Satterwhite, Patrick B. Mullen, and Alan B. Govenar, 41–47. Publication of the Texas Folklore Society No. 54. Denton: University of North Texas Press, 1996.

_______. "Once Upon a Time in Houston." In *Waiting in Line at the Drugstore and Other Writings of James Thomas Jackson*, collected by June Acosta, 7–10. Denton: University of North Texas Press, 1993.

_______. "Of Roses and a Black Family's Unusual Visitor." In *Waiting in Line at the Drugstore and Other Writings of James Thomas Jackson*, collected by June Acosta, 11–14. Denton: University of North Texas Press, 1993.

_______. "On Learning Values, and People." In *Waiting in Line at the Drugstore and Other Writings of James Thomas Jackson*, collected by June Acosta, 23–28. Denton: University of North Texas Press, 1993.

Jarboe, Jan. "Dog Ghosts and Bottle Trees." *Texas Monthly* 20 (January 1992): 104–111.

Jones, G. William. *Black Cinema Treasures: Lost and Found.* Denton: University of North Texas Press, 1991.

_______. "Black Filmmaking." In *The New Handbook of Texas*, edited by Ron Tyler, Douglas E. Barnett, Roy R. Barkley, Penelope C. Anderson, and Mark F. Odintz, vol. 1, 567. Austin: Texas State Historical Association, 1996.

Jones, Nancy N. "'Be' in Dallas Black English." Ph.D. dissertation, North Texas State University, 1972.

Jubera, Drew. "Donald Curry vs. the World." *Texas Monthly* 15 (July 1987): 130–133, 159–163.

Katz, William Loren. "Sutton E. Griggs: A Black Son of Texas Lifts His Pen." In *Black People Who Made the Old West*, 170–174. Trenton, N.J.: Africa World Press, 1992.

Keeling, Hightower T. *History of African Methodism in Texas.* Waco: C. F. Blanks Publisher, 1885.

Law, Robert Adger. "A Note on Four Negro Words." In *Texas and Southwestern Lore*, edited by J. Frank Dobie, 119–120. Austin: Texas Folklore Society, 1927.

Lewis, J. Vance. *Out of the Ditch: A True Story of an Ex-Slave*. Houston: Rein and Sons, 1910.

Lipsitz, George. "'Goin' On: Afro-American Imagery in Texas Film and Folklore." *Southwest Media Review* 3 (Spring 1985): 42–45.

Lomax, John A., and Alan Lomax, eds. *Negro Folk Songs as Sung by Leadbelly.* New York: Macmillan, 1936.

Lomax, Joseph F. "Zydeco—Must Live On!" In *What's Going On (In Modern Texas Folklore)*, edited by Francis Edward Abernethy, 205–223. Austin: Encino Press, 1976.

Lornell, Kip, and Charles Wolfe. *The Life and Legend of Leadbelly*. New York: HarperCollins, 1992.

Loud, I. B. "Methodism and the Negroes." In *History of Texas Methodism, 1900–1960*, edited by Olin W. Nail, 87–112. Austin: Capital Print, 1961.

Lovingood, Penman. *A Negro Seer: The Life and Work of Dr. R. S. Lovingood, Educator, Churchman and Race Leader*. Compton: The Lovingood Company, 1963.

Lowrey, Flora. "The Dallas Negro Players." *Southwest Review* 16 (1931): 373–382.

Lundy, Anne. "Conversation with . . . Ernestine Jessie Covington Dent." *Black Perspective in Music* 12 (Fall 1984): 244–263.

Mardis, Jas., ed. *KenteCloth: Southwest Voices of the African Diaspora, The Oral Tradition Comes to the Page*. Denton: University of North Texas Press, 1997.

Margot, Louis III. "The *Dallas Express*: A Negro Newspaper: Its History, 1892–1971, and Its Point of View." Master's thesis, East Texas State University, 1971.

Mays, Fayrene Neuman. "A History of Public Library Service to Negroes in Houston, Texas, 1907–1962." Master's thesis, Atlanta University, 1964.

McGuire, Kathryn S., and James Ward Lee, eds. *New Texas 94: Poetry and Fiction*. Denton: Center for Texas Studies, 1994. [Special issue on Afro-Texans]

McQueen, Clyde. *Black Churches in Texas: A Guide to Historic Congregations*. College Station: Texas A&M University Press, 2000.

Minton, John. "Creole Community and 'Mass' Communication: Houston Zydeco as a Mediated Tradition." *Journal of Folklore Research* 32 (1995): 1–19.

_______. "Houston Creoles and Zydeco: The Emergence of an African American Urban Popular Style." *American Music* 14 (1996): 480–526.

_______. "West African Fiddles in Deep East Texas." In *Juneteenth Texas: Essays in African-American Folklore*, edited by Francis E. Abernethy, Carolyn Fiedler Satterwhite, Patrick B. Mullen, and Alan B. Govenar, 291–312. Publication of the Texas Folklore Society No. 54. Denton: University of North Texas Press, 1996.

Montgomery, William E. "African-American Churches." In *The New Handbook of Texas*, edited by Ron Tyler, Douglas E. Barnett, Roy R. Barkley, Penelope C. Anderson, and Mark F. Odintz, vol. 1, 43–46. Austin: Texas State Historical Association, 1996.

Moring, Margaret Carol. "Brave Nigger Brit." Master's thesis, University of Texas at Austin, 1972. [Fiction]

Morrison, Dorothy, and Rebecca Buard. *The Black Citizen in American Democracy: Black Culture in Harrison County, Past, Present, and Future*, 2 volumes. Marshall, Tex.: Marshall Public Library, 1976, 1979.

Morthland, John. "Soul Survivor (Johnnie Taylor)." *Texas Monthly* 26 (July 1998): 50, 52–53.

Moutoussamy-Ashe, Jeanne. "Elizabeth 'Tex' Williams." In *Viewfinders: Black Women Photographers*, 98–100. New York: Dodd, Mead, 1986.

Mullen, Harryette. *Tree Tall Woman: Poems by Harryette Romell Mullen*. Austin: Red River Women's Press, 1978.

Mullen, Patrick B. "'Bongo Joe': A Traditional Street Performer." In *Juneteenth Texas: Essays in African-American Folklore*, edited by Francis E. Abernethy, Carolyn Fiedler Satterwhite, Patrick B. Mullen, and Alan B. Govenar, 273–288. Publication of the Texas Folklore Society No. 54. Denton: University of North Texas Press, 1996.

_______. "The Function of Folk Belief among Negro Fisherman of the Texas Coast." *Southern Folklore Quarterly* 33 (1969): 80–91.

_______. "A Negro Street Performer: Tradition and Innovation." *Western Folklore* 29 (1970): 91–103.

_______. "The Prism of Race: Two Texas Folk Performers." *Southern Folklore* 54.1 (1997): 13–25.

Nash, Sunny. *Bigmama Didn't Shop at Woolworth's*. College Station: Texas A&M University Press, 1996.

_______. "A Mission Completed for Doll." In *State Lines*, edited by Ken Hammond, 40–44. College Station: Texas A&M University Press, 1993.

Nye, Naomi Shihab. "Field Trip." In *State Lines*, edited by Ken Hammond, 91–94. College Station: Texas A&M University Press, 1993.

O'Brien, Florence Bradshaw. "Adequacy of Texas History Texts in Reporting Negro Achievements." Master's thesis, Stephen F. Austin State Teachers College, 1939.

Oliphant, Dave. "Eddie Durham and the Texas Contribution to Jazz History." *Southwestern Historical Quarterly* 96 (1993): 490–525.

_______. "From Bebop to Hard Bop and Beyond: The Texas Jazz Connection." In *Juneteenth Texas: Essays in African-American Folklore*, edited by Francis E. Abernethy, Carolyn Fiedler Satterwhite, Patrick B. Mullen, and Alan B. Govenar, 153–164. Publication of the Texas Folklore Society No. 54. Denton: University of North Texas Press, 1996.

_______. *Texas Jazz*. Austin: University of Texas Press, 1996.

Owens, William A. "Seer of Corsicana." In *And Horns on the Toads*, edited by Mody C. Boatright, 14–31. Dallas: Southern Methodist University Press, 1959.

_______. "Writing A Novel—Problem and Solution." *Southwest Review* 40 (1955): 254–261.

Parks, Carole A. "J. E. Franklin, Playwright." *Black World* 21 (April 1972): 49–50.

Pemberton, Doris. *Juneteenth at Comanche Crossing*. Austin: Eakin Press, 1983.

Peter, Duane, Marsha Prior, Melissa Green, and Victoria Green Clow (editors). *A Legacy of a Pioneer Black Community in Dallas, Texas: Freedman's Cemetery*. Special Publication No. 6. Austin: Archaeological Studies Program, Environmental Affairs Division, Texas Department of Transportation, 2000.

Pickens, William. "Death Detail: Trial and Execution of Thirteen Negro Soldiers at Fort Sam Houston, Texas, December, 1917." *World Tomorrow* 13 (April 1930): 162–165.

_______. "Jim Crow in Texas." *The Nation* 117 (August 15, 1923): 155–156.

_______. "Wiley University and Texas." In *Bursting Bonds,* 169–188. Boston: The Jordan and More Press, 1923.

Pinsky, Robert. "On 'Eve Tempted By the Serpent' by Defendente Ferrari, and in Memory of Congresswoman Barbara Jordan of Texas." *Salmagundi* 113 (Winter 1997): 174–175.

Pipkin, Loretta. "Loretta Pipkin: Finding My Place." *International Review of African American Art* 13 (1996): 34–36.

Pitts, Walter Franklin. "Linguistic Variation as a Function of Ritual Frames in the Afro-Baptist Church in Central Texas." Ph.D. dissertation, University of Texas at Austin, 1986.

Posey, John R. "Ebony Voices Harmonizing Across the Texas Prairie." In *New Texas 94: Poetry and Fiction*, edited by Kathryn S. McGuire and James Ward Lee, 1–10. Denton: Center for Texas Studies, 1994.

Powell, Leah Carson, and Helen Danzeiser Dockall. "Folk Narratives and Archaeology: An African American Cemetery in Texas." *Journal of Field Archaeology* 22 (1995): 349–353.

Pruett, Jakie L., and Everett B. Cole. *As We Lived: Stories by Black Story Tellers*. Burnet, Tex.: Eakin Press, 1982.

Pryor, LaRita Booth. *The African-American Writer's Digest: How and Where to Sell What You Write*. Austin: Princess Press, 1994.

Pyle, Philip Alan, and George McElroy. "The Black Press in Texas: A Short Overview." *The Black Presence in the Texas Sesquicentennial*, edited by Jesse E. Gloster and Hunter O. Brooks, 33–47. Houston: D. Armstrong Company, 1986.

Rand, Earl Wadsworth. *The Journey of Earl Wadsworth Rand: From There to Here, From Then until Now*. New York: Vintage Press, 1992.

Redwine, W.A. "Brief History of the Negro in Five Counties." *Chronicles of Smith County* [Texas] 11 (Fall 1972): 13–70. Originally published as a book (Tyler, Tex.: Privately printed, 1901).

Robinson, Dorothy Redus. *The Bell Rings at Four: A Black Teacher's Chronicle of Change*. Austin: Madrona Press, 1978.

Rodenberger, Lou Halsell. "A Developing Tradition: African-American Writers." In *Texas Women Writers: A Tradition of Their Own*, edited by Sylvia Ann Grider and Lou Halsell Rodenberger, 247–252. College Station: Texas A&M University Press, 1997.

Ross, Donald R. "Black Sacred Harp Singing Remembered in East Texas." In *Juneteenth Texas: Essays in African-American Folklore*, edited by Francis E. Abernethy, Carolyn Fiedler Satterwhite, Patrick B. Mullen, and Alan B. Govenar, 15–19. Publication of the Texas Folklore Society No. 54. Denton: University of North Texas Press, 1996.

Rosson, Chester. "Juneteenth." *Texas Monthly* 16 (June 1988): 110.

Russell, Jan. "Harriet and Harmon Kelley: Collecting Their Culture." *Texas Monthly* 24 (September 1996): 118–119, 179.

Sackler, Howard. *The Great White Hope*. New York: Dial, 1968.

Sample, Albert Race. *Racehoss: Big Emma's Boy*. Austin: Eakin Press, 1984.

Sanders, Helen. "Antioch Baptist Church." *Black Focus* (December–January 1977): 6–8.

Sapper, Neil G. "Black Culture in Urban Texas: A Lone Star Renaissance." *Red River Valley Historical Review* 6 (Spring 1981): 56–77.

Scarborough, Dorothy. "The 'Blues' as Folk-Songs." In *Coffee in the Gourd*, edited by J. Frank Dobie, 52–66. Dallas: Southern Methodist Press, 1979.

_______. *On the Trail of Negro Folksong*. Cambridge: Harvard University Press, 1925.

Shange, Ntozake. "Recipes from the Gypsy Cowgirl." *American Visions* 13 (February/March 1998): 33–35.

Sheeler, J. Reuben. "Negro History Week in the Houston Area." *Negro History Bulletin* 19 (October 1955): 2, 21.

Shorkey, Clay. "Texas Music Museum Studies African-American Contributions to Texas Music." *Texas Journal of Ideas, History and Culture* 10 (Fall/Winter 1987): 28–29.

Simond, Ada DeBlanc. "The Discovery of Being Black: A Recollection." *Southwestern Historical Quarterly* 76 (1973): 440–447.

_______. "A History of African-American Catholicism in Texas." In *Bricks Without Straw: A Comprehensive History of African Americans in Texas*, edited by David A. Williams, 309–322. Austin: Eakin Press, 1997.

Smallwood, James M. "Texas." In *The Black Press in the South, 1865–1979*, edited by Henry Lewis Suggs, 357–377. Westport, Conn.: Greenwood Publishers, 1983.

Smith, Riley Blake. "Some Phonological Rules in the Negro Speech of East Texas." Ph.D. dissertation, University of Texas at Austin, 1973.

Solomon, Marva. "The Voices of Black Texans." *Texas Highways* 40 (September 1993): 26–31.

Stanley, Oma. "Negro Speech of East Texas." *American Speech* 16 (February 1941): 3–16.

Steagall, Archie. "The Voodoo Man of the Brazos." *Texian Stomping Grounds*, edited by J. Frank Dobie, Mody C. Boatright, and Harry H. Ranson, 113–114. Austin: Texas Folk-Lore Society, 1941.

Stimpson, Eddie Jr. *My Remembers: A Black Sharecropper's Recollections of the Depression*, edited by James W. Byrd. Denton: University of North Texas Press, 1996.

Tathan, Campbell. "Sutton Griggs' *Imperium in Imperio*." *Studies in Black Literature* 4 (1974): 7–15.

Terrell, Suzanne. *This Other Kind of Doctors: Traditional Medical Systems in Black Neighborhoods in Austin, Texas*. New York: AMS Press, 1990.

Thomas, Gates. "South Texas Negro Work-Songs: Collected and Uncollected. In *Rainbow in the Morning*, edited by J. Frank Dobie, 154–180. Hatboro, Pa.: Folklore Association, 1965.

Thomas, Jesse O. *Negro Participation in the Texas Centennial Exposition*. Boston: Christopher Publishing House, 1938.

Thomas, Lorenzo. "The African-American Folktale and J. Mason Brewer." In *Juneteenth Texas: Essays in African-American Folklore*, edited by Francis E. Abernethy, Carolyn Fiedler Satterwhite, Patrick B. Mullen, and Alan B. Govenar, 223–234. Publication of the Texas Folklore Society No. 54. Denton: University of North Texas Press, 1996.

_______. "From Gumbo to Grammys: The Development of Zydeco Music in Houston." In *Juneteenth Texas: Essays in African-American Folklore*, edited by Francis E. Abernethy, Carolyn Fiedler Satterwhite, Patrick B. Mullen, and Alan B. Govenar, 139–150. Publication of the Texas Folklore Society No. 54. Denton: University of North Texas Press, 1996.

_______. "Gathering Like Heat: Black Writing in Texas." *Texas Humanist* 2 (April 1980): 4–5, 9.

Thomas, Matt. *Hopping on the Border (The Life Story of a Bellboy)*. San Antonio: Naylor, 1951.

Thomas, W. H. *Some Current Folk-Songs of the Negro*. n.p.: Folk-lore Society of Texas, 1912.

Thompson, James B. "King Star Baptist Church: A Guiding Light." *Journal of South Texas* 6 (1993): 72–79.

Totten, Herman L. "A Survey of the Use of the Carnegie Library of Wiley College Students, 1964." Master's thesis, University of Oklahoma, 1964.

_______. "The Wiley College Library: The First Library for Negroes West of the Mississippi. *Negro History Bulletin* 32 (1969): 6–10.

Trantham, Carrie P. "An Investigation of the Unpublished Negro Folk-Songs of Dorothy Scarborough." Master's thesis, Baylor University, 1941.

Truett, Luther J. "The Negro Element in the Life and Work of Dorothy Scarborough." Master's thesis, Baylor University, 1967.

Truvillion, Jesse. "Henry Truvillion of the Big Thicket: A Song Worth Singing." In *Juneteenth Texas: Essays in African-American Folklore*, edited by Francis E. Abernethy, Carolyn Fiedler Satterwhite, Patrick B. Mullen, and Alan B. Govenar, 21–38. Publication of the Texas Folklore Society No. 54. Denton: University of North Texas Press, 1996.

Turner, Darwin T. "J. Mason Brewer: Vignettes." *CLA Journal* 18 (June 1975): 570–577.

Turner, Douglas. "The *Dallas Express* as a Forum on Lynching, 1919–1921." Master's thesis, Southern Methodist University, 1974.

Turner, Kenneth William. "Negro Collectors of Negro Folklore: A Study of J. Mason Brewer and Zora Neale Hurston." Master's thesis, East Texas State College, 1964.

Twomey, Dannehl M. "Into the Mainstream: Early Black Photography in Houston." *The Houston Review* 9.1 (1987): 39–48.

Verheyden, Cindy Bland. "Grieving for Their Dead: Mother Nature and Human Neglect Threaten Austin's Historic Black Cemeteries." In *Bricks Without Straw: A Comprehensive History of African Americans in Texas*, edited by David A. Williams, 111–113. Austin: Eakin Press, 1997.

Vlach, John Michael. "Afro-American Folk Crafts in Nineteenth Century Texas." *Western Folklore* 40 (1981): 149–161.

_______. "Black Folk Crafts in Antebellum Texas." In *Texana I: The Frontier*, Proceedings of a Humanities Forum Held at Round Top, Texas, May 1–3, 1980, edited by LeRoy Johnson Jr., 33–36. Austin: Texas Historical Commission, 1983.

Ward, James Wesley. "Judges' Attitudes toward Standard English and Black English in the State of Texas." Ph.D. dissertation, Wayne State University, 1989.

Wardlaw, Alvia J. *The Art of John Biggers: View from the Upper Room.* Houston: Museum of Fine Arts, 1995.

_______. "John Biggers—Artist: Traditional Folkways of the Black Community." In *Juneteenth Texas: Essays in African-American Folklore*, edited by Francis E. Abernethy, Carolyn Fiedler Satterwhite, Patrick B. Mullen, and Alan B. Govenar, 208–221. Publication of the Texas Folklore Society No. 54. Denton: University of North Texas Press, 1996.

Wardlaw, Frank H. "John Biggers, Artist." In *Black Leaders: Texans for Their Times*, edited by Alwyn Barr and Robert A. Calvert, 191–220. Austin: Texas State Historical Association, 1981.

Ware, Ural F. "The History of the Church of the Living God from 1906 to 1971." Master's thesis, Texas Southern University, 1972.

Watriss, Wendy. "Celebrate Freedom: Juneteenth." *Southern Exposure* 5 (1977): 80–85.

Watts, Jill. "African American Churches." In *Encyclopedia of the American West*, edited by Charles Phillips and Alan Axelrod, vol. 1, 7–8. New York: Simon and Schuster, 1996.

Weatherford, Carole Boston. *Juneteenth Jamboree.* New York: Lee and Low Books, 1995.

Werden, Frieda. "Bernice Love Wiggins." In *American Women Writers*, edited by Lina Mainiero, vol. 4, 414–415. New York: Ungar Publishing Company, 1982.

Wheat, John. "'Lightnin' Hopkins: Blues Bard of the Third Ward." In *Juneteenth Texas: Essays in African-American Folklore*, edited by Francis E. Abernethy, Carolyn Fiedler Satterwhite, Patrick B. Mullen, and Alan B. Govenar, 255–271. Publication of the Texas Folklore Society, No. 54. Denton: University of North Texas Press, 1996.

White, C. C., and Ada Morehead Holland. *No Quittin' Sense.* Austin: University of Texas Press, 1969.

Wiggins, William H. Jr. "Juneteenth: A Red Spot Day on the Texas Calendar." In *Juneteenth Texas: Essays in African-American Folklore*, edited by Francis E. Abernethy, Carolyn Fiedler Satterwhite, Patrick B. Mullen, and Alan B. Govenar, 237–252. Publication of the Texas Folklore Society, No. 54. Denton: University of North Texas Press, 1996.

_______. "Juneteenth: They Closed the Town Up, Man!" *American Visions* 1 (May/June 1986): 40–45.

Williams, Lorece P. "Country Black." In *The Folklore of Texan Cultures*, edited by Francis Edward Abernethy and Dan Beaty, 118–129. Austin: Encino Press, 1974.

Williams, Patricia R. "Literary Traditions in Works by African-American Playwrights." In *Texas Women Writers: A Tradition of Their Own*, edited by Sylvia Ann Grider and Lou Halsell Rodenberger, 253–255. College Station: Texas A&M University Press, 1997.

Winegarten, Ruthe. "Culture and Social Life." *Black Texas Women: 150 Years of Trial and Triumph,* 123–151. Austin: University of Texas Press, 1995.

14. Economics

Exterior of Porter F. Roberts Grocery Store located at 301 Victoria, San Antonio, ca. 1910s.

The UT Institute of Texan Cultures, No. 92-381
Courtesy of Henrietta Roberts Stevenson

Adams, Allene Archia. "The Development of the Oil Industry in the Baytown Area, especially as it affects the Employment and Welfare of Negroes." Master's thesis, Prairie View State Normal and Industrial College, 1944.

Adams, Fred Elester. "The Variations of Socio-Economic Characteristics of Counties According to the Per Cent Negro Population of Each County." Master's thesis, Prairie View Agricultural and Mechanical College, 1948.

Allen, Ruth A. "The Negro Woman." In *The Labor of Women in the Production of Cotton,* 174–208. Bureau of Research in the Social Sciences. Austin: University of Texas, 1931.

_______. "A Peculiar People." In *East Texas Lumber Workers: An Economic and Social Picture, 1870–1950*, 51–68. Austin: University of Texas Press, 1961.

_______. "A Psychological Problem of Southern Labor." In *Chapters in the History of Organized Labor in Texas* 187–218. Austin: University of Texas Publication, 1941.

Atkinson, Lillie E. "Slavery in the Economy of Colorado County, 1822–1863." Master's thesis, Prairie View Agricultural and Mechanical College, 1954.

Barrett, Faydell Lomma. "Slavery in the Economy of San Augustine County, 1822–1863." Master's thesis, Prairie View Agricultural and Mechanical College, 1963.

Boyce, James Henry Jr. "Change in Socio-Economic Status of Negroes as a Result of Residential Invasion." Master's thesis, Texas Southern University, 1951.

Brewer, Rose M. "Black Women Workers: Yesterday and Today." In *Women in the Texas Workforce: Yesterday and Today*, edited by Richard Croxdale and Melissa Hields, 35–48. Austin: People's History in Texas, 1979.

Brophy, William Joseph. "Black Business Development in Texas Cities, 1900–1950." *Red River Valley Historical Review* 6 (Spring 1981): 42–55.

Bullard, Robert D. *Black Houston Business Survey.* Houston: Texas Southern University Publication, 1983.

_______. *Houston's Third Ward: A Center of Black Business.* Houston: Texas Southern University, 1982.

Bullock, Henry Allen. *Pathways to the Houston Negro Market.* Ann Arbor: J. N. Edwards, 1957.

_______. *Profile of Houston's Negro Business Enterprises: A Survey and Directory of Their Attitudes.* Houston: Negro Chamber of Commerce, 1962.

_______. "Racial Attitudes and the Employment of Negroes." *American Journal of Sociology* 56 (March 1951): 448–457.

Burns, Richard Allen. "Afro-American Blacksmithing in East Texas." Master's report, University of Texas at Austin, 1984.

Calvert, Robert A., ed. "The Freedmen and Agricultural Prosperity." *Southwestern Historical Quarterly* 76 (1973): 461–472.

Cary, Reby. "The Development of the Negro Chamber of Commerce Movement in Texas." Master's thesis, Prairie View Agricultural and Mechanical College, 1948.

Chumley, Leo Bertice. "Negro Labor and Property Holdings in Shelby County, Texas, 1870–1945." Master's thesis, Prairie View Agricultural and Mechanical College, 1948.

Coleman, Alvin L. "A Proposed Program for Improving Farm Family Incomes in District Five, Marion County, Texas." Master's thesis, Hampton Institute, 1951.

Conner, Jeffie O. Allen. "A Study of Four Hundred and Sixty Negro Farm Families in Three Texas Counties." Master's thesis, Prairie View State Normal and Industrial College, 1944.

Fine, Bernice Rash. "Agrarian Reform and the Negro Farmer in Texas, 1886–1896." Master's thesis, North Texas State University, 1971.

Fish, Mary Martha. "Comparative Study of the Economic Status of the Negroes and Latin Americans in Midland, Texas." Master's thesis, Texas Technological College, 1957.

Gallagher, Arthur Jr. *The Negro and Employment Opportunities in the South—Houston*. Atlanta Southern Regional Council, 1961.

Gersh, Gabriel. "The Economic Advances of the American Negro." *Contemporary Review* 207 (September 1965): 134–139.

Gite, Lloyd. "Texas." *Black Enterprise* 24 (June 1994): 192–198.

Hicks, Doris A. "Career Opportunities for Negroes in Texas Libraries, 1957." Master's thesis, University of Texas, 1959.

Hill, Forest Garrett. "The Negro in the Texas Labor Supply." Master's thesis, University of Texas, 1946.

Housewright, George Maxwell. "The Changing Economic Status in Texas of the Latin-American and the Negro, 1950–1960." Ph.D. dissertation, University of Arkansas, 1972.

Humphreys, Drucie Ray, and Lenora Althia Johnson. "A Study of the Employment Status of the Negro Deaf in Texas." Master's thesis, Hampton Institute, 1951.

Hunter, Irene P. "Slavery in the Economy of Cherokee County, Texas, 1846–1860." Master's thesis, Prairie View Agricultural and Mechanical College, 1956.

Jackson, Larry J. "The Development of Black Business in Texas, 1919–1969: From a Houston Perpective." Master's thesis, Texas Tech University, 1979.

Jefferson, Calvin B. "Tenancy as it affects the Negro Farmer in Brazos County, Texas." Master's thesis, Prairie View Agricultural and Mechanical College, 1956.

Jenkins, Carolyn. "Business and Economic Development in the Black Community: Houston's Third Ward." Master's thesis, Texas Southern University, 1982.

Jones, Vonciel. "Born a Black Bastard . . . The Education and Organization of Houston's Black Lawyers, 1947–1967." Master's thesis, Rice University, 1976.

Kaplan, Barry J. "Race, Income, and Ethnicity: Residential Change in a Houston Community, 1920–1970." *The Houston Review* 3 (Winter 1981): 178–202.

Kinsey, Winston Lee. "Negro Labor in Texas, 1865–1876." Master's thesis, Baylor University, 1965.

Linsley, Judith W. "Main House, Carriage House: African-American Domestic Employees at the McFaddin-Ward House in Beaumont, Texas, 1900–1950." *Southwestern Historical Quarterly* 103 (1999): 17–51.

Mathis, Annie Maie. "Negro Public Health Nursing in Texas." *Southern Workman* 56 (July 1927): 302–303.

Maxwell, Robert S. "Lumbermen of the East Texas Frontier." *Forest History* 9 (1965): 12–16.

Mitchell, Tommye Mayes. "A Study of the Occupational Status of the Prairie View Home Economics Graduates, 1922–48." Master's thesis, Prairie View Agricultural and Mechanical College, 1949.

Montgomery, Ellie Walls. *Possibilities of Improving Negro Business through Better Business Methods*. Houston: Webster Printing, 1935.

Morgan, Fletcher Jr. "A Study of the Economic Status of Fifty Negro Farmers of Matagorda County, Texas." Master's thesis, Prairie View University, 1946.

Obadele-Starks, Ernest M. B. "Black Labor, the Black Middle Class, and Organized Protest along the Upper Texas Gulf Coast, 1883–1945." *Southwestern Historical Quarterly* 103 (1999): 53–65.

_______. *Black Unionism in the Industrial South*. College Station: Texas A&M University Press, 2000.

_______. "The Road to Jericho: Black Workers, The Fair Employment Practice Commission, and the Struggle for Racial Equality on the Upper Texas Gulf Coast, 1941–1947." Ph.D. dissertation, University of Houston, 1996.

Olien, Roger M., and Diana Davids Olien. "Black and Mexican Americans." In *Oil Booms: Social Change in Five Texas Towns*, 109–126. Lincoln: University of Nebraska Press, 1982.

Owens, Emiel Wade. "A Study of the Economical Status of Fifty Negro Farmers in Leon County, Texas." Master's thesis, Prairie View Agricultural and Mechanical College, 1948.

Pierce, Ellise. "Anthony Mark Hankins: Fashionably Affordable." *Texas Monthly* 24 (September 1996): 127, 180.

Randle, Charles F. "A Study of the Farm Management Practices of Fifty Negro Farmers in McLennan County, Texas." Master's thesis, Prairie View State Agricultural and Mechanical College, 1950.

Reece, Froncell. "A Study of the Economic Status of Fifty Negro Farm Families of Montgomery County, Texas." Master's thesis, Prairie View Agricultural and Mechanical College, 1950.

Reese, James V. "The Early History of Labor Organizations in Texas, 1838–1876." *Southwestern Historical Quarterly* 72 (1968): 1–20.

Reynolds, James Talmadge. "The Preretirement Educational Needs of Retired Black Women who were Domestic Workers in Dallas, Texas." Ph.D. dissertation, East Texas State University, 1981.

Reynolds, Lois Arnell. "Sustenance Position of Texas Negro Domestic Servants in the Texas Economy." Master's thesis, Prairie View State Normal and Industrial College, 1942.

Robbins, Hal. "Slavery in the Economy of Matagorda County, Texas, 1839–1860." Master's thesis, Prairie View Agricultural and Mechanical College, 1952.

Sargent, Frederick O. "Economic Adjustments of Negro Farmers in East Texas." *Southwestern Social Science Quarterly* 42 (1961): 32–39.

Shannon, Mary Gamble. "An Occupational Study of Negro Maids in Dallas." Master's thesis, Southern Methodist University, 1941.

Slaton, William J. "Negro Businesses in Texas." *Texas Business Review* 43 (July 1969): 194–198.

Smallwood, James M. "Perpetuation of Caste: Black Agricultural Workers in Reconstruction Texas." *Mid-America* 61 (1979): 5–23.

Smith, Bernice Daviss. "A Study of the Business Work Experience of Business Teachers in Selected Class AA High Schools in Texas." Master's thesis, Texas Southern University, 1959.

Smith, Robert Lloyd. "Elevation of Negro Farm Life." *Independent* 1 (August 30, 1900): 2103– 2106.

_______. "The Farmers' Improvement Society of Texas." *AME Review* (January 1909): 289–296.

_______. "An Uplifting Negro Cooperative Society in Texas." *The World's Work* 16 (July 1908): 10462–10466.

_______. "Village Improvement among the Negroes." *Outlook* 64 (March 31, 1900): 733–736.

SoRelle, James M. "The Emergence of Black Business in Houston, Texas: A Study of Race and Ideology, 1919–1945." In *Black Dixie: Afro-Texan History and Culture in Houston*, edited by Howard Beeth and Cary D. Wintz, 103–115. College Station: Texas A&M University Press, 1992.

_______. "'An de Po Culled Man is in de Wuss Fix uv Awl:' Black Occupational Status in Houston, Texas, 1920–1940." *The Houston Review* 1 (Spring 1979): 15–26.

Sorenson, Donald E. "The Effects of Industry Deregulation on Black-Owned Banks." *Midwestern Business and Economic Review* 16 (Fall 1992): 33–36.

Sparks, Randy J. "'Heavenly Houston' or 'Hellish Houston'? Black Unemployment and Relief Efforts, 1929–1936." *Southern Studies* 25 (Winter 1986): 353–366.

Spurlin, Virginia Lee. "The Conners of Waco: Black Professionals in Twentieth Century Texas." Ph.D. dissertation, Texas Tech University, 1991.

Sterling, Ernest S. "Economic Patterns of the Rural Negro Families of Smith County." Master's thesis, Texas College, 1953.

Stewart, Jacob Thomas. "Characteristics of Negro-Owned and-Operated Business Establishments in Houston." Ph.D. dissertation, University of Texas, 1956.

Stiles, Jo Ann P. "The Changing Economic and Educational Status of Texas Negroes, 1940–1960." Master's thesis, University of Texas, 1966.

Strange, Tempie Virginia. "The Dallas Negro Chamber of Commerce: A Study of a Negro Institution." Master's thesis, Southern Methodist University, 1945.

Teel, Robert Eli. "Discrimination against Negro Workers in Texas: Extent and Effects." Master's thesis, University of Texas, 1947.

Terrell, Wendell Phillips. "A Short History of the Negro Longshoreman." Bachelor's essay, Houston College for Negroes, 1936.

_______. "A Study of the Employment of the Graduates of Ten Negro High Schools of Texas." Master's thesis, Colorado State College, 1937.

Thomas, Matt. *Hopping on the Border (The Life Story of a Bellboy)*. San Antonio, Naylor Publishing, 1951.

Toyer, Frances Aurelia. "A Survey of Negro Business Units and the Employment Opportunities afforded by such Units in Houston, Texas." Master's thesis, Atlanta University, 1942.

Ulrich, Ora Emma. "A Study of the Expenditure of Urban Negro Work Relief Families in Travis County, Texas as compared to an Adequate Diet." Master's thesis, University of Texas, 1935.

Webber, Carolyn Cott. "The Negro in the Texas Industrial Labor Market, 1940–1947." Master's thesis, University of Texas, 1948.

Webeshete, Asefa. "Level of Education and Job Satisfaction: The Case of Ethiopian Refugees and Defacto Refugees in Houston, Texas." Ed.D. dissertation, Texas Southern University, 1985.

Yancy, C. D. "Negro Participation in the Agricultural Adjustment Agency Program in Texas." Master's thesis, Colorado A&M College, Fort Collins, 1946.

15. Education

Original sewing class of St. Philip's College, San Antonio, Texas, in the spring of 1898.

The UT Institute of Texan Cultures, No. 74-1227
Courtesy of Dr. Clarence W. Norris

Adair, J. B. "A Study of the Negro Schools of Hunt County, 1943–44." Master's thesis, East Texas State Teachers College, 1945.

Adams, Claude R. "The Historical Development of Education for Negroes in Texas." Master's thesis, Prairie View Agricultural and Mechanical College, 1949.

Alexander, Genevieve Tarlton. "An Historical Analysis of Catholic Educational Integration in Texas." Master's thesis, University of Texas, 1959.

Allen, Irving Henry. "A Comparative Study of Alumni Attitude toward their Alma Mater at Selected Small Black Church Related Colleges in Texas." Ph.D. dissertation, Kansas State University, 1981.

Allen, Jewell. "The History of Negro Education at Wiley College." Master's thesis, East Texas State Teachers College, 1940.

Andrews, Robert Samuel. "The Availability of Education to Negroes in Waller County, Texas." Master's thesis, Prairie View State Normal and Industrial College, 1941.

Armstrong, Ira E. "A Historical Study of Public Elementary Schools in San Antonio, Texas with Special Emphasis on Elementary Schools for Negroes from 1910 to 1940." Master's thesis, Prairie View State Normal and Industrial College, 1941.

Atkins, Florine J. "Analysis of Health Education Programs in the Negro Schools of Marion County, Texas." Master's thesis, Tuskegee Institute, 1950.

Bailey, Edward Lee. "Survey of the Negro Schools in Brazos County, Texas." Master's thesis, Texas Agricultural and Mechanical College, 1931.

Baker, Orestes Jeremiah. "A Study of Senior College Library Facilities for Negroes in Texas." Master's thesis, Columbia University, 1936.

Baker, T. Lindsay. "Holy Rosary School and Church, 1887–1914: A Pioneer Catholic Effort Among African American Texans." *Journal of Texas Catholic History and Culture* 6 (1995): 16–34.

Balester, Valerie M. *Cultural Divide: A Study of African-American College-Level Writers*. Portsmouth, N.H.: Boynton/Cook, 1993.

Barchus, Gale Leslie. "The Dynamics of Black Demands and White Responses for Negro Higher Education in Texas, 1945–1950." Master's thesis, University of Texas at Austin, 1970.

Bartley, Ruby Ruth. "A Brief Survey of the Historical Background and of the Present Status of Music Education in the Negro Schools of Texas." Master's thesis, Southwest Texas State Teachers College, 1950.

Batts, William Malcolm. "What the General Baptists of Texas (Negro) want Educationally with Suggestions for Improvement of the Educational Program." Master's thesis, Prairie View University, 1946.

Bell, Gail K. "James Leonard Farmer: Texas' First African American Ph.D." *East Texas Historical Journal* 36.1 (1998): 18–25.

Benson, Lula J., comp. *Beaumont Colored Schools, 1880–1926.* Beaumont, Tex.: American Printing Company, [1926].

Blackman, Bernard H. "An Occupational Survey of the Students and their Parents of Lincoln High School, Dallas, Texas." Master's thesis, University of Southern California, 1960.

Blackshear, E. L. "Industrial Training and the Race Question." *Southern Workman* 35 (1906): 396–401.

Board, Edna Theresa. "The Historical Development of the Public Schools for Negroes in Liberty County, Texas from 1918 to 1948." Master's thesis, Prairie View Agricultural and Mechanical College, 1949.

Bonner, Josey Lee. "A Study of the Nutritional Effectiveness of Cafeterias in the Negro Public Schools of Texas." Master's thesis, Howard University, 1946.

Bowden, Artemisia. "Education, Negro." *The Handbook of Texas*, edited by Walter Prescott Webb, vol. 1, 544–545. Austin: Texas State Historical Association, 1952.

Bowman, Myrtle E. "A Comparative Study of the Vocabularies of White and Colored Children." Master's thesis, Baylor University, 1936.

Bradley, Charles C. "A Study of the Duties of Negro Principals in Angelina County, Texas." Master's thesis, Prairie View Agricultural and Mechanical College, 1949.

Brawner, Anne. "Guadalupe College: A Case History in Negro Higher Education, 1884–1936." Master's thesis, Southwest Texas State University, 1980.

Brewer, J. Mason, ed. *A History of Dallas High School for Negroes*. Reprint. Dallas: Friends of the Dallas Public Library, 1991.

Brewer, Junett. "An Ecological Study of the Psychological Environment of a Negro College and the Personality Needs of its Students." Ph.D. dissertation, University of Texas, 1963.

Briscoe, Dorothy Lee. "A Survey of the Materials Collection of the Texas Southern University Library, Houston, Texas." Master's thesis, Atlanta University, 1957.

Bryant, Ira B. Jr. "Administration of Vocational Education in Negro High Schools of Texas." Ed.D. dissertation, University of Southern California, 1948.

_______. *The Development of the Houston Negro Schools.* Houston: Webster Publishing Company, 1935.

_______. *Texas Southern University: Its Antecedents, Political Origin, and Future.* Houston: D. Armstrong Company, 1975.

_______. "Vocational Education in Negro High Schools in Texas." *The Journal of Negro Education* 18 (1949): 9–15.

Bullock, Henry Allen. "The Availability of Education in the Texas Negro Separate School." *The Journal of Negro Education* 16 (1947): 425–432.

Bullock, Merle L. A. "A Personality Study of Student Leaders at Prairie View College." Master's thesis, University of Michigan, 1939.

Byrd, James S. "A Comparative Study of the Duties of Forty Negro High School Principals in Class AA Schools of Texas." Master's thesis, Prairie View Agricultural and Mechanical College, 1949.

Byrne, David D. "A Comparison of the White and Negro Schools of Montgomery County, Texas." Master's thesis, University of Colorado, 1931.

Cadwell, John A. "The Status of Physical Education for Boys in the State Accredited Class A High Schools for Negroes in Texas." Master's thesis, University of Michigan, 1938.

Campbell, Emmanuel. *The Development of Negro Education in El Paso*. El Paso: Public Schools Press, 1945.

Campbell, W. R. "The Present Status of the Principals in the Accredited Negro High Schools in Texas." Master's thesis, University of Michigan, 1940.

Cash, Christine Benton. "An Evaluation of the Grade Achievement of the Pupils over a Period of Six Years, 1937–1943, at the Center Point School, Pittsburg, Texas." Master's thesis, Atlanta University, 1944.

Christopher, Nehemiah McKinley. "The History of Negro Public Education in Texas, 1865–1900." Ed.D. dissertation, University of Pittsburgh, 1948.

Chunn, Prentis Walter. "Education and Politics, A Study of the Negro in Reconstruction Texas." Master's thesis, Southwest Texas State College, 1957.

Clark, Virginia Melton. "A Study of Attitudes held by Whites toward Admitting Negroes into Institutions of Higher Learning in Texas." Master's thesis, Texas State College for Women, 1951.

Clater, B. Daniel. "A Study of Selected Factors of the Sunday Church Schools of the Baptist Missionary and Educational Convention of Texas." Master's thesis, Bishop College, 1951.

Clay, S. C. "Brief Survey of Guidance Work in Blackshear High School, San Angelo, Texas." Master's thesis, Prairie View Agricultural and Mechanical College, 1948.

Cobb, Willie Lenox. "Provisions for Vocational Education for Negroes in the High Schools of Texas." Master's thesis, University of Southern California, 1940.

Collins, William M. "A Study to Determine Practices in Secondary Student Teaching Programs in Nine Negro Colleges and Universities in Texas and the Improvements that are needed." Ph.D. dissertation, Cornell University, 1957.

Cooper, Matthew N. "To determine the Nature and Significance, if any, of Certain Differences in the Social and Personal Adjustment of Fifty-One Successful and Fifty-One Non-Successful Students at Texas Southern University." Ph.D. dissertation, New York University, 1955.

Corley, Rex Spencer. "A Comparative Study of the Public Schools for Whites and Negroes in the Independent School Districts of Falls County, Texas." Master's thesis, University of Texas, 1950.

Cornelius, Sandra Faye. "Board of Regents' and Board of Trustees' Perceptions of Current and Desired Goals of Black Colleges and Universities in the State of Texas." Ed.D. dissertation, Texas Southern University, 1987.

Crump, Oliver Wendell. "Community Activities of Negro Rural Teachers in Texas." Ed.D. dissertation, University of Northern Colorado, 1945.

Culwell, Paul Ross. "A Survey of the Financial Support of Negro Education in Three Counties of Texas." Master's thesis, University of Texas, 1942.

Dagler, Winona Alvilda. "The Status of Secondary Mathematics in the Larger Negro Schools of the State of Texas." Master's thesis, University of Minnesota, 1945.

Darden, Rose Etta. "The Occupational Status of Prairie View's Sociology Major and Minor Graduates, 1929–1949." Master's thesis, Prairie View Agricultural and Mechanical College, 1950.

Davis, William R. *The Development and Present Status of Negro Education in East Texas*. New York: Columbia University Teachers College, 1934.

Debes, Robert Randolph. "A Sociological Study of Paul Quinn College, Waco, Texas." Master's thesis, Baylor University, 1949.

Denton, Lynn C. "Comparison of the White and Negro Schools of Lamar County." Master's thesis, East Texas State Teachers College, 1949.

Deon, Harding Thorean. "A Study of the Sunday Schools of the Negro Baptist Churches in Orange, Texas." Master's thesis, Bishop College, 1948.

Dodd, Beulah D. "An Appraisal of the English Language Arts Instructional Program of the Dunbar School with Implications for Improvement." Master's thesis, Bishop College, 1954.

Dodgen, Mary. "The Slave Plantations as an Educational Institution." Master's thesis, University of Texas, 1932.

Doggett, Dorothy Lasseter. "Survey of Fort Worth's Negro Schools." Master's thesis, Texas Christian University, 1927.

Dometrius, Nelson C., and Lee Sigelman. "The Cost of Quality: Teacher Testing and Racial-Ethnic Representativeness in Public Education." *Social Science Quarterly* 69 (March 1988): 70–82.

Downs, Travis. "A Study of Certain Factors Affecting the Educational Status of Grade Eight, Dunbar Elementary School, Marshall, Texas." Master's thesis, Bishop College, 1952.

Duren, Almetris Marsh, and Louise Iscoe. *Overcoming: A History of Black Integration at the University of Texas at Austin.* Austin: University of Texas at Austin, 1979.

Durvan, Katherine I. Greene. "Status of Guidance in the Thirteen Negro Colleges of Texas with a Proposed Program for St. Phillip's Junior College." Master's thesis, University of Colorado, 1940.

Eby, Frederick. "Negro Education." In *The Development of Education in Texas*, 263–280. New York: Macmillan, 1925.

Echols, Jack Wendell. "Criteria for Evaluating Teacher Education in the Negro Colleges of Texas." Ed.D. dissertation, University of Denver, 1954.

Eilers, William August. "Negro Education in Lavaca County, Texas." Master's thesis, Southwest Texas State Teachers College, 1938.

Ellison, Frances Anna. "Choral Development in the Negro High Schools of Houston, Texas." Master's thesis, University of Colorado, 1941.

Eustace, Stella Jeanne. "The Present Status of Extracurricular Activities in the Secondary Schools for Negroes in the State of Texas." Master's thesis, University of Colorado, 1938.

Evans, Maud West. "The Early History and Present Status of Negro Education in Coleman County, Texas." Master's thesis, Hardin-Simmons University, 1949.

Fair, Eugene Lawrence. "Factors that Contribute to the Failure of Negro Teachers of Vocational Agriculture in Texas." Master's thesis, Iowa State College, 1943.

Ferguson, William. "A Reading Survey of Negro Homes of Beaumont, Texas." Master's thesis, George Peabody College for Teachers, 1932.

Forward, Barney Grover. "History of Education in Jasper County." Master's thesis, Prairie View Agricultural and Mechanical College, 1949.

Franklin, Theophilus Clay. "The Development of the George Washington Carver High School, Karnack, Texas, as a Consolidated School." Master's thesis, Prairie View Agricultural and Mechanical College, 1948.

Gadlin, Felmon U. "A Study of the Administrative and Supervisory Duties of Negro Principals in Titus County, Texas." Master's thesis, Texas College, 1953.

Gaines, Jean Foley. "An Evaluative Analysis of Job Opportunities for Negro Students of Business Education in Houston, Texas." Master's thesis, University of Colorado, 1956.

Gates, Samuel Houston. "Negro Secondary Education in Texas." Master's thesis, University of Colorado, 1936.

Gee, Ruth Ella. "The History and Development of the Prairie View Training School, 1916–1946." Master's thesis, Prairie View University, 1946.

Gibson, Marye Bland. "A Comparative Study of the Present Status of Business Education for Negroes and for Whites in Selected Secondary Schools in Texas." Master's thesis, University of Texas, 1960.

Gillespie, Dair Lindsay. "The Texas Southern University Incident: A Case Study of Local Newspaper Coverage of Racial Conflict." Master's thesis, University of Houston, 1968.

Gillette, Michael L. "Blacks Challenge the White University." *Southwestern Historical Quarterly* 86 (1982): 393–416.

Gould, Lewis L., and Melissa R. Sneed. "Without Pride or Apology: The University of Texas at Austin, Racial Integration, and the Barbara Smith Case." *Southwestern Historical Quarterly* 103 (1999): 67–87.

Grant, Baston Phillip. "An Evaluation of the Vocational Guidance Program in the San Marcos, Texas, Negro High School." Master's thesis, Colorado State College of Education, Greeley, 1943.

Gray, Phineas Young. "The Development of the Negro Schools of Morris County, Texas from 1924–1925 to 1949–1950." Master's thesis, Bishop College, 1951.

Green, George E. "A Comparison of Negro and White Secondary Education and Plan for Reorganization of Negro Schools in Shelby County." Master's thesis, Stephen F. Austin State College, 1950.

Green, Nina Mae. "Development of a School [O.J. Thomas School in Cameron]." *Texas Historian* 33.5 (May 1973): 18–25.

Greene, Carrie Etta. "The History of Education Provided for Negroes in San Angelo, Texas, from Inception to Integration, September, 1955." Master's thesis, Texas Southern University, 1956.

Gregory, J. D. Jr. "Black School Board Members of Texas: A Social, Economic, and Political Profile (History, Election)." Ed.D. dissertation, Texas Southern University, 1985.

Hackney, Vivian Howard. "Adjustment Problems of the Pupils of Pemberton High School (Colored), Marshall, Texas." Master's thesis, Southern Methodist University, 1949.

Harper, Bradly C. "The Frederick Douglass School and Early Black Education in Kingsville, Texas (1909–1969)." *Journal of South Texas* 6 (1993): 80–88.

Harrison, Generale Lamar. "A Program of Teacher Training by Prairie View State College for the Improvement of the Rural Negro Schools of Texas." Ph.D. dissertation, Ohio State University, 1936.

Harvey, McClennon Phillip, comp. *A Brief History of Paul Quinn College*. Waco: Smith Printing Company, 1965.

Heintze, Michael R. "Black Colleges." In *The New Handbook of Texas*, edited by Ron Tyler, Douglas E. Barnett, Roy R. Barkley, Penelope C. Anderson, and Mark F. Odintz, vol. 1, 562–565. Austin: Texas State Historical Association, 1996.

_______. "A History of the Black Private Colleges in Texas, 1865–1954." Ph.D. dissertation, Texas Tech University, 1981.

_______. *Private Black Colleges in Texas, 1865–1954.* College Station: Texas A&M University Press, 1985.

Hines, Lillie Bell Corley. "A Comparative Study of some Current Practices in Elementary Education as found in Negro Schools in Travis County." Master's thesis, Prairie View Agricultural and Mechanical College, 1944.

Holden, Percy H. "After-School Careers of Negro High School Graduates of Houston, Texas for 1933." Master's thesis, University of Colorado, 1936.

Holley, Thomas L. "A Vocational Training Program for Negroes in San Antonio, Texas." Master's thesis, Colorado State College, 1947.

Hollins, Arntie Edward. "The Colored Teachers State Association of Texas as revealed in the Texas Press." Master's thesis, Prairie View Agricultural and Mechanical College, 1948.

Holmes, Charles Murphy. "A Study of Physical Education Programs of Negro Elementary Schools of Texas." Master's thesis, North Texas State University, 1964.

Hornsby, Alton Jr. "The 'Colored Branch University' Issue in Texas—Prelude to *Sweatt v. Painter*." *Journal of Negro History* 61 (1976): 51–60.

_______. "The Freedmen's Bureau Schools in Texas, 1865–1870." *Southwestern Historical Quarterly* 76 (1973): 397–417.

_______. "Negro Education in Texas, 1865–1917." Master's thesis, University of Texas, 1962.

Howard-Waters, Odessa Ladenia. "Personal Problems Brought to Counselors of Jarvis Christian College During 1944–1945." Master's thesis, Atlanta University, 1946.

Jackson, Charles Emerson. "A Study of Educational Provisions for Negroes in Gregg County." Master's thesis, Prairie View University, 1945.

Jackson, Leslie Samuel. "A Study of Curriculum Offerings in Certain West Texas High Schools for Negroes." Master's thesis, University of Texas, 1957.

Jackson, William Clarence. "The History of Negro Public Education in Galveston County, Texas." Master's thesis, State University of Iowa, 1948.

Johnson, Basco. "Venereal Disease Health Education Project for Negroes in Texas." *Journal of Social Hygiene* 30 (February 1944): 72–75.

Johnson, Clarence J. "A Study of Health Facilities in Thirty Schools in Harris County, Texas." Master's thesis, Texas Southern University, 1952.

Johnson, David Horace. "Student Influence in Selected Administrative Policies: An Empirical Study of Three Predominantly Negro Colleges in East Texas." Ph.D. dissertation, Texas A&M University, 1972.

Johnson, Ethel Mae Downs. "A Survey of the Material Resources of the Negro Schools in Walker County, Texas." Master's thesis, Hampton Institute, 1941.

Johnson, Norman J. "A Comparative Study of the Interest Patterns of Students Enrolled in Selected Curricula at Prairie View Agricultural and Mechanical College, Texas, 1956–1958." Ph.D. dissertation, University of Michigan, 1961.

Johnson, Scott Edwin. "A Survey of Educational Resources for the Negro Youth of the Huntsville Independent School District." Master's thesis, Hampton Institute, 1944.

Johnson, W. L. D. "Organization of the Public Schools in Houston, Texas, 1905–1940." Master's thesis, Prairie View University, 1943.

Jones, Douglas L. "The Sweatt Case and the Development of Legal Education for Negroes in Texas." *Texas Law Review* 47 (March 1969): 677–693.

Jones, Laura N. A. "A Survey of the Visual Aids in Waller County Schools." Master's thesis, Prairie View State Normal and Industrial College, 1941.

Jones, Walter Benson. "A Study of the Graduates of Douglas High School, Sulphur Springs, Texas, 1924 to 1937, with a View to Curricular Revision along Vocational Lines." Master's thesis, Hampton Institute, 1938.

Junkin, Sara Caroline. "The Independent Negro College in Texas: Change and Challenge." Master's thesis, University of Texas at Austin, 1969.

Kattner, Bruno A. "A Comparison of the White and the Colored Schools of Texas." Master's thesis, North Texas State Teachers College, 1938.

Ketch, Clarence Willard. "A Study of Changes in Expressed Attitudes in the Realm of Negro-White Relations of Texas A&M Freshmen." Master's thesis, Agricultural and Mechanical College of Texas, 1955.

Kimble, Westerfield T. "An Analysis of the Methods of Teaching History in the Seventeen High Schools for Negroes in Texas Accredited by the Southern Association of Colleges and Secondary Schools." Master's thesis, Prairie View University, 1952.

Kirk, W. Aston, and John T. Q. King. "Desegregation of Higher Education in Texas." *Journal of Negro Education* 27 (1958): 318–323.

Kuhr, Nancy Jane Newton. "Segregated Public Schools in Texas, 1876–1940." Master's thesis, University of Texas at Austin, 1971.

Kuykendall, Ralph B. "A Comparison of the Educational Opportunities of the Whites and the Negroes of Walker County." Master's thesis, North Texas State Teachers College, 1938.

LaGrone, Cyrus Wilson. "History of Negro Education at Marshall, Texas." Master's thesis, Southern Methodist University, 1927.

Lane, Harry B. "The Present Status of Secondary Education for Negroes in Texas." Master's thesis, University of Southern California, 1932.

Lanier, Raphael O. "The History of Higher Education for Negroes in Texas, 1930–1955, with Particular Reference to Texas Southern University." Ph.D. dissertation, New York University, 1957.

Lanier, Roy H. "Church-Related Colleges for Negroes in Texas." Master's thesis, Hardin-Simmons University, 1950.

Lash, John S., Hortense W. Dixon, and Thomas F. Freeman. *Texas Southern University: From Separation to Special Designation*. Houston: Texas Southern University, 1975.

Linton, Dolores Burton. "The Growth and Development of the West San Antonio Heights School in District I." Master's thesis, Our Lady of the Lake College, 1952.

Long, John A. "A Brief History of the Development of Negro Education in Houston County, Texas." Master's thesis, Sam Houston State Teachers College, 1943.

Lott, Mable Smith. "An Analysis of the Extra-Curricular Activities Program in the Booker T. Washington High School, Houston, Texas." Master's thesis, Atlanta University, 1945.

Luter, Buckner Sythias. "A Historical and Educational Analysis of the Administration and Curriculum of the Hempstead Negro School from 1867 to 1938: Inclusive." Master's thesis, Prairie View State Normal and Industrial College, 1939.

MacKenna, David Warren. "Development Recommendations for a Select Texas Black College." Ph.D. dissertation, North Texas State University, 1972.

Manning, Newton. "A Study of the Status of Negro Education in Grayson County, Texas." Master's thesis, Southern Methodist University, 1940.

McBay, Willie Earlene. "Adequacy of the Secondary and Adult Homemaking Program of Dunbar High School, Mexia, Texas, in View of Certain Sanitary Conditions of Negro Homes." Master's thesis, Iowa State College, 1949.

McDaniel, Vernon. *History of the Teachers State Association of Texas.* Washington, D.C.: National Education Association, 1977.

_______. "Negro Publicly-Supported Higher Institutions in Texas." *Journal of Negro Education* 31 (1962): 349–353.

McDavid, Percy Hiram. "A Social and Economic Survey of the Community served by the Phillis Wheatley High School in Houston, Texas." Master's thesis, University of Southern California, 1940.

McDonald, Jack Arthur. "Higher Education for Negroes in Texas." Master's report, University of Southern California, 1947.

McDowell, Rosetta. "A Study of School Libraries in Negro Elementary Schools of Navarro County, Texas." Master's thesis, Texas College, 1959.

McNeely, Lois Towles. "The History of Music Education at Wiley University." Master's thesis, State University of Iowa, 1942.

Mitchell, Tommye Mayes. "A Study of the Occupational Status of the Prairie View Home Economics Graduates, 1922–48." Master's thesis, Prairie View Agricultural and Mechanical College, 1949.

Montgomery, Ellie Walls. *A Survey of Negro Youths Not in School—Houston, Texas.* Houston: Houston College for Negroes, 1936.

Montgomery, Ruby Marie. "A Guidance Program for the Negro High Schools of Houston, Texas." Master's thesis, University of Colorado, 1941.

Mooring, Kittye Dale Samuels. "A Study of the Graduates, Department of Business Administration, Prairie View Agricultural and Mechanical College, May 1946–January 1968." Ed.D. dissertation, University of Houston, 1969.

Morgan, Leon. *Public Education for Blacks in Galveston, 1838–1968.* Galveston: Old Central Cultural Center, 1978.

Morgan, Leon Augustus. "A Study of Pupil Participation in School Control in the Negro High Schools of Texas Accredited by Southern Association of Colleges and Secondary Schools." Master's thesis, University of Michigan, 1938.

Morse, Arthur D. "When Negroes entered a Texas School: Del Mar College." *Harper's* 209 (September 1954): 47–49.

Nelson, John M. "A Study of Administrative and Supervisory Duties of Negro Principals in Hunt County, Texas." Master's thesis, Texas Southern University, 1951.

Nelum, Junior Nathaniel. "A Study of the First Seventy Years of the Colored Teachers State Association of Texas." Ed.D. dissertation, University of Texas, 1955.

Nichols, Ruby Marion. "An Appraisal of the Gilmer-Aiken Laws upon Fifteen Schools in Texas that have Negro Superintendents or Supervising Principals." Master's thesis, University of Southern California, 1945.

Noe, Minnie Alice. "History of Jarvis Christian College." Master's thesis, Texas Christian University, 1966.

Norman, Delia Mae Adams. "A Study to determine the Health Knowledge of 627 Pupils of the Fourth, Fifth, Sixth, Seventh and Eighth Grades of Twenty-one Negro Public Schools of Morris and Camp Counties, Texas." Master's thesis, Atlanta University, 1944.

Norris, Clarence W. Jr. "St. Phillip's College: A Case Study of a Historically Black Two-Year College." Ph.D. dissertation, University of Southern California, 1975.

Oliver, Joseph Green. "Availability of Educational Opportunities for Negroes in Leon County, Texas." Master's thesis, Prairie View Agricultural and Mechanical College, 1949.

Ottinger, Sam J. "A Study of Industrial Arts Programs in Negro High Schools of Texas." Master's thesis, North Texas State College, 1953.

Pannell, Orvella Tatum. "A Study of the Duties of Negro Principals in Bell County, Texas." Master's thesis, Prairie View Agricultural and Mechanical College, 1949.

_______. "A Study of the Status of Negro Schools in Bell County, Texas." Master's thesis, Prairie View Agricultural and Mechanical College, 1948.

Paradis, Robert L. "Comparison of Physical Fitness Scores of Anglo, Latin-American and Negro Students of Equal Socioeconomic Level." Master's thesis, Texas Technological College, 1967.

Pender, William M. "Curriculum and Instructional Problems of the Smaller Secondary Schools for Negroes in East Texas." Ed.D. dissertation, University of Texas, 1960.

Perpener, John O. Jr. "The Effects of the Gilmer-Aiken Laws Upon Fifteen Schools in Texas that have Negro Superintendents or Supervising Principals." Ph.D. dissertation, University of Colorado, 1953.

Phelps, Ralph A. Jr. "The Struggle for Public Higher Education for Negroes in Texas." D.D. dissertation, Southwest Baptist Theological Seminary, 1949.

Platt, Hazel. "Negro Education in Texas." Master's thesis, University of Texas, 1917.

Pollan, Madlyn Evelyn Schuchardt. "A Speech Survey of the Colored Children in the Elementary and Junior High School of Austin, Texas." Master's thesis, University of Texas, 1950.

Pollock, Juanice N. "The Development of Public Secondary Education for Negroes in the State of Texas." Master's thesis, Howard University, 1948.

Posey, E. B. Jr. "The History of Negro Education in Nolan County, Texas." Master's thesis, Hardin-Simmons University, 1952.

Powell, John Roosevelt. "A Study of the Development of Education for Negroes in Walker County." Master's thesis, Prairie View Agricultural and Mechanical College, 1948.

Preston, Allie. "Some of the Misconceptions of Modern Education in the Negro Public School and Community of Ladonia, Texas." Master's thesis, Texas College, 1954.

Pruitt, George. "Factors Affecting Educational Advancement in Shelby County, Texas." Master's thesis, Stephen F. Austin State College, 1941.

Randle, Irene Ethelind. "A Comparative Study of Common Schools for Negroes in Brazos County." Master's thesis, Prairie View State Normal and Industrial College, 1944.

Reese, Drew H. "The Historical Development and Present Status of Negro Education in DeWitt County, Texas." Master's thesis, Southwest Texas State Teachers College, 1949.

Robertson, Alberta Carl. "A Survey of Certain Aspects of the Negro High Schools in Leon County, Texas." Master's thesis, University of Southern California, 1941.

Robertson, Ruby Burton. "Educational Opportunities Available to Negro Youth in the United States: A Study of Bowie County, Texas, as a Particular Unit." Master's thesis, Texas State College for Women, 1948.

Sampson, Cornelius Carl. "The Status of Negro Education in Texas." Master's thesis, University of Chicago, 1949.

Schupack, Charles W. "A Comparative Study of White and Negro Schools in Fayette and Eight Adjoining Counties." Master's thesis, University of Texas, 1953.

Scourton, Lillie Renfro. "A Study of the Educational Program for Negro Exceptional Children in the South Park District of Beaumont, Texas." Master's thesis, University of Texas, 1960.

Shabazz, Amilcar. "The Opening of the Southern Mind: The Desegregation of Higher Education in Texas, 1865–1965." Ph.D. dissertation, University of Houston, 1996.

Shackelford, Richard Gary. "Advertising as a Profession as Perceived by Black and White Texas High School Seniors." Master's thesis, Texas Tech University, 1972.

Shackles, Chrystine I. *Reminiscences of Huston-Tillotson College*. Austin: n.p., 1973.

Sims, Van E. "The Willette Rutherford Banks' Administration: A Study in the Historical Development of Prairie View Agricultural and Mechanical College." Master's thesis, Prairie View Agricultural and Mechanical College, 1950.

Smith, Bernice Daviss. "A Study of the Business Work Experience of Business Teachers in Selected Class AA High Schools in Texas." Master's thesis, Texas Southern University, 1959.

Smith, James R. "How can the Educational Opportunities be improved for the Colored Children of Rusk County, Texas?" Master's thesis, North Texas State Teachers College, 1939.

Smith, Laura B. "A Survey of Negro Schools in Wood County, Texas." Master's thesis, University of Southern California, 1936.

Stewart, Iva Mae. "A Study of Music in the Negro Secondary Schools of Houston, Texas." Master's thesis, State University of Iowa, 1943.

Stoker, Winfred M. "A Comparison of White and Negro Elementary School Teachers in Galveston County. " Ed.D. dissertation, University of Houston, 1958.

Stone, Pearle Pippen. "An Analysis of the Changes and the Development of Negro Education in Rural Harrison County, 1940–1950." Master's thesis, North Texas State College, 1950.

Tarrow, Willie Andrew. "A University for Negroes of Texas—A Promise Unfulfilled." Master's thesis, Prairie View University, 1946.

Taylor, Douglas Barnes. "Negro Education in Texas." Master's thesis, University of Texas, 1927.

Terrell, Wendell Phillips. "A Study of the Employment of the Graduates of Ten Negro High Schools of Texas." Master's thesis, Colorado State College, 1937.

Terry, William E. "Origin and Development of Texas Southern University, Houston, Texas." Ed.D. dissertation, University of Houston, 1968.

_______. *Origin and Development of Texas Southern University, Houston, Texas*. Houston: W. E. Terry, 1978.

Thomas, Bessie Aleda. "A Study of the Advantages and Disadvantages of the Consolidated Negro Schools in Waller County, Texas." Master's thesis, Prairie View State Normal and Industrial College, 1942.

Thompson, Ester Lane. "The Influence of the Freedmen's Bureau on the Education of the Negro in Texas." Master's thesis, Texas Southern University, 1972.

Thompson, Hortense Smith. "A Study of the Status of Negro Education in Liberty County, Texas." Master's thesis, Southern Methodist University, 1935.

Thompson, James E. "A History of Negro Colleges of East Texas." Master's thesis, Stephen F. Austin State College, 1951.

Thompson, Lloyd Kay. "The Origin and Development of Black Religious Colleges in East Texas." Ph.D. dissertation, North Texas State University, 1976.

Todd, William Clyde. "The Attitudes of the Negroes of Texas toward Higher Education." Master's thesis, University of Texas, 1929.

Tompkins, George Washington Jr. "Racial Discrimination and the Equalization of Negro and White Teachers' Salaries in the Dallas Public Schools." Master's thesis, North Texas State University, 1974.

Totten, Herman L. "A Survey of the use of the Carnegie Library of Wiley College Students, 1964." Master's thesis, University of Oklahoma, 1964.

_______. "The Wiley College Library: The First Library for Negroes West of the Mississippi. *Negro History Bulletin* 32 (1969): 6–10.

Traughber, Clark R. "A Study of Negro Public Schools of Smith County, Texas." Master's thesis, East Texas State Teachers College, 1940.

Travis, Ray Polk. "The Status of the Teaching of Negro History in the Public High Schools of Texas." Ed.D. dissertation, North Texas State University, 1972.

Trezevant, Adlee Houston. "A Comparative Survey of Music in the Larger Negro High Schools of Texas." Master's thesis, Northwestern University, 1948.

Tullis, David S. "A Comparative Study of Negro, Latin, and Anglo Children in a West Texas Community." Ed.D. dissertation, Texas Technological College, 1964.

Urquhart, George Richard. "The Status of Secondary and Higher Education of Negroes in Texas." Master's thesis, University of Texas, 1931.

Vowell, Raymond Woodrow. "The Need and Suggested Areas for the Location of Public Junior Colleges for Negroes in the State of Texas." Master's thesis, University of Texas, 1948.

Wallace, Frances Willard Blake. "A Study of Intelligence, Some Personality Traits and Adjustments of Seventy Negro Teachers of Panola County, Texas." Master's thesis, Atlanta University, 1943.

Walsh, Jennie Russell. "An Analysis of Attitudes of Teachers in Selected Texas Public Schools Toward the Negro." Master's thesis, Texas A&M University, 1966.

Washington, Jordan Thomas. "Adequacy of Public Education for Negroes of Jasper County, Texas." Master's thesis, Prairie View State Normal and Industrial College, 1943.

Washington, Samuel N. "The Land-Grant Colleges for Negroes, 1914–1945." Master's thesis, Prairie View Agricultural and Mechanical University, 1949.

Watkins, Jocelyn Henderson. "The History and Development of the Colored State Teachers' Association of Texas." Master's thesis, University of Southern California, 1941.

Watkins, Pauline Melonee. "An Investigation of Negro Elementary Schools in the State of Texas." Master's thesis, University of Southern California, 1937.

Webb, John Compton. "Personal Problems of Negro Students in High Schools of East Texas." Ph.D. dissertation, Texas A&M University, 1971.

Whatley, Calvin Arthur. "A Study of the Intelligence of 1,285 Negro Children in Texas Public Schools." Master's thesis, Southern Methodist University, 1926.

White, Annie Mae Vaught. "The Development of the Program of Studies of the Prairie View State Normal and Industrial College." Master's thesis, University of Texas, 1938.

White, Leslie J. "A Study of Recent Efforts to Equalize Educational Opportunities for Negroes in Texas." Master's thesis, Fisk University, 1945.

Williams, David Alvernon. "A History of African-American Higher Education in Austin and Travis County, Texas." In *Bricks Without Straw: A Comprehensive History of African Americans in Texas*, edited by David A. Williams, 279–308. Austin: Eakin Press, 1997.

_______. "A History of Higher Education for African-American Texans, 1872–1977." In *Bricks Without Straw: A Comprehensive History of African Americans in Texas*, edited by David A. Williams, 208–278. Austin: Eakin Press, 1997.

_______. "The History of Higher Education for Black Texans, 1872–1977." Ed.D. dissertation, Baylor University, 1978.

Williams, Ethel M. "A Comparative Study of the School Facilities offered White and Colored Pupils in Selected Schools in Eleven Counties in Southeast Texas in 1948–1949." Ph.D. dissertation, University of Houston, 1954.

Williams, Leonora Barbara. "Relationship of Certain Factors to Superstitious Beliefs of Negro and White High School Pupils in Texas." Master's thesis, University of Colorado, 1938.

Williams, L. V. "Teaching Negro Life and History in Texas High Schools." *Journal of Negro History* 20 (1935): 13–18.

Williams, Mabel Crayton. "The History of Tillotson College, 1881–1952." Master's thesis, Texas Southern University, 1967.

Williams, Mamie Edditha. "A Study of the Health Programs in Selected Elementary Schools as a Basis for the Development of Health Programs in Eight Negro Elementary Schools of Anderson County, Texas." Master's thesis, Texas College, 1959.

Williams, Walter Sam Jr. "A Study of the Status of the Area of Health, Physical Education, and Recreation in the Colleges and Universities of Texas for Negro Students during the Session of 1953–1954." Master's thesis, North Texas State College, 1955.

Williams, W. T. B. "Colored Public Schools of Texas." *Southern Workman* 53 (October 1924): 445–448.

Willingham, William Oliver. "Progress of Negro Education in Texas." Master's thesis, Texas Technological College, 1932.

Wilson, Anna Victoria. "Forgotten Voices: Remembered Experiences of Cross-over Teachers during Desegregation in Austin, Texas, 1964–1971." Ph.D. dissertation, University of Texas at Austin, 1997.

Wood, Curtis A. "A Proposed Plan to Coordinate and Extend Services in Health Education at Prairie View A&M College to Schools and Communities of Texas." Ph.D. dissertation, Columbia University, 1956.

Woods, L. A. *Negro Education in Texas, 1934–1935*. Austin: Texas Department of Education, 1935.

Woolfolk, George R. *Prairie View: A Study in Public Conscience, 1878–1946*. New York: Pageant Press, 1962.

Worley, Charles Dinzle. "Six Years of Advance of Negro Public School Education in Texas, 1943–1948." Master's thesis, Southwest Texas State College, 1949.

Young, Horace Alexander Jr. "A History and Appraisal of the Colored Teachers' State Association of Texas." Master's thesis, University of New Mexico, 1949.

16. Fiction

Two cowboys, Mose and Nat, near windmill and tank preparing camp dinner on James F. Welder Ranch, ca. 1950.

The UT Institute of Texan Cultures, No. 80-490 Courtesy of the Estate of Roger Fleming

akimbo, nia. "Speaking in Tongues." In *Texas Short Stories II*, edited by Billy Bob Hill and Laurie Champion, 481–496. Dallas: Browder Springs Publishing, 2000.

Allen, Phyllis W. "The Crown." *Tex: A Magazine of Texas Fiction, Poetry, and Art* (1998): 4–5.

_______. "Mama Minnie and Me." In *Texas Short Stories*, edited by Billy Bob Hill, 306–314. Dallas: Browder Springs Publishing, 1997.

_______. "The Red Swing." In *KenteCloth: Southwest Voices of the African Diaspora, The Oral Tradition Comes to the Page*, edited by Jas. Mardis, 141–146. Denton: University of North Texas Press, 1997.

_______. "The Shopping Trip." In *KenteCloth: African American Voices in Texas,* edited by Sherry McGuire and John R. Posey, 60–65. Denton: Center for Texas Studies, University of North Texas, 1995.

_______. "Blood on the Moon." In *Texas Short Stories II*, edited by Billy Bob Hill and Laurie Champion, 49–59. Dallas: Browder Springs Publishing, 2000.

Blair, Yvette. "The Wooden Box." In *Texas Short Stories II,* edited by Billy Bob Hill and Laurie Champion, 551–556. Dallas: Browder Springs Publishing, 2000.

Brister, Bob. "Moss, Mallards, and Mules." In *Moss, Mallards and Mules, and Other Hunting and Fishing Stories*, 1–7. New York: Winchester Press, 1973.

_______. "Of Perches and Pleasures." In *Moss, Mallards and Mules, and Other Hunting and Fishing Stories,* 33–39. New York: Winchester Press, 1973.

Bunkley, Anita Richmond. *Black Gold.* New York: Dutton, 1994.

_______. *Emily, The Yellow Rose: A Texas Legend.* Houston: Rinard Publishing, 1989.

_______. *Wild Embers*. New York: Dutton, 1995.

Carhart, J. W. *Under Palmetto and Pine*. Cincinnati: Editor Publishing Company, 1899. [Short stories]

Carstarphen, Meta G. "Point of Departure." In *KenteCloth: African American Voices in Texas,* edited by Sherry McGuire and John R. Posey, 151–157. Denton: Center for Texas Studies, University of North Texas, 1995.

Cooper, J. California. *The Wake of the Dead.* New York: Doubleday, 1998.

Crawford, Marc. "Willie T. Washington's Blues." *Black World* 21 (May 1972): 54–66.

Crenshaw, Vernita. *Black Girl.* Missouri City, Tex.: Privately printed, 1992.

Dawson, Curtis Dale. "Mayday at Northeast Mall." In *KenteCloth: African American Voices in Texas*, edited by Sherry McGuire and John R. Posey, 193–200. Denton: Center for Texas Studies, University of North Texas Press, 1995.

Dionne, Wanda. *A Yank among Us.* Austin: Eakin Press, 1997. [Children's book]

Dobie, Charles Caldwell. *Less Than Kin; A Novel.* New York: John Day, 1926.

Dove, Rita. "Damon and Vandalia." In *Fifth Sunday*, 30–39. Charlottesville: University Press of Virginia, 1985.

Du Bois, W. E. B. "Jesus Christ in Texas." 1920. In *Darkwater: Voices from the Veil,* 123–133. New York: Schocken Books, 1969.

_______. "On Being Crazy." 1907. In *From the Roots: Short Stories by Black Americans*, edited by Charles L. James, 43–45. New York: Dodd, Mead, 1970.

Fahrenthold, Lisa. "Roberta." In *Common Bonds: Stories by and about Modern Texas Women,* edited by Suzanne Comer, 12–25. Dallas: Southern Methodist University Press, 1990.

Faulk, John Henry. "A Glorious Fourth." In *Unknown Texas,* edited by Jonathan Eisen and Harold Straughn, 208–215. New York: Collier Books, 1988.

Fleming, David L. "The Sun Gone Down, Darkness Be Over Me." In *Careless Weeds: Six Texas Novellas,* edited by Tom Pilkington, 141–186. Dallas: Southern Methodist University Press, 1993.

Ford, Nick Aaron. "No Room in the Inn." In *Best Short Stories By Afro-American Writers (1925–1950)*, edited by Nick Aaron Ford and H. L. Faggett, 19–24. New York: Meador Publishing Company, 1950.

Griggs, Sutton E. *Imperium in Imperio.* New York: Arno Press, 1969. Reprint of 1899 edition.

Himes, Chester. "One More Way to Die." *Negro Story* 3 (1946): 10–14. Also in *The Collected Stories of Chester Himes*, 375–380. New York: Thunder's Mouth Press, 1990.

_______. "A Penny for Your Thoughts." *Negro Story* 1 (March-April 1945): 14–17. Also in *The Collected Stories of Chester Himes*, 56–60. New York: Thunder's Mouth Press, 1990.

Jackson, Guida. *Passing Through.* New York: Simon and Schuster, 1979.

Jackson, James Thomas. "Waiting in Line at the Drugstore." In *KenteCloth: Southwest Voices of the African Diaspora, The Oral Tradition Comes to the Page*, edited by Jas. Mardis, 117–120. Denton: University of North Texas Press, 1997.

Jimoh, A. Yemisi. "Peace Be Still." In *Sisterfire: Black Womanist Fiction and Poetry*, edited by Charlotte Watson Sherman, 54–56. New York: HarperPerennial, 1994.

Jones, Gayl. *Mosquito.* Boston: Beacon Press, 1999.

Kelton, Elmer. "Man on the Wagontongue." In *They Won Their Spurs*, edited by Nelson Nye, 129–143. New York: Avon Books, 1962.

_______. *Wagontongue*. New York: Bantam Books, 1972.

_______. *The Wolf and the Buffalo*. Fort Worth: Texas Christian University Press, 1986.

Kidd, Harry Jr. "Low Road Go Down." *Southwest Review* 33 (1948): 385–393.

Lee, Bob. "A Hunt in the Big Thicket." In *KenteCloth: Southwest Voices of the African Diaspora, The Oral Tradition Comes to the Page*, edited by Jas. Mardis, 121–124. Denton: University of North Texas Press, 1997.

Lewis, Arthur H. *The Day they Shook the Plum Tree*. New York: Bantam Books, 1963.

Majors, Michelle. "The Taxi Ride Home." In *KenteCloth: African American Voices in Texas,* edited by Sherry McGuire and John R. Posey, 179–182. Denton: Center for Texas Studies, University of North Texas, 1995.

Mardis, Jas. "The Arsenic Biscuits." *Tex: A Magazine of Texas Fiction, Poetry, and Art* (1998): 24–25.

_______. "Clayton and Bungalo." In *Texas Short Stories II*, edited by Billy Bob Hill and Laurie Champion, 113–126. Dallas: Browder Springs Publishing, 2000.

McElroy, Njoki. "The Ninth Day of May." In *Common Bonds: Stories by and about Modern Texas Women*, edited by Suzanne Comer, 40–42. Dallas: Southern Methodist University Press, 1990.

McGuire, Sherry, and John R. Posey, eds. *KenteCloth: African American Voices in Texas*. Denton: Center for Texas Studies, University of North Texas, 1995.

McKinley, Georgia. *Follow the Running Grass*. Boston: Houghton Mifflin, 1969.

McKnight, Reginald. "The Kind of Light that Shines on Texas." In *The Kind of Light that Shines on Texas*, 20–40. Boston: Little, Brown, 1992.

_______. "Who Big Bob?" In *Moustapha's Eclipse,* 37–42. Pittsburgh: University of Pittsburgh Press, 1988.

McMurtry, Larry. *Anything for Billy*. New York: Simon and Schuster, 1988.

Modupe, Talibah Folami. "Inmate 93274." In *Texas Short Fiction: A World in Itself II,* edited by Mike Hennech and Billy Bob Hill, 20–31. Redmond, Wash.: ALE Publishing, 1995.

_______. "Is the Other Man's Ice Really Colder?" In *Texas Short Stories*, edited by Billy Bob Hill, 361–363. Dallas: Browder Springs Publishing, 1997.

_______. "The Right Reverend James." In *New Texas 94: Poetry and Fiction*, edited by Kathryn S. McGuire and James Ward Lee, 159–162. Denton: Center for Texas Studies, 1994.

Mullen, Harryette. "Bad Girls." In *Her Work: Stories by Texas Women*, edited by Lou Halsell Rodenberger, 204–206. Bryan, Tex.: Shearer Publishing, 1992.

_______. "Pica." In *Her Work: Stories by Texas Women*, edited by Lou Halsell Rodenberger, 200–203. Bryan, Tex.: Shearer Publishing, 1992.

_______. "Tenderhead." In *Common Bonds: Stories by and about Modern Texas Women*, edited by Suzanne Comer, 69–78. Dallas: Southern Methodist University Press, 1990.

_______. "What Can't Be Measured." In *South By Southwest: 24 Stories from Modern Texas,* edited by Don Graham, 203–213. Austin: University of Texas Press, 1986.

Nash, Sunny. "Amen." *Southwestern American Literature* 20 (Spring 1995): 85–96.

_______. "The Ladies' Room." In *Common Bonds: Stories by and about Modern Texas Women,* edited by Suzanne Comer, 183–189. Dallas: Southern Methodist University Press, 1990.

_______. "Too High for Birds." In *New Growth/2: Contemporary Short Stories by Texas Writers*, edited by Mark Busby, 153–159. San Antonio: Corona Publishing, 1993.

Norris, Adrienne. "Dreams Befitting." In *KenteCloth: Southwest Voices of the African Diaspora, The Oral Tradition Comes to the Page*, edited by Jas. Mardis, 242–249. Denton: University of North Texas Press, 1997.

Owens, William A. "Hangerman John." *Southwest Review* 32 (1947): 124–132.

_______. *Walking on Borrowed Land.* Fort Worth: Texas Christian University Press, 1988.

Patterson, Lindsay. "A New Understanding." In *KenteCloth: Southwest Voices of the African Diaspora, The Oral Tradition Comes to the Page*, edited by Jas. Mardis, 14–18. Denton: University of North Texas Press, 1997. [First published in *Tarnished Hero* (Modern Black Man, 1986)].

Pickens, William. "Jim Crow in Texas." *The Nation* 117 (August 15, 1923): 155–156.

Pinson, Hermine. *Ashe.* Houston: Wings Press, 1992.

_______. "Kris/Crack/Kyle." In *KenteCloth: African American Voices in Texas*, edited by Sherry McGuire and John R. Posey, 36–39. Denton: Center for Texas Studies, University of North Texas, 1995.

_______. "Someday My Prince." In *Common Bonds: Stories by and about Modern Texas Women,* edited by Suzanne Comer, 294–298. Dallas: Southern Methodist University Press, 1990.

Posey, John R. "Ticket to Freedom." In *Texas Short Fiction: A World in Itself II,* edited by Mike Hennech and Billy Bob Hill, 203–217. Redmond, Wash.: ALE Publishing, 1995.

Reid, Jan. "Second Saddle." In *Texas Short Stories*, edited by Billy Bob Hill, 267–278. Dallas: Browder Springs Publishing, 1997.

Sackler, Howard. *The Great White Hope*. New York: Dial, 1968.

Shange, Ntozake. *Betsey Brown*. New York: St. Martin's Press, 1985.

_______. "Ridin' the Moon in Texas." In *Ridin' the Moon in Texas: Word Paintings*, 5–11. New York: St. Martin's Press, 1987.

Simond, Ada DeBlanc. *Let's Pretend: Mae Dee and Her Family and the First Wedding of the Year*. Austin: Stevenson Press, 1979. [Children's book]

_______. *Let's Pretend: Mae Dee and Her Family Go to Town*. Austin: Stevenson Press, 1977. [Children's book]

_______. *Let's Pretend: Mae Dee and Her Family in the Merry, Merry Season*. Austin: Stevenson Press, 1978. [Children's book]

_______. *Let's Pretend: Mae Dee and Her Family Join the Juneteenth Celebration*. Austin: Stevenson Press, 1978. [Children's book]

_______. *Let's Pretend: Mae Dee and Her Family on a Weekend in May*. Austin: Stevenson Press, 1977. [Children's book]

_______. *Let's Pretend: Mae Dee and Her Family Ten Years Later*. Austin: Stevenson Press, 1980. [Children's book]

Singley, Bernestine. "Heat." *Tex: A Magazine of Texas Fiction, Poetry, and Art* (1998): 18.

_______. "Take Me to the Water." In *Texas Short Stories II*, edited by Billy Bob Hill and Laurie Champion, 301–307. Dallas: Browder Springs Publishing, 2000.

Story, Rosalyn M. "Quiet As Its Kept." In *New Texas 94: Poetry and Fiction*, edited by Kathryn S. McGuire and James Ward Lee, 67–86. Denton: Center for Texas Studies, 1994.

Tolliver, Ruby C. *Muddy Banks*. Fort Worth: Texas Christian University Press, 1987.

Truvillion, Jesse Garfield. "A Child's Life in the Big Thicket: A Love of Blackberries." In *KenteCloth: Southwest Voices of the African Diaspora, The Oral Tradition Comes to the Page*, edited by Jas. Mardis, 136–140. Denton: University of North Texas Press, 1997.

_______. "A Stray Dog's Great Day." In *KenteCloth: Southwest Voices of the African Diaspora, The Oral Tradition Comes to the Page*, edited by Jas. Mardis, 113–116. Denton: University of North Texas Press, 1997.

Wald, Malvin. "Keys to the City." *Negro Story* 1 (December-January 1944–1945): 19–22.

Watt, Donley. "Caddo." In *Can You Get There From Here?*, 83–96. Dallas: Southern Methodist University Press, 1994.

Weatherford, Carole Boston. *Juneteenth Jamboree.* New York: Lee and Low Books, 1995. [Children's book]

Wheaton, Elizabeth Lee. *Mr. George's Joint.* New York: E. P. Dutton, 1941.

Wiespape, Betty. "Canned Peaches." In *New Texas '99: A Center for Texas Studies Book,* edited by Donna Walker-Nixon and James Ward Lee, 248–257. Belton, Tex.: University of Mary Hardin-Baylor, 1999.

Williams, Margaret. "Grazing in Good Pastures." *The Crisis* 48 (1941): 42–43, 59.

Wright, Lawrence. "Escape." In *Texas Bound: 19 Texas Stories*, edited by Kay Cattarulla, 211–236. Dallas: Southern Methodist University Press, 1994.

Yerby, Frank. "Health Card." *Harper's Magazine* 188 (May 1944): 548–553.

17. Urban Communities

Staff of the Maternity Home and Hospital at 716 Sherman Street, San Antonio, Texas, 1925.

The UT Institute of Texan Cultures, No. 87-193
Courtesy of Luther S. Lee

Agnew, Peter W. "Making Dallas Moral: Two Baptist Pastors." *Heritage News* 12 (Summer 1987): 19–25.

Ahlfield, Danny Lee. "Fraternalism Gone Awry: The Ku Klux Klan in Houston, 1920–1925." Master's thesis, University of Texas at Austin, 1984.

Amin, Julius. "Black Lubbock: 1955 to the Present." *West Texas Historical Association Year Book* 65 (1989): 24–35.

Barr, Alwyn. "Black Migration into Southwestern Cities, 1865–1900." In *Essays on Southern History: Written in Honor of Barnes F. Lathrop*, edited by Gary W. Gallagher, 15–38. Austin: General Libraries of University of Texas, 1980.

_______. "Occupational and Geographical Mobility in San Antonio, 1870–1900." *Social Science Quarterly* 51 (1970): 396–403.

Barr, Alwyn, and Robert L. Foster. "Black Lubbock." *West Texas Historical Association Year Book* 54 (1978): 20–31.

Beeth, Howard. "A Black Elite Agenda in the Urban South: The Call for Political and Racial Economic Solidarity in Houston during the 1920s." *Essays in Economic and Business History* 10 (June 1992): 41–55.

_______. "Houston and History, Past and Present: A Look at Black Houston in the 1920's." *Southern Studies* 25 (Summer 1986): 172–186.

Beeth, Howard, and Cary D. Wintz, eds. *Black Dixie: Afro-Texan History and Culture in Houston*. College Station: Texas A&M University Press, 1992.

Botson, Michael. "Jim Crow Wearing Steel-Toed Shoes and Safety Glasses: Duel Unionism at the Hughes Tool Company, 1918–1942." *The Houston Review* 16.2 (1994): 101–116.

_______. "No Gold Watch for Jim Crow's Retirement: The Abolition of Segregated Unionism at Houston's Hughes Tool Company." *Southwestern Historical Quarterly* 101 (1998): 497–521.

Breed, Warren. *Beaumont, Texas: College Desegregation without Popular Support*. New York: Anti-Defamation League of B'nai B'rith, 1957.

Brewer, J. Mason, ed. *A History of Dallas High School for Negroes*. Reprint. Dallas: Friends of the Dallas Public Library, 1991.

Brophy, William Joseph. "Active Acceptance—Active Containment: The Dallas Story." In *Southern Businessmen and Desegregation*, edited by Elizabeth Jacoway and David R. Colburn, 137–150. Baton Rouge: Louisiana State University Press, 1982.

_______. "Black Business Development in Texas Cities, 1900–1950." *Red River Valley Historical Review* 6 (Spring 1981): 42–55.

Bryan, Marilyn T. "The Economic, Political and Social Status of the Negro in El Paso." *Password* 13 (1968): 74–86.

Bryson, Conrey. "El Paso and the Poll Tax." *Password* 4 (1959): 46–52.

Bullard, Robert D. "Black Housing in the Golden Buckle of the Sunbelt." *Free Inquiry* 8 (November 1980): 169–172.

_______. *Black Houston Business Survey*. Houston: Texas Southern University Publication, 1983.

_______. "Blacks in Heavenly Houston." In *In Search of the New South: The Black Urban Experience in the 1970s and 1980s*, edited by Robert D. Bullard, 16–44, 176–178. Tuscaloosa: University of Alabama Press, 1989.

_______. "Dispute Resolution and Toxics: Case Studies." In *Dumping in Dixie: Race, Class, and Environmental Quality*, second edition, 37–74. Boulder: Westview Press, 1994.

_______. "Endangered Environs: The Price of Unplanned Growth in Boomtown Houston." *California Sociologist* 7 (Summer 1984): 84–102.

_______. "Housing Problems and Prospects in Contemporary Houston." In *Black Dixie: Afro-Texan History and Culture in Houston*, edited by Howard Beeth and Cary D. Wintz, 236–252. College Station: Texas A&M University Press, 1992.

_______. *Houston's Third Ward: A Center of Black Business*. Houston: Texas Southern University, 1982.

_______. *Invisible Houston: The Black Experience in Boom and Bust*. College Station: Texas A&M University Press, 1987.

_______. "Solid Waste Sites and the Black Houston Community." *Sociological Inquiry* 53 (1983): 273–288.

Bullard, Robert D., and Odessa L. Pierce. "Black Housing in a Southern Metropolis: Competition for Housing in a Shrinking Market." *Black Scholar* 11 (November/December 1979): 60–67.

Bullard, Robert D., and Donald L. Tryman. "Competition for Decent Housing: A Focus on Housing Discrimination in a Sunbelt City." *Journal of Ethnic Studies* 7 (Winter 1980): 561–563.

_______. "Housing Segregation in the Sunbelt, 1960s–1970s." In *Peoples of Color in the American West*, edited by Sucheng Chan, Douglas Henry Daniels, Mario T. Garcia, and Terry P. Wilson, 345–351. Lexington, Mass.: D.C. Heath, 1994.

Bullard, Robert D., and Beverly H. Wright. "Dumping Grounds in a Sunbelt City." *Urban Resources* 2 (Winter 1985): 37–39.

Bullock, Henry Allen. *Pathways to the Houston Negro Market.* Ann Arbor: J. N. Edwards, 1957.

_______. *Profile of Houston's Negro Business Enterprises: A Survey and Directory of Their Attitudes.* Houston: Negro Chamber of Commerce, 1962.

_______. "Significance of the Racial Factor in the Length of Prison Sentences." *Journal of Criminal Law, Criminology, and Police Science* 52 (1961): 411–417.

_______. "Urban Homicide in Theory and Fact." *Journal of Criminal Law, Criminology, and Police Science* 45 (1955): 565–575.

Burran, James A. "Violence in an 'Arsenal of Democracy': The Beaumont Race Riot, 1943." *East Texas Historical Review* 14.1 (1976): 39–51.

Christian, Garna L. "Texas Beginnings: Houston in the World of Jazz." *The Houston Review* 12.3 (1990): 144–156.

Cole, Thomas. *No Color is My Kind: The Life of Eldrewey Stearns and the Integration of Houston.* Austin: University of Texas Press, 1997.

Condon, Cynthia G., Joy L. Becker, Heather Edgar, James Davidson, Juerena Hoffman, Patricia Kalima, Daniel Kysar, Susan Moorehead, Victoria Owens, and Keith Condon. *Freedman's Cemetery: Site 41DL316, Dallas, Texas, Assessments of Sex, Age-at Death, Stature and Date of Interment.* Report No. 9. Austin: Archaeological Studies Program, Environmental Affairs Division, Texas Department of Transportation, 1998.

Crouch, Barry A. "Seeking Equality: Houston Black Women during Reconstruction." In *Black Dixie: Afro-Texan History and Culture in Houston*, edited by Howard Beeth and Cary D. Wintz, 54–73. College Station: Texas A&M University Press, 1992.

Dailey, Nancy. "History of the Beaumont, Texas, Chapter of the National Association for the Advancement of Colored People, 1918–1970." Master's thesis, Lamar University, 1971.

Davidson, Chandler. *Biracial Politics: Conflict and Coalition in the Metropolitan South.* Baton Rouge: Louisiana State University Press, 1972.

_______. "Negro Politics and the Rise of the Civil Rights Movement in Houston, Texas." Ph.D. dissertation, Princeton University, 1968.

Davidson, James M. "Freedman's Cemetery (1869–1907): Establishing a Chronology for Exhumed Burials from an African-American Burial Ground, Dallas, Texas". *African-American Archaeology, Newsletter of the African-American Archaeology Network* 26 (Early Winter 1999): 4–5.

_______. "Freedman's Cemetery: A Chronological Reconstruction of an Excavated African-American Burial Ground, Dallas, Texas." Master's thesis, University of Arkansas, 1999

_______. The Old Dallas Burial Ground: A Forgotten Cemetery. *Southwestern Historical Quarterly* 102.2 (1998):162–184.

_______. "The Oldest Cemetery in Dallas Rediscovered: The Lost Location of Dallas's Slave Burials." *African-American Archaeology, Newsletter of the African-American Archaeology Network* 22 (Fall 1998): 4, 7.

Delta Sigma Theta Sorority. *The Black Heritage Exhibit: A Pictorial History of Austin, Travis County, Texas' Black Community, 1839–1920.* Austin: Delta Sigma Theta Sorority, c. 1973.

Dodson, Jack. "Minority Group Housing in Two Texas Cities." In *Studies in Housing and Minority Groups*, edited by Nathan Glazer and Davis McEntire, 84–110. Berkeley: University of California Press, 1960.

Doggett, Dorothy Lasseter. "Survey of Fort Worth's Negro Schools." Master's thesis, Texas Christian University, 1927.

Dressman, Frances. "'Yes We Have No Jitneys!': Transportation Issues in Houston's Black Community, 1914–1924." *The Houston Review* 9.2 (1987): 69–81.

Dulaney, W. Marvin. "Multiculturalism in Dallas, Texas: The Legacy for Sharing Political Power in the 1990s." *Journal of Multicultural Studies* 1 (1991): 1–12.

_______. "The Progressive Voters' League: A Political Voice for African Americans in Dallas." *Legacies* 3 (Spring 1991): 27–35.

_______. "Whatever Happened to the Civil Rights Movement in Dallas, Texas?" In *Essays on the American Civil Rights Movement*, edited by W. Marvin Dulaney and Kathleen Underwood, 66–95. College Station: Texas A&M University Press, 1993.

Engerand, Steven W. "Black and Mulatto Mobility and Stability in Dallas, Texas, 1880–1910." *Phylon* 39 (1978): 203–215.

Fairbanks, Robert B. "From Consensus to Controversy: The Rise and Fall of Public Housing in Dallas." *Legacies* 1 (Fall 1989): 37–43.

Ferguson, William. "A Reading Survey of Negro Homes of Beaumont, Texas." Master's thesis, George Peabody College for Teachers, 1932.

Foster, Robert L. "Black Lubbock: A History of Negroes in Lubbock, Texas, to 1940." Master's thesis, Texas Tech University, 1974.

Foster, Robert L., and Alwyn Barr. "Black Lubbock." *West Texas Historical Association Year Book* 54 (1978): 20–31.

Gallagher, Arthur Jr. *The Negro and Employment Opportunities in the South—Houston*. Atlanta Southern Regional Council, 1961.

Gee, Sadye, comp., and Darnell Williams, ed. *Black Presence in Dallas: Historic Black Dallasites*. Dallas: Museum of African-American Life and Culture, 1986.

Greene, A. C. "The Durable Society: Austin in the Reconstruction." *Southwestern Historical Quarterly* 72 (1969): 492–519.

Greene, Carrie Etta. "The History of Education Provided for Negroes in San Angelo, Texas, from Inception to Integration, September, 1955." Master's thesis, Texas Southern University, 1956.

Gunter, Margaret Jane. "Race and the Generations: A Comparative Study of Racial Prejudice in Two Generations in Amarillo, Texas." Master's thesis, West Texas State University, 1971.

Haynes, Robert V. "Black Houstonians and the White Democratic Primary, 1920–45." *Black Dixie: Afro-Texan History and Culture in Houston*, edited by Howard Beeth and Cary D. Wintz, 192–210. College Station: Texas A&M University Press, 1992.

________. "The Houston Mutiny and Riot of 1917." *Southwestern Historical Quarterly* 76 (1973): 418–439.

________. *A Night of Violence: The Houston Riot of 1917*. Baton Rouge: Louisiana State University Press, 1976.

Hickman, R. C. *Behold the People: R. C. Hickman's Photographs of Black Dallas, 1949–1961*. Austin: Texas State Historical Association, 1994.

Hilliard, Roby Waldo. "Juvenile Delinquency among Negroes in Houston, Texas." Master's thesis, University of Wisconsin, 1936.

Ivy, Charlotte. "Forgotten Color: Black Families in Early El Paso." *Password* 35 (1990): 5–18.

Jackson, Charles Christopher. "A Southern Black Community Comes of Age: Black San Antonio in the Great Depression, 1930–1941." Master's thesis, Texas A&M University, 1989.

Jackson, James Thomas. "Houston's Fourth Ward." In *Juneteenth Texas: Essays in African-American Folklore*, edited by Francis E. Abernethy, Carolyn Fiedler Satterwhite, Patrick B. Mullen, and Alan B. Govenar, 41–47. Publication of the Texas Folklore Society No. 54. Denton: University of North Texas Press, 1996.

Jackson, Kenneth T. "Dallas: Dynamo of the Southwest." In *The Ku Klux Klan in the City, 1915–1930*, 66–80, 265–266. New York: Oxford University Press, 1967.

Jackson, Larry J. "The Development of Black Business in Texas, 1919–1969: From a Houston Perpective." Master's thesis, Texas Tech University, 1979.

Jackson, Robena Estelle. "East Austin: A Socio-Historical View of a Segregated Community." Master's thesis, University of Texas at Austin, 1979.

Jenkins, Carolyn. "Business and Economic Development in the Black Community: Houston's Third Ward." Master's thesis, Texas Southern University, 1982.

Johnson, W. L. D. "Organization of the Public Schools in Houston, Texas, 1905–1940." Master's thesis, Prairie View University, 1943.

Johnston, O. G. "A Sociological Study of Standards of Living of Families in the Waco Negro Housing Project." Master's thesis, Baylor University, 1951.

Jones, Carolyn. *Volma. . .My Journey: One Man's Impact on the Civil Rights Movement in Austin, Texas*. Austin: Eakin Press, 1998.

Jones, Howard. *The Red Diary: A Chronological History of Black Americans in Houston and Some Neighboring Harris County Communities—122 Years Later*. Austin: Nortex Press, 1991.

Justice, Blair. *Violence in the City*. Fort Worth: Texas Christian University Press, 1969.

Kaplan, Barry J. "Race, Income, and Ethnicity: Residential Change in a Houston Community, 1920–1970." *The Houston Review* 3 (Winter 1981): 178–202.

Keir, Scott S. "Middle Class Black Families in Austin, Texas: An Exploratory Analysis of Husbands and Wives." Ph.D. dissertation, University of Texas at Austin, 1987.

Kilmer, Rita Kathryn McCoulskey. "Residential Movement of Blacks in Austin, Texas, 1950–1970." Master's thesis, University of Texas at Austin, 1974.

LaGrone, Cyrus Wilson. "A Sociological Study of the Negro Population of Marshall, Texas." Master's thesis, University of Texas, 1932.

Laine, Alice K. "An In-Depth Study of the Black Political Leadership in Houston, Texas." Ph.D. dissertation, University of Texas at Austin, 1978.

Lamkin, Patricia E. "Blacks in San Angelo: Relations between Fort Concho and the City, 1875–1889." *West Texas Historical Association Year Book* 66 (1990): 26–37.

_______. "A History of Blacks in San Angelo, 1869–1930." Master's thesis, Angelo State University, 1990.

Landon, Johnnie A. Jr. "The N.A.A.C.P. in El Paso: An Instrument for Political Involvement." Master's thesis, University of Texas at El Paso, 1972.

Lay, Shawn. *War, Revolution, and the Ku Klux Klan: A Study of Intolerance in a Border City*. El Paso: Texas Western Press, 1985.

Linden, Glenn. *Desegregating Schools in Dallas*. Dallas: Three Forks Press, 1995.

Lindsey, Walter. "Black Houstonians Challenge the White Democratic Primary, 1921–1944." Master's thesis, University of Houston, 1969.

Mason, Kenneth. *African Americans and Race Relations in San Antonio, Texas, 1867–1937.* New York: Garland Publishing, 1998.

_______. "Paternal Continuity: African-Americans and Race Relations in San Antonio, 1867–1937." Ph.D. dissertation, University of Texas at Austin, 1994.

Massaquoi, Hans J. "Introducing Ron Kirk: First Black Mayor of Dallas." *Ebony* 50 (September 1995): 32–34.

Maxwell, Louise Passey. "Freedmantown: The Evolution of a Black Neighborhood in Houston: 1865–1880." Master's thesis, Rice University, 1993.

McCord, William, et al. *Life Styles in the Black Ghetto.* New York: W. W. Norton, 1969.

McGowan-Johnson, Cernoria. "A Study in the History and Development of the Urban League Program in Fort Worth, Texas, 1944–1945." Master's thesis, Atlanta University, 1946.

McKnight, Mamie. *African American Families and Settlements of Dallas: On the Inside Looking Out.* Dallas: Black Dallas Remembered, 1990.

_______. *First African American Families of Dallas: Creative Survival.* Dallas: Black Dallas Remembered, 1990.

Meltzer, Mildred Huber. "Chapters in the Struggle for Negro Rights in Houston, 1944–1962." Master's thesis, University of Houston, 1963.

Merseburger, Marion. "A Political History of Houston, Texas, during the Reconstruction Period as recorded by the Press: 1868–1873." Master's thesis, Rice University, 1950.

Miles, Charles M. "Voting Habits and Political Attitudes of Negroes in Austin, Texas." Master's thesis, North Texas State University, 1963.

Minton, John. "Houston Creoles and Zydeco: The Emergence of an African American Urban Popular Style." *American Music* 14 (1996): 480–526.

Morgan, Leon. *Public Education for Blacks in Galveston, 1838–1968.* Galveston: Old Central Cultural Center, 1978.

Morris, Mark Noland. "Saving Society Through Politics: The Ku Klux Klan in Dallas, Texas, in the 1920s." Ph.D. dissertation, University of North Texas, 1997.

Munchus-Forde, Lady George. "History of the Negro in Fort Worth—Syllabus for a High School Course." Master's thesis, Fisk University, 1941.

Norris, Clarence Windzell. "A Comparative Study of Selected White and Negro Youth of San Antonio, Texas, with Special Reference to Certain Basic Social Attitudes." Ph.D. dissertation, University of Southern California, 1950.

Olson, James S., and Sharon Phair. "The Anatomy of a Race Riot: Beaumont, Texas, 1943." *Texana* 11 (1973): 64–72.

Olson, Virgil Jerome. "A Comparative Study of Negro Slum Dwellers, Public Housing Project Dwellers, and Project Move-outs in Dallas, Texas." Master's thesis, Southern Methodist University, 1953.

Park, Phocion Samuel Jr. "The Twenty-Fourth Infantry Regiment and the Houston Riot of 1917." Master's thesis, University of Houston, 1971.

Perry, Wilhelmina Elaine. "The Urban Negro with Special Reference to the Universalism-Particularism Pattern Variable." Ph.D. dissertation, University of Texas at Austin, 1967.

Peter, Duane, Marsha Prior, Melissa Green, and Victoria Green Clow (editors). *A Legacy of a Pioneer Black Community in Dallas, Texas: Freedman's Cemetery.* Special Publication No. 6. Austin: Archaeological Studies Program, Environmental Affairs Division, Texas Department of Transportation, 2000.

Pitre, Merline. "Black Houstonians and the 'Separate but Equal' Doctrine: Carter W. Wesley versus Lulu B. White." *The Houston Review* 12 (1990): 23–36.

_______. "Richard Allen: The Chequered Career of Houston's First Black State Legislator." In *Black Dixie: Afro-Texan History and Culture in Houston*, edited by Howard Beeth and Cary D. Wintz, 74–83. College Station: Texas A&M University Press, 1992.

Reynolds, James Talmadge. "The Preretirement Educational Needs of Retired Black Women Who Were Domestic Workers in Dallas, Texas." Ph.D. dissertation, East Texas State University, 1981.

Ringheim, Karin. "Investigating the Structural Determinants of Homelessness: The Case of Houston." *Urban Affairs Quarterly* 28 (1993): 617–640.

Sapper, Neil G. "Black Culture in Urban Texas: A Lone Star Renaissance." *Red River Valley Historical Review* 6 (Spring 1981): 56–77.

Schuler, Edgar A. "The Houston Race Riot, 1917." *Journal of Negro History* 29 (1944): 300–338.

Schutze, Jim. *The Accommodation: The Politics of Race in an American City.* Secaucus, N.J.: Citadel, 1986.

Scott, Emmett J. *The Red Book of Houston: A Compendium of Social, Professional, Religious, Educational and Industrial Interests of Houston's Colored Population.* Houston: Sotex Publishing, [1915].

Shannon, Mary Gamble. "An Occupational Study of Negro Maids in Dallas." Master's thesis, Southern Methodist University, 1941.

Sheeler, J. Reuben. "Negro History Week in the Houston Area." *Negro History Bulletin* 19 (October 1955): 2, 21.

Simond, Ada DeBlanc. *Looking Back: A Black Focus on Austin's Heritage*. Austin: Austin Independent School District, 1984.

Smith, C. Calvin. "On the Edge: The Houston Riot of 1917 Revisited." *The Griot* 10 (Spring 1991): 3–12.

_______. "The Houston Riot of 1917, Revisited." *The Houston Review* 13 (1991): 84–102.

Smith, Rogers Melton. "The Waco Lynching of 1916: Perspective and Analysis." Master's thesis, Baylor University, 1971.

Smith, Thomas H. "Blacks in Dallas: From Slavery to Freedom." *Heritage News* 10 (Spring 1985): 18–22.

_______. "'Cast Down Your Bucket': A Black Experiment in Dallas." *Heritage News* 12 (Spring 1987): 13–18.

SoRelle, James M. "The Darker Side of 'Heaven': The Black Community in Houston, Texas, 1917-1945." Ph.D. dissertation, Kent State University, 1980.

_______. "'An de Po Culled Man is in de Wuss Fix uv Awl:' Black Occupational Status in Houston, Texas, 1920–1940." *The Houston Review* 1 (Spring 1979): 15–26.

_______. "The Emergence of Black Business in Houston, Texas: A Study of Race and Ideology, 1919–1945. In *Black Dixie: Afro-Texan History and Culture in Houston*, edited by Howard Beeth and Cary D. Wintz, 103–115. College Station: Texas A&M University Press, 1992.

_______. "Race Relations in 'Heavenly Houston', 1919–1945." In *Black Dixie: Afro-Texan History and Culture in Houston,* edited by Howard Beeth and Cary D. Wintz, 175–191. College Station: Texas A&M University Press, 1992.

_______. "The 'Waco Horror:' The Lynching of Jesse Washington." *Southwestern Historical Quarterly* 86 (1983): 517–536.

Sparks, Randy J. "'Heavenly Houston' or 'Hellish Houston'? Black Unemployment and Relief Efforts, 1929–1936." *Southern Studies* 25 (Winter 1986): 353–366.

Spurlin, Virginia Lee. "The Conners of Waco: Black Professionals in Twentieth-Century Texas." Ph.D. dissertation, Texas Tech University, 1991.

Stewart, Jacob Thomas. "Characteristics of Negro-Owned and-Operated Business Establishments in Houston." Ph.D. dissertation, University of Texas, 1956.

Stowers, Kevin Ross. "Residential Segregation in Dallas County, Texas: A Comparison of Two Stratification Models." Master's thesis, Texas A&M University, 1973.

Strange, Tempie Virginia. "The Dallas Negro Chamber of Commerce: A Study of a Negro Institution." Master's thesis, Southern Methodist University, 1945.

Terrell, Suzanne. *This Other Kind of Doctors: Traditional Medical Systems in Black Neighborhoods in Austin, Texas*. New York: AMS Press, 1990.

Thomas, Jesse O. *A Study of the Social Welfare Status of the Negroes in Houston, Texas*. Houston: National Urban League, 1929.

Tollerson, Tandy III. "The Negro in Politics in Houston, Texas." Master's thesis, Texas Southern University, 1952.

Toyer, Frances Aurelia. "A Survey of Negro Business Units and the Employment Opportunities afforded by such Units in Houston, Texas." Master's thesis, Atlanta University, 1942.

Waide, C. D. "When Psychology Failed: An Unbiased Fact-Story of the Houston Race Riot of 1917." *Houston Gargoyle*, May 15, 22, 29, 1928; June 5, 12, 1928.

Walker, May. *The History of the Black Police Officers in the Houston Police Department, 1878–1988*. Dallas: Taylor Publishing Company, 1988.

Wassenich, Paul Green. "A Social Study of the Negro Population of Austin, Texas, 1928–1935." Master's thesis, University of Texas, 1936.

Watley, Sarah Beal. "The Power Structure in the Negro Sub-Community in Lubbock, Texas." Master's thesis, Texas Tech University, 1970.

Watson, Dwight David. "Change Did Come: The Transformation of the Houston Police Department, 1930–1984." Ph.D. dissertation, University of Houston, 1999.

West, Richard. "Only the Strong Survive." *Texas Monthly* 7 (February 1979): 94–105.

Williams, David Alvernon. "A History of African-American Higher Education in Austin and Travis County, Texas." In *Bricks Without Straw: A Comprehensive History of African Americans in Texas*, edited by David A. Williams, 279–308. Austin: Eakin Press, 1997.

Williams, J. Allen Jr. "The Effects of Urban Renewal upon a Black Community [Kealing Section of Austin, Texas]: Evaluation and Recommendations." *Social Science Quarterly* 50 (1969): 703–712.

Williams, Joyce E. *Black Community Control: A Study of Transition in a Texas Ghetto*. New York: Praeger, 1973.

_______. "Black Community in Transition: Issues and Leadership in a Texas Ghetto." Ph.D. dissertation, Washington University, St. Louis, Missouri, 1971.

Wilson, Jessie Mae. "A Study of the Community Resources for the Negro of Austin, Texas, 1944–1945." Master's thesis, Atlanta University, 1945.

Wilson, William H. "Desegregation of the Hamilton Park School, 1955–1975." *Southwestern Historical Quarterly* 95 (1991): 43–63.

_______. *Hamilton Park: A Planned Black Community in Dallas*. Baltimore: Johns Hopkins University Press, 1998.

_______. "Private Planning for Black Housing in Dallas, Texas, 1945–1955." *Proceedings of the Second National Conference on American Planning History*, 67–84. Columbus, Ohio: Society for American City and Regional Planning History, 1988.

_______. "'This Negro Housing Matter:' The Search for a Viable African-American Residential Subdivision in Dallas, 1945–1950." *Legacies* 4 (Fall 1994): 28–40.

Wintz, Cary D. "Blacks." In *The Ethnic Groups of Houston*, edited by Fred R. von der Mehden, 9–40. Houston: Rice University Studies, 1984.

_______. *Blacks in Houston*. Houston: Center for the Humanities, 1982.

_______. "The Emergence of a Black Neighborhood: Houston's Fourth Ward, 1865–1915." In *Urban Texas: Politics and Development*, edited by Char Miller and Heywood T. Sanders, 96–109, 194–196. College Station: Texas A&M University Press, 1990.

Xie, Jingjing. "The Black Community in Waco, Texas: A Study of Place, Family, and Work, 1880–1900." Master's thesis, Baylor University, 1988.

Yates, Donald Lee. "Correlates of Attitudes toward the Police: A Comparison of Black and White Citizens in Austin, Texas." Ph.D. dissertation, University of Texas at Austin, 1984.

Yates, Rutherford B. H., and Paul L. Yates. *The Life and Efforts of Jack Yates*. Houston: Texas Southern University Press, 1985.

18. Women

Bessie Russell holding her baby sister, Lucille Russell, on a front porch, Floresville, Texas, 1910–1911.

The UT Institute of Texan Cultures, No. 95-105
Courtesy of Jamie L. Harris

Allen, Ruth A. "The Negro Woman." In *The Labor of Women in the Production of Cotton*, 174–208. Bureau of Research in the Social Sciences. Austin: University of Texas, 1931.

Armstead, Johnnie M. "Black Women and Texas History." In *Bricks Without Straw: A Comprehensive History of African Americans in Texas,* edited by David A. Williams, 114–124. Austin: Eakin Press, 1997.

Asbaugh, Carolyn. *Lucy Parsons, American Revolutionary*. Chicago: Kerr, 1976.

Atkinson, M. Jourdan. "Familialism in Texas: A Texan View." In *The Extended Family in Black Societies*, edited by Demitri B. Shimkin, Edith M. Shimkin, and Dennis A. Frate, 355–362. The Hague: Mouton Publishers, 1978.

Brandenstein, Sherilyn. "Prominent Roles of Black Womanhood in *Sepia Record*, 1952–1954." Master's thesis, University of Texas at Austin, 1989.

_______. "*Sepia Record* as a Forum for Negotiating Women's Roles." In *Women and Texas History: Selected Essays*, edited by Fane Downs and Nancy Baker Jones, 143–157. Austin: Texas State Historical Association, 1993.

Brewer, Rose M. "Black Women Workers: Yesterday and Today." In *Women in the Texas Workforce: Yesterday and Today*, edited by Richard Croxdale and Melissa Hield, 35–48. Austin: People's History in Texas, 1979.

Brooks, Christopher. "Coming Home: An Interview with Sippie Wallace." *Texas Humanist* 7 (July-August 1985) : 30–31.

Brown, Olive D., and Michael R. Heintze. "Mary Branch: Private College Educator." In *Black Leaders: Texans for Their Times*, edited by Alwyn Barr and Robert A. Calvert, 112–127. Austin: Texas State Historical Association, 1981.

Broyles, William. "The Making of Barbara Jordan." *Texas Monthly* 4 (October 1976): 33–47.

Bryant, Ira B. Jr. *Barbara Charline Jordan: From the Ghetto to the Capitol.* Houston: D. Armstrong Company, 1977.

Burka, Paul. "Major Barbara [Jordan]." *Texas Monthly* 24 (March 1996): 88–89, 110–111.

Burrow, Rachel Northington. "Juanita Craft." Master's thesis, Southern Methodist University, 1994.

Byrd, James W. "Aunt Dicy: Legendary Black Lady." In *Legendary Ladies of Texas*, edited by Francis Edward Abernethy, 123–131. Dallas: E-Heart Press, 1981.

Campbell, Randolph B. "'My Dear Husband': A Texas Slave's Love Letter, 1862." *Journal of Negro History* 65 (1980): 361–364.

Cartwright, Marguerita. "Etta Moten: Glamorous Grandmother." *Negro History Bulletin* 18 (March 1955): 137–138.

Crawford, Ann Fears, and Crystal Sasse Ragsdale. "Congresswoman from Texas [Barbara Jordan]." In *Women in Texas: Their Lives, Their Experiences, Their Accomplishments*, 296–307. Burnet, Tex.: Eakin Press, 1982.

Crouch, Barry A. "The 'Cords of Love': Legalizing Black Marital and Family Rights in Postwar Texas." *Journal of Negro History* 79 (1994): 334–351.

_______. "Seeking Equality: Houston Black Women during Reconstruction." In *Black Dixie: Afro-Texan History and Culture in Houston*, edited by Howard Beeth and Cary D. Wintz, 54–73. College Station: Texas A&M University Press, 1992.

Crouch, Barry A., and Larry Madaras. "Reconstructing Black Families: Perspectives from the Texas Freedmen's Bureau Records." *Prologue* 18 (1986): 109–122.

Curlee, Kendall. "White, Mattie B. Haywood." In *The New Handbook of Texas*, edited by Ron Tyler, Douglas E. Barnett, Roy R. Barkley, Penelope C. Anderson, and Mark F. Odintz, vol. 6, 930. Austin: Texas State Historical Association, 1996.

Davis, Alecia. "Christia V. Adair: Servant of Humanity." *Texas Historian* 38 (September 1977): 1–7.

de Graaf, Lawrence B. "Race, Sex, and Region: Black Women in the American West, 1850–1920." *Pacific Historical Review* 49 (1980): 285–313.

Ealy, Rachel Ann. "Dr. Paulene Hopkins: The History of a Community Leader." *Texas Historian* 53 (September 1992): 18–19.

Eckerman, Jo. "Artemesia Bowden: Dedicated Dreamer." *Texas Passages* 2 (Winter 1987): 1–2.

Evans, Eola Adeline. "Activity of Black Women in the Woman Suffrage Movement, 1900–1920." Master's thesis, Lamar University, 1987.

Faust, Drew Gilpin. "Trying to do a Man's Business: Gender Violence and Slave Management in Civil War Texas." In *Southern Stories in Peace and War*, edited by Drew Gilpin Faust, 174–192. Columbia: University of Missouri Press, 1992.

Flandreau, Suzanne. "Victoria Spivey." In *Black Women in America: An Historical Encyclopedia*, edited by Darlene Clark Hine, vol. 2, 1098–1099. Brooklyn: Carlson Publishing Company, 1993.

Franklin, J. E. *"Black Girl": From Genesis to Revelations*. Washington, D.C.: Howard University Press, 1973.

Freydberg, Elizabeth A. H. *Bessie Coleman: The Brownskin Lady Bird.* New York: Garland Publishing, 1994.

Gooch, Jane P. "Barbara C. Jordan: Her First Forty Years; A Rhetorical Analysis." Master's thesis, Baylor University, 1977.

Goodall, N. H. "Arizona Juanita Dranes." In *Black Women in America: An Historical Encyclopedia*, edited by Darlene Clark Hine, vol. 1, 355–356. Brooklyn: Carlson Publishing Company, 1993.

Greenfield, Meg. "The New Lone Star of Texas [Barbara Jordan]." *Newsweek* (March 3, 1975): 31.

Hall, Josie Briggs. *Hall's Moral and Mental Capsule for the Economic and Domestic Life of the Negro, as a Solution of the Race Problem.* Dallas: Rev. F. S. Jenkins, 1905.

Halsell, Grace. *In Their Shoes: A White Woman's Journey Living as a Black, Navajo, and Mexican Illegal.* Fort Worth: Texas Christian University Press, 1996.

Harrigan, Stephen. "The Yellow Rose of Texas." *Texas Monthly* 12 (April 1984): 152.

Harris, Trudier. "'The Yellow Rose of Texas': A Different Cultural View." In *Juneteenth Texas: Essays in African-American Folklore*, edited by Francis Edward Abernethy, Carolyn Fiedler Satterwhite, Patrick B.Mullen, and Alan B. Govenar, 315–333. Publication of the Texas Folklore Society No. 54. Denton: University of North Texas Press, 1996.

Henson, Margaret. "She's the Real Thing." *Texas Highways* 33 (April 1986): 60–61.

Howard, Vicki. "The Courtship Letters of an African American Couple: Race, Gender, Class, and the Cult of True Womanhood." *Southwestern Historical Quarterly* 100 (1996): 65–80.

Hunter, J. Marvin. "Negress Died at Age of 125." *Frontier Times* 9 (1932): 200.

_______. "Negress 106 Dies." *Frontier Times* 11 (1934): 524.

_______. "Old Slave Mammy Becomes Wealthy." *Frontier Times* 5 (1928): 295.

Ivy, Charlotte. "Forgotten Color: Black Families in Early El Paso." *Password* 35 (1990): 5–18.

Jackson, Lela. "Rachel Whitfield (1814–1908)." In *Women in Early Texas*, edited by Evelyn M. Carrington, 288–293. Austin: Jenkins Publishing Company, 1975.

James, Allie Winifred. "The Homemaking Activities of a Selected Group of Negro Homemakers in East Texas." Master's thesis, Kansas State College, Manhattan, 1939.

Jones, Nancy Baker. "Dupree, Anna Johnson." In *The New Handbook of Texas*, edited by Ron Tyler, Douglas E. Barnett, Roy R. Barkley, Penelope C. Anderson, and Mark F. Odintz, vol. 2, 732–733. Austin: Texas State Historical Association, 1996.

Jones, Nancy Baker, and Ruthe Winegarten. "Eddie Bernice Johnson." *Capitol Women: Texas Female Legislators, 1923–1999*, 169–173. Austin: University of Texas Press, 2000.

_______. "Senfronia Paige Thompson" *Capitol Women: Texas Female Legislators, 1923–1999*, 176–179. Austin: University of Texas Press, 2000.

_______. "Wilhelmina Ruth Fitzgerald Delco" *Capitol Women: Texas Female Legislators, 1923–1999*, 182–186. Austin: University of Texas Press, 2000.

Jones, Yvette. "Seeds of Compassion." *Texas Historian* 37 (November 1976): 16–21.

Jordan, Barbara, and Shelby Hearon. *Barbara Jordan: A Self-Portrait.* Garden City: Doubleday, 1979.

Jordan, Julia K. Gibson, and Charlie Mae Brown Smith. *Beauty and the Best: Frederica Chase Dodd, the Story of a Life of Love and Dedication.* Dallas: Delta Sigma Theta Sorority, 1985.

Katz, William Loren. "Texas." In *Black Women of the Old West*, 48–50. New York: Atheneum Books, 1995.

Keir, Scott S. "Middle Class Black Families in Austin, Texas: An Exploratory Analysis of Husbands and Wives." Ph.D. dissertation, University of Texas at Austin, 1987.

Kirk, Rita G. "Barbara Jordan: The Rise of a Black Woman Politician." Master's thesis, University of Arkansas, 1978.

Lede, Naomi W. *Precious Memories of a Black Socialite: A Narrative of the Life and Times of Constance Houston Thompson.* Houston: D. Armstrong Company, 1991.

Lewis, Linda. "Young, Gifted and Black." In *No Apologies: Texas Radicals Celebrate the '60s*, edited by Daryl Janes, 62–71. Austin: Eakin Press, 1992.

Lundy, Anne. "Conversation with . . . Ernestine Jessie Covington Dent." *Black Perspective in Music* 12 (Fall 1984): 244–263.

Malone, Ann Patton. "Black Women." In *Women on the Texas Frontier: A Cross-Cultural Perspective*, 26–52, 63–78. Southwestern Studies no. 70. El Paso: Texas Western Press, 1983.

Mathis, Annie Maie. "Negro Public Health Nursing in Texas." *Southern Workman* 56 (July 1927): 302–303.

Miles, Merle Yvonne. "'Born and Bred' in Texas: Three Generations of Black Females: A Critique of Social Science Perceptions on the Black Female." Ph.D. dissertation, University of Texas at Austin, 1986.

Moutoussamy-Ashe, Jeanne. "Elizabeth 'Tex' Williams." In *Viewfinders: Black Women Photographers*, 98–100. New York: Dodd, Mead, 1986.

Mullen, Harryette. *Tree Tall Woman: Poems by Harryette Romell Mullen.* Austin: Red River Women's Press, 1978.

Nash, Sunny. *Bigmama Didn't Shop at Woolworth's*. College Station: Texas A&M University Press, 1996.

_______. "A Mission Completed for Doll." In *State Lines*, edited by Ken Hammond, 40–44. College Station: Texas A&M University Press, 1993.

Neeley, Sarah LeVahn. "A Study of the Rehabilitation Program at Crockett State School for Girls." Master's project, Texas Southern University, 1958.

Owens, William A. "Seer of Corsicana." In *And Horns on the Toads*, edited by Mody C. Boatright, 14–31. Dallas: Southern Methodist University Press, 1959.

Paley, Lillie M. "The Education and Responsibilities of Negro Home Demonstration Agents in Texas." Master's thesis, Kansas State College of Agriculture and Applied Science, 1941.

Parks, Carole A. "J. E. Franklin, Playwright." *Black World* 21 (April 1972): 49–50.

Pinsky, Robert. "On 'Eve Tempted By the Serpent' by Defendente Ferrari, and in Memory of Congresswoman Barbara Jordan of Texas." *Salmagundi* 113 (Winter 1997): 174–175.

Pitre, Merline. "White, Lulu Belle Madison." In *The New Handbook of Texas*, edited by Ron Tyler, Douglas E. Barnett, Roy R. Barkley, Penelope C. Anderson, and Mark F. Odintz, vol. 6, 929. Austin: Texas State Historical Association, 1996.

Reynolds, James Talmadge. "The Preretirement Educational Needs of Retired Black Women who were Domestic Workers in Dallas, Texas." Ph.D. dissertation, East Texas State University, 1981.

Reynolds, Lois Arnell. "Sustenance Position of Texas Negro Domestic Servants in the Texas Economy." Master's thesis, Prairie View State Normal and Industrial College, 1942.

Rich, Doris L. *Queen Bess: Daredevil Aviator*. Washington, D.C.: Smithsonian Institution Press, 1993.

Riley, Glenda. "African American Women in the West." In *A Place to Grow: Women in the American West*, 43–57, 262–266. Arlington Heights: Harlan Davidson, 1992.

_______. "American Daughters: Black Women in the West." *Montana: The Magazine of Western History* 38 (Spring 1988): 14-27.

Robinson, Dorothy Redus. *The Bell Rings at Four: A Black Teacher's Chronicle of Change*. Austin: Madrona Press, 1978.

Rodenberger, Lou Halsell. "A Developing Tradition: African-American Writers." In *Texas Women Writers: A Tradition of Their Own*, edited by Sylvia Ann Grider and Lou Halsell Rodenberger, 247–252. College Station: Texas A&M University Press, 1997.

Rodriguez, Roberto. "Mamie McKnight: Promoting Education and Preserving Black Dallas History." *Black Issues in Higher Education* 10 (December 16, 1993): 24–25.

Rogers, B. Ann, and Linda Schott. "'My Mother Was a Mover': African American Seminole Women in Bracketville, Texas, 1914–1964." In *Writing the Range: Race, Class, and Culture in the Women's West*, edited by Elizabeth Jameson and Susan Armitage, 585–599. Norman: University of Oklahoma Press, 1997.

Rogers, Mary Beth. *Barbara Jordan: American Hero*. New York: Bantam Books, 1998.

Sanders, Charles L. "Barbara Jordan: Texan is a New Power on Capitol Hill." *Ebony* 30 (February 1975): 136–142.

Scarborough, Dorothy. *On the Trail of Negro Folksong*. Cambridge: Harvard University Press, 1925.

Schaffer, Ruth C. "The Health and Social Functions of Black Midwives on the Texas Brazos Bottom, 1900–1985." *Rural Sociology* 56 (Spring 1991): 89–105.

Shannon, Mary Gamble. "An Occupational Study of Negro Maids in Dallas." Master's thesis, Southern Methodist University, 1941.

Sharpless, Rebecca. *Fertile Ground, Narrow Choices: Women on Texas Cotton Farms, 1900–1940*. Chapel Hill: University of North Carolina Press, 1999.

Simond, Ada DeBlanc. "The Discovery of Being Black: A Recollection." *Southwestern Historical Quarterly* 76 (1973): 440–447.

Smallwood, James. "Black Freedwomen after Emancipation: The Texas Experience." *Prologue* 27 (1995): 303–317.

_______. "Emancipation and the Black Family: A Case Study in Texas." *Social Science Quarterly* 57 (1977): 849–857.

Smith, Gloria Lawsha. "Bessie Coleman: From the Cotton Fields to the Airfields." In *KenteCloth: African American Voices in Texas,* edited by Sherry McGuire and John R. Posey, 160–167. Denton: Center for Texas Studies, University of North Texas, 1995.

Smith, Melinda. "Minority Women Attorneys Share Their Thoughts and Experiences." *Texas Bar Journal* 53 (October 1990): 1050–1056.

Snapp, Elizabeth, and Harry F. Snapp, eds. "African American Women." In *Read All About Her!: Texas Women's History, A Working Bibliography,* 9–11. Denton: Texas Woman's University Press, 1995.

Stanley, William David. "Southern Black Women's Orientation toward Interracial Relations: Study of a Small Nonmetropolitan-Urban East Texas Town, 1970–1977." Master's thesis, Texas A&M University, 1982.

Turner, Martha Anne. *The Life and Times of June Long*. Waco: Texian Press, 1969.

_______. *The Yellow Rose of Texas: Her Saga and Her Song*. Austin: Shoal Creek Publishers, 1976.

_______. *The Yellow Rose of Texas: The Story of a Song*. El Paso: Texas Western Press, 1971.

Werden, Frieda. "Bernice Love Wiggins." In *American Women Writers*, edited by Lina Mainiero, vol. 4, 414–415. New York: Ungar Publishing Company, 1982.

White, Clarence Cameron. "Maud Cuney Hare." *Journal of Negro History* 21 (1936): 239–240.

Wiggins, Bernice Love. *Tuneful Tales*. El Paso: Privately printed, 1925.

Williams, Lorece. "[Untitled]." In *Growing Up in Texas: Recollections of Childhood*, 111–118. Austin: Encino Press, 1972.

Williams, Patricia R. "Literary Traditions in Works by African-American Playwrights." In *Texas Women Writers: A Tradition of Their Own,* edited by Sylvia Ann Grider and Lou Halsell Rodenberger, 253–255. College Station: Texas A&M University Press, 1997.

Winegarten, Ruthe. *Black Texas Women: 150 Years of Trial and Triumph*. Austin: University of Texas Press, 1994.

_______. "Black Texas Women: 150 Years of Trial and Triumph." *Medallion* 29 (February 1992): 8–9.

_______. *Black Texas Women: A Sourcebook: Documents, Biographies, Time Line*. Austin: University of Texas Press, 1996.

_______, ed. *I am Annie Mae, an Extraordinary Woman in Her Own Words: The Personal Story of a Black Texas Woman*. Austin: Rosegarden Press, 1983.

_______. "Texas Slave Families." *Texas Humanist* 7 (March-April 1985): 29–30, 33.

Winegarten, Ruthe, and Sharon Kahn. *Brave Black Women: From Slavery to the Space Shuttle*. Austin: University of Texas Press, 1996.

Winegarten, Ruthe, and Debra Winegarten. *Strong Family Ties: The Tiny Hawkins Story*. Austin: SocioSights Press, 1999.

Yerwood, Ada Marie. "Certain Housing Conditions and Activities of Negro Girls Enrolled in Federally Aided Schools in Texas as One Index of Their Educational Needs." Master's thesis, Iowa State College, 1936.

Author Index

AFTERWORD

We all know that a Bibliography is never complete; that it is a living, breathing, growing organism with a life of its own—and I recently was reminded of that quite vividly. The weekend succeeding my review of the manuscript page copy prepared by Kelly García of the Center for Big Bend Studies, in discussions with Alwyn Barr, Paul Carlson, and Ed Eakin, I learned of items not included in the Bibliography (see below). I also received an email from Barry Crouch wondering whether I had located his contributions to black Texas history (probably not all, unfortunately). Each day the list grows—adequate reason for publishing this bibliography. Studies continue—Douglas Hales on Norris Wright Cuney, Bernadette Pruitt on Black Migration to Houston, Bruce Glasrud and Merline Pitre on Black Texas Women (with contributions from Angela Boswell, Barry Crouch, James Smallwood, Rebecca Sharpless, Stefanie Decker, and Jewel Prestage), Maceo Dailey on Bernice Love Wiggins, James SoRelle on Cimbee, a humorist for *The Houston Informer*, and Laurie Champion and Bruce Glasrud on Chester Himes' use of Texas as a racial foil. Enjoy and use this bibliography, but recognize that it is already a little bit out-of-step. On the other hand, I hope it makes all of our research tasks a little easier.

Bruce A. Glasrud

Barr, Alwyn. "Advancing from History's Hollow to History's Mountain: Sources on African American History in Texas." *East Texas Historical Journal* 38.1 (2000): 28–34.

Beard, Marty. "The Right to Learn: Desegregation in a West Texas Town (Alpine)." *Texas Historian* 52 (May 1992): 9–12.

Beil, Gail K. "Sowing the Seeds of the Civil Rights Movement: Dr. J. Leonard Farmer and Wiley College, Marshall, Texas, as Case Studies of the Educational Influence on Modern Civil Rights Leaders." Master's thesis, Stephen F. Austin State University, 1999.

_______. "Dr. James Leonard Farmer: Texas' First Black Ph.D." *East Texas Historical Journal* 36.1 (1998): 18–25.

Burton, Art B. "Seminole Negro Indian Scouts." *Black, Buckskin, and Blue: African-American Scouts and Soldiers on the Western Frontier*, 87–102. Austin, Tex.: Eakin Press, 1999.

Crouch, Barry A. "The Freedmen's Bureau in Beaumont." *Texas Gulf Coast Historical and Biographical Record* 29 (1993): part 2, 8–29.

_______. "The Freedmen's Bureau in Colorado County, Texas, 1865–1868." *Nesbitt Memorial Library Journal* 5 (May 1995): part 1, 71–104.

_______. "The Freedmen's Bureau in Colorado County, Texas, 1865–1868." *Nesbitt Memorial Library Journal* 7 (September 1997): part 2, 147-175.

_______. "The Freedmen's Bureau in Colorado County, Texas, 1865–1868." *Nesbitt Memorial Library Journal* 8 (January 1998): part 3, 3–31.

_______. "The Fetters of Justice: Black Texans and the Penitentiary During Reconstruction." *Prologue* 28 (Fall 1996): 183–193.

_______. "'To Enslave the Rising Generation': The Freedmen's Bureau and the Texas Black Code." In *The Freedmen's Bureau and Reconstruction: Reconsiderations*, edited by Paul A. Cimbala and Randall M. Miller, 261–287. New York: Fordham University Press, 1999.

Ealy, Rachel Ann. "Mack Hopkins: One of the First Black Air Force Pilots." *Texas Historian* 51 (November 1990): 12–14.

Fink, Robert C. "African-American Baseball in Texas." Master's thesis, Texas Tech University, 1999.

Hales, Douglas. "Black Cowboy: Daniel Webster '80 John' Wallace." In *The Cowboy Way: An Exploration of History and Culture*, edited by Paul H. Carlson, 33–43. Lubbock: Texas Tech University Press, 2000.

Humble, Berenda J. "Farmer Before King: The Non-violent Civil Rights Movement." *Texas Historian* 52 (September 1991): 5–7.

Kosary, Rebecca A. "Regression to Barbarism in Reconstruction Texas: An Analysis of White Violence Against African-Americans From the Texas Freedmen's Bureau Records, 1965–1868." Master's thesis, Southwest Texas State University, 1999.

Parks, Katie, comp. *Remember When? A History of African Americans in Lubbock, Texas*. Lubbock, Tex.: Friends of the Library/Southwest Collection, 1999.

Pruitt, Bernadette. "Exodus, the Movement: People of African Descent and Their Migrations to Houston, 1914–1945." Ph. D. dissertation, University of Houston, 2000.

_______. "The Urban Transformation of the MacGregor Area, 1950–1970." Master's thesis, Texas Southern University, 1991.

Robertson, Robert J. "Congressman Jack Brooks, the Civil Rights Act of 1964, and the Desegregation of Public Accommodations and Facilities in Southeast Texas: A Preliminary Inquiry." *Texas Gulf Historical and Biographical Record* 35 (November 1999): 18–31.